Thinking Person's Guide to Autism

First Edition November 2011

Cover design by Amy Freels

Logo artwork by Will Hornaday, Hornaday Designs

ISBN-13:9780-692-01055-6

Library of Congress Cataloging-in-Publication Data has been applied for.

For my bright shining boy Leo. Thank you for spreading joy so freely.

—Shannon Des Roches Rosa

To Jack, who shapes my character daily, and Katie, who loves so deeply, and to Shawn, whom I would pick again for this island.

—Jennifer Byde Myers

I dedicate this book to the countless adults with undiagnosed autism, in the hopes that the future will be brighter for them as autism awareness and acceptance grow.

—Liz Ditz

To the Viking, without whom it would all seem ashes, and to our little Vikings, who grace our days with their generous and loving spirits.

—Emily Willingham

To my husband, John, my most excellent source of strength and joy. To Arren, whose beauty and grit leave me breathless.

—Carol Greenburg

Introduction

This is the book we wish we'd been given when autism first became part of our lives: a toolkit bursting with carefully curated, evidence-based information from autism parents, autistics, and autism professionals.

The goal of *Thinking Person's Guide to Autism* is to help you fast-forward past society's rampant autism fabrications and negativity by providing clear, thoughtfully presented, balanced, and referenced information. We also want you to understand that autism awareness and acceptance are not merely noble but also necessary attitudes—and are separate matters from the autistic and other autism communities' never-ending fights for medical, legal, social, and educational accommodation.

While this book contains experienced perspectives and well-researched evidence, our goal is not to tell you what to do. We believe the best thing we can do for ourselves and for our children—out of love and out of common sense—is to acquire the most reliable autism information available. Like a good, wise friend, the essays in this collection simply lay out information that will help you sift through media and Internet noise, or even the autism perspectives you encounter in your daily life.

Some people in the autism communities are sincerely passionate about what they believe are successful interventions for autism, or ardent in their beliefs about what causes autism. Their emotion and sincerity can be powerfully attractive and powerfully convincing. Other, less-sincere people in the autism intervention community target loving, desperate parents—and take advantage of that desperation.

Our belief is that all autism approaches should mirror the physicians' credo "First, do no harm." But how do you determine when benefits outweigh potential damage? The pseudoscience so often promoted as "autism treatments" has a handful of consistent identifying characteristics. Ask yourself:

- Does this practitioner or vendor promise miracles that no one else seems to achieve?

- Is the person promising the outcome also asking me for money?

- Do I find any scientific research supporting the claims, or are there only individual (often emotional) testimonials of effects?

- Does the practitioner or vendor promise a blanket "cure" for unrelated disorders, grouping together, for example, allergies and autism; or autism and ADHD; or autism, diabetes, cancer, and allergies?

- Does the practitioner or vendor have strong credentials as an expert in the therapies promised or in the field of autism?

Many practitioners of autism pseudoscience know their market well and are uninhibited about exploiting autism families and autistics. Because only you can let yourself be exploited, the best defense against pseudoscience is to apply your best critical evaluation skills. Thinking critically is one of the most important actions we can take for those we love, and for ourselves.

Thinking critically starts with listening critically. You will find frank autistic voices in this book, sharing insights on a wide range of topics, including rights, needs, aging, sexuality, and employment. They deserve your full attention, consideration, and respect. You may also notice that several autistic contributors appear in dual or triple roles as autism parents and/or autism professionals, too, and that some people prefer to capitalize the term Autistic.

We hope that, with the support of the contributors to *Thinking Person's Guide to Autism*, you will find your rational self—and embrace the best, fact-based autism approaches and attitudes. At the same time, we trust you will never lose sight of the emotions and love that propel your every autism-related decision and action. Ideally, your rational and emotional selves will merge, and you will be able to declare, "I love someone with autism *and...*" rather than "I love someone with autism *but...*" Whether that person you love is your child—or yourself.

—The Editors

Disclaimer

This book is not intended as, nor implied to be, a substitute for professional medical or mental health advice. Always seek the advice of your physician or qualified care provider before trying any new therapy or remedy for your or your child's personal health. Information contained here should not be considered professional legal advice. Please seek licensed counsel if you need legal help.

Each essay is the opinion of the particular author of that essay. It should not be construed that any other contributor shares the same opinion, although he or she might. Although our fact and source checking is thorough, the editors of *Thinking Person's Guide to Autism* do not guarantee or warrant that any information written by individuals is correct and disclaim any liability for any loss or damage resulting from reliance on any such information.

The editorial board of *Thinking Person's Guide to Autism* currently consists of five editors: Shannon Des Roches Rosa, Jennifer Byde Myers, Liz Ditz, Emily Willingham, and Carol Greenburg. *Thinking Person's Guide to Autism* is a project of the Myers-Rosa Foundation, which is dedicated to autism advocacy, education, and community support. Funds received through activities and direct donations support autism research and the autistic community. We are a recognized 501(c)3 non-profit organization, effective June 2011. All donations to this organization are tax-deductible.

Table of Contents

1 After the Autism Diagnosis: First Steps

You will never, ever take progress for granted. Every milestone met, no matter what the timing, will be cause for celebration. Every baby step will be a quantum leap. You will find the people who understand that. You will revel in their support and love and shared excitement.

—Jess at *Diary of a Mom*

Bring Everyone Out

Kyra Anderson

In the summer of 2006, I attended a session at the Autism Science of America (ASA) Conference led by a panel of parents who identified themselves as on the autism spectrum raising kids on the autism spectrum. With the exception of one person, they had Asperger's. They got their diagnoses after their children were diagnosed. They had spouses and children. Most had jobs. They were making their way in the world. I don't say that to take anything away from their experience, from their frustration with the fear, ignorance, and limited vision of those suffering from neurotypicality. But I did note there was an assumption that all kids on the spectrum are experiencing the same thing when they're not. And neither are their parents.

One of the many things they talked about was the invisibility of this disability and the way society responds to those with autism compared to those with visible, physical disabilities. To the latter, society says, "We must adapt and adjust!" To the former, society says, "You must adapt and adjust!"

They saw their children's strengths as strengths and even some of their struggles as strengths. Their children didn't play the game, didn't know how to fake it, couldn't read subtle social clues. They wore these things as almost a badge of pride. It was enlightening to hear parents talk from this perspective. Most conferences and Internet forums at the time were dominated by neurotypical parents' concerns about their spectrum kids. I'd been one of those voices. But rather than uniting in a common quest to provide for our spectrum kids, the chorus of voices was at odds, often divisive, driving us into opposing camps.

I left wondering how a neurotypical parent could talk about their experience, their worries and fears, without offending adults on the spectrum. It isn't a lament of raising a child with autism; it's a struggle to give them a good life, an independent life. I'm all for expanding the breadth of acceptable neurology. I'm all for respecting and broadening the scope of acceptable behavior. But when I hear angry calls to get away from the "grief model of diagnosis," for aggressive slaps of "Congratulations! Your child has Autism!" I tell you, I pause. What has happened to acknowledging the process, the human process of moving through the unexpected to a new understanding?

It reminded me of when my ex-husband left me. I met a woman who had been through a divorce years earlier. I barely knew her but when she found out about my situation, she flashed a clown smile and practically shouted,

"Oh, I'm so excited for you!" I wanted to punch her in the face. She danced around, boogying to the pulse of my new life. The freedom! The choices! The discoveries! But I was in the middle of the explosion and I needed time to sort through the mess, to step around and feel what I needed to feel, grieve what was lost, and then slowly see what was now possible. My life eventually got better than I ever imagined, my new relationship happier and more realized. But I had to go through something to get there. Many people were uncomfortable with my process, with my dark feelings—my fear, my sadness, my anger. They wanted me to clean it up, get over it! Or at least suck it up long enough so that they didn't have to see it, so they didn't have to let it rustle up anything in them.

Now, discovering your child has autism is not the same thing. But, as with any profound change, there is a shift, and in that shift, a loss, and in that loss, grief, and in that grief, a process, and through that process, an expansion or at least the possibility of an expansion that makes for more room, for greater sight. Why the rush to brush it under the rug? What is threatening about it? Because I can only think it must be threatening for there to be this reaction. If it were only a matter of not relating or identifying with this process, wouldn't there be more curiosity?

I don't hear people acknowledging enough that autism is a spectrum disorder. Okay, right there. I should not say disorder? I may say spectrum, yes? It is a wide spectrum with a wide band of expression, of—for lack of better word—severity. It often (always?) comes with co-occurring conditions that increase the challenge both for the child and the parent raising the child, who is trying their best to provide what that child needs most, for their happiness, for their actualization, because that is what parents are trying to do, help their child actualize. They have a role that lasts a certain length of time (usually) before they pass the baton, and they want to do their best. The confusion and difficulty made by the perplexing nature of their child's unusual neurology coupled with the paucity of services and supports out there in the world and the level of misinformation bombarding our circuitry, well, it's a lot to deal with.

Some kids on the spectrum are socializing and communicating and moving on their own, dressing themselves, developing relationships, walking, talking, using the potty. Others are blind and having seizures, unable to physically navigate, still in diapers, eating through a feeding tube, struggling to communicate their feelings, thoughts, and needs, and unable to connect to others easily for a whole host of reasons. It's clear to me that these children are every bit as blessed and precious and valued as any other child, that they need and deserve respect, love, education, care, attention, and that their lives are as important as every other life.

Isn't this obvious? And isn't it also obvious that their care is more complicated? That their parents are moving through something very different from most, certainly different than what they anticipated? That the parents in the first group, on one end of the spectrum, the families on the opposite end, and all the families in between are experiencing something that is hard? Couldn't it be possible that these parents experience a kind of worry and concern about their children every day? About their future? About who will care for them when they are no longer alive? Let's not sweep our arms across the room in a blind gesture of mild irritation, impatience, and judgment for those that are, at the very least, experiencing stress and anxiety about providing for their children who require something more and different because they are not of typical neurology.

Autism is not just a disability issue but also a diversity issue. We can and ought to shift the message from tragedy to hope, shift the focus from a pressure to have our kids be "indistinguishable from their peers" to a genuine and serious effort to educate society.

One panelist said, "What's so awful about hand flapping? Why isn't it okay to hand flap in this world? Why can't we take the stigma out of the autism diagnosis and the expression of unusual behaviors?" Yes! I want to stand up and say, "Hand flapping is fine with me! Stimming is a stupid word! We all stim! Why do we have interests and passions and those with autism have obsessions?" And, "Why don't we look more closely at our language and choose our words more carefully to use words of acceptance and inclusion rather than rejection and exclusion?" One goal, spoken by an autistic activist, was to grow a feeling of competence in those with autism, to help them better navigate the social interactions that are a very real and everyday part of life. Yes, again!

While we're working to take the stigma out of an autism diagnosis, let's also take the stigma out of talking about what's hard in dealing with autism. Let's stop pushing away the necessary process of acceptance that occurs when your child is diagnosed with autism. This process is not the same as having a roundtable discussion of whiny parents complaining about how hard it is to care for their children. And it's certainly not the same as having thoughts of harming or killing one's child. That is mental illness.

But for me, there's a tiny elephant in the room and it looks sort of like this: There is a difference between those on the spectrum who mostly "pass" and those that stand out. That is just the truth. It's harder if you stand out. If you sound funny when you talk or if you don't talk at all. If your pants are up around your armpits and your fingers are in your ears. If you look at things sideways. If you scream and hit rather than say, no thank you. If your typical stroll through the mall is following your tongue as it drags against shiny metal surfaces. It is. I want to live in a world where all of that is okay, where it isn't harder, where no one scowls or laughs or wishes "it" would all just go away. I really truly do. In the meantime, we live in a society where wearing size six is a sign of being a fatty pants, where nursing in public is considered lewd and disgusting, where stepping inches out of the narrow and ever-changing target zone of hip and cool and acceptable is cause for ridicule and, sometimes, terrible violence. How close are we to embracing hand flapping? Really?

Still, we must create the change we want to see. We must create a society that extends equality, respect, and acceptance to all.

What and who is society? According to Barbara T. Doyle, one of the ASA conference presenters, it is: Everyone. Everywhere. All The Time. Society is the one lady who sees how you treat your struggling child in the checkout line; society is the class who observes the teacher responding to a child's dysregulation in the hallway; society is the group at the neighboring table who watches how you interact with your sensory-overloaded child in the restaurant. Society is everyone who sees you resist the urge to hurry up or hide when the going gets rough and instead use the opportunity of being looked at to demonstrate the child's unconditional value and worth. Every time. As best you can.

Doyle suggests coming up with your own definition of autism that is simple enough to say in an instant so others can begin to digest it. Here is mine: Autism is a developmental issue that makes dealing with social situations and sensory information harder than for the typical person.

She said many other wonderful things. Here are just a few:

- Put the relationship ahead of compliance. Do we really want our kids completely compliant? Consider someone saying this: Get in the car. Drink that up. Take off your clothes.
- See all behavior as communication. Don't seek to extinguish behavior until you at least understand what is trying to be communicated.
- Respond to all communicative signals as quickly as you can.
- When you feel stuck, choose a respectful response that minimizes the tension.

Help eliminate the Us versus Them mentality that is reinforced every time someone says something like, you are so patient to deal with that every day! You are such a special person! God chose you because such and such and la la la! Phooey. We are not divided that way, or we ought not to be. We are we. I do what I do with my son because I love him, I rejoice in my time with him, I learn from him, and I am compelled to be the best mom I can because it's important to me.

What is this world we want to create? The one we don't have because, in part, we've never tried to create it? Because up until now, we haven't seen the "affected." We've been busy keeping them in, keeping them away. But now it's time to bring them out. Bring everyone out. And here is what everyone needs:

To be safe.

To belong.

To be valued.

To make a contribution.

And if we experience difficulty in creating this for our children, let us keep making the space to talk honestly about it.

—

A version of this essay originally appeared at
www.kyraanderson.wordpress.com.

What Is Neurodiversity?

Mike Stanton

When I attended the (United Kingdom's) National Autism Society's first International Autism Conference in London in 2005, I heard Professor David Amaral tell the story of a young man with Asperger's who visited the MIND Institute at the University of California, Davis. The young man was asked what he would do if they could develop a pill to cure autism. He thought for a while before replying that he would take half the pill.

I think this illustrates a real difference within the autism community. There are many who pathologize autism as a disorder that afflicts an otherwise healthy individual. If you hold this idea, you naturally look to understand the causes of autism in order to find that "autism pill."

The idea of neurodiversity was developed by autistic people in opposition to the pathologizing model. According to them, autistic people are not disordered. They have a different sort of order. Their brains are differently wired. They think differently. They do not want to be cured. They want to be understood.

This is not to deny that autistic people often face real difficulties. That is why the young man at the MIND Institute told David Amaral he would take half the pill, but not the whole pill.

What does neurodiversity mean for parents?

The cure mentality places great pressure on parents to rush into interventions. Then there is the guilt. Was there something I did or didn't do that caused the autism in my child? Can I put it right? How can I not put it right? Instead of raising your child, you can spend all your time trying to fix him or her. The story of Liz Astor[1] and her approach to her daughter Olivia's autism illustrate this.

Olivia was four when Liz finally faced up to the diagnosis. She was wracked with guilt that, having given birth to Olivia at the age of 42, she was somehow responsible for her child's problems, either directly or as a result of a prenatal diagnostic test (amniocentesis) that went wrong.

Lady Astor's way of dealing with this lonely burden was to take action. "I wanted to rip the autism out of Olivia with my bare hands," she says. In the years that followed, she whirled her daughter from one therapist to another, trying everything from cranial osteopathy and "brushing" her nerve endings, to Portage, a method of teaching everything in tiny steps.

In a 2006 interview, Lady Astor said, "Every practitioner is convinced that his or her treatment is the one and you feel compelled to try everything to find the one that will open up your child. I have seen children who have made remarkable improvements, but I would never say they have been cured or recovered."

The reporter went on to write, "Having reached a state of mind where, even if she could, she would not change Olivia, she tries to concentrate on the good qualities that come with autism—honesty, uncompetitiveness, and absence of spite."

Embracing neurodiversity allows you to stop looking for a cure because there isn't one. I agree with the eight autism organizations that signed an open letter to CBS and Dr. Phil McGraw (January 27, 2006), stating that "Most of the enlightened world knows that autism is at its root, genetic, and therefore by definition it is not something that can be considered 'curable' or a 'disease.'"

Giving up on a cure is not the same as giving up on your child. In fact, it can help you to take a more balanced approach. It is easier to reflect on your child's strengths as well as his or her difficulties and take up Lorna Wing's advice that "...an autistic child can only be helped if a serious attempt is made to see the world from his point of view."

Sometimes our biggest problem lies with other people. One mother gave me permission to quote something she wrote in an email about autism and acceptance:

> I think that it's a bit insulting sometimes for people, especially family and friends, to try to give me information about how to make my son be a "bit less autistic." It makes me think they want a shortcut to make him more acceptable. I'd prefer it if they tried to connect with him and enjoy him as he is. Then they'd really be able to help him to progress.

This is the essence of neurodiversity. First accept the difference. Then find ways to work together. And it is not all about problems, either. We all had a favorite subject at school that we were good at and something else we really struggled with. Imagine being told that you had to drop your best subject and have double lessons in your worst subject.

That is not so far from the experience of lots of autistic children whose interests and talents are sidelined while we concentrate on their difficulties. This can send all the wrong messages to our kids. They learn about their limitations but rarely get the chance to achieve. So they put up barriers to protect what is left of their self-esteem. You try and offer constructive criticism. They take it as a mortal insult.

If we accept people and work with their strengths, we can help them to find ways of dealing with their problems that work for them. I spent a lot of time trying to solve my son's problems and making choices for him. The turning point came when Dave, a clinical psychologist, asked him to think about what he wanted. Prior to this, my son had always been encouraged to meet other people's demands and expectations. Dave was the first person to give my son explicit permission to put his desires before our expectations.

When does neurodiversity give way to disability?

It is a common mistake to believe that neurodiversity is only for people who are "high-functioning" or are "mildly autistic" or any other synonym for "not my child." The argument goes that neurodiversity is all right for you. You can talk. You can write. You are intelligent. My kid is nonverbal, self-injures, and needs constant care.

A whole set of problems comes with being "high-functioning." People expect you to be normal or at least to act normal. So you expend a lot of mental energy pretending to be "normal," which leaves you wide open to stress-related problems like depression, obsessive-compulsive disorder, and social anxiety disorder. You may be paralyzed by panic attacks or have uncontrollable bouts of anger. This can get you in trouble with the law or trapped in the psychiatric system. Being "high-functioning" is not a soft option.

Does the demand for tolerance and understanding mean ignoring children in distress, doing nothing about autism, denying the need for scientific research? Of course not. We support the need for decent peer-reviewed research into the problems associated with autism. It is by no means clear what constitutes the core features that are fundamental to autism, and what are secondary factors. We just do not see any justification for seeing all of a child's problems as being because of autism and imagining that there is a magic bullet to solve them all.

Who will speak for my child?

This is a real concern, especially for parents of children who are highly dependent on others. We are all mortal and when we die, who will speak for our children then? Neurodiversity is a way of thinking about human difference that has the potential to change the world for autistic people in ways that are comparable to the impact of the liberation movements for women, or people who are black or gay. When society speaks for my child, then I can die happy.

The National Autistic Society (NAS) recently changed its constitution. We are no longer a parent-led organization. Previously there had to be a majority of parents elected to our National Council. Now there has to be a majority of family members—parents, siblings, and people with autism. Many parents of severely autistic children were worried that this dilution of control would weaken their voice as the only effective advocates for their children. Some were worried that high-functioning autistics would take over the NAS and their children would be forgotten.

I pointed out at the NAS's Annual General Meeting that in my experience, autistic people who were willing and able to campaign and hold office were concerned for the rights of all autistic people. They take neurodiversity seriously and value everyone on the autistic spectrum. The parents of children with Asperger's syndrome were far more likely to push the NAS down the path of providing mainstream support for their children at the expense of those who needed more expensive care and protection.

Neurodiversity, like freedom, is indivisible. And its benefits are being seen within the NAS as the professionals in our care homes and schools strive to create mechanisms whereby all autistic people within our structures are able to self-advocate, make choices, and exercise personal autonomy.

What does neurodiversity mean for professionals?

By listening to autistic adults, I have changed my practice in relation to the autistic children with severe learning difficulties in the special school where I teach. I no longer expect eye contact. Instead of demanding, "Look at me when I am talking to you!" I ask, "Are you listening?" When I speak to a child, I give them extra time to process my words and formulate a response. If someone is acting strangely, instead of stepping in to prevent the behavior, I ask myself, "Why is he doing that?"

Okay, I am only human. Sometimes I have bad days. I make mistakes. I mess up. So do the kids in my class. They make allowances for me. I make allowances for them. Some people do not get it. They think I am "letting them get away with it." Yes, like they are being autistic on purpose.

The most important thing a professional can do is to help a person understand and accept that they are autistic and then decide what they are going to do about it. A lot of autistic people spend a lot of time trying to change themselves to fit in with the world as it is. It is important for autistic people to learn how to get by in this world. But they will not do that if we try to manage the way they think. I often say that we should not teach autistic people to manage their behavior; we should teach them to manage ours. And between us we may make the world a bit more manageable for all of us.

What does neurodiversity mean for autistic people?

I am a parent and a professional. I am not autistic and therefore would not presume to speak for autistic people. There are many who can speak for themselves. You can find a really good sample at the *Autism Hub*, a place where autistic people, parents, and professionals meet with no distinction and anyone is welcome, providing you share our respect for the condition of being autistic. We seek no fundamental alteration to this state of being, but we do seek to intervene sometimes should the situation require it. And when we do intervene, we should remember the words of a very wise person with autism, my son:

> My autism is not a problem. It creates problems. But it is not going to go away.

> I want help with my problems, not with who I am.

> I want you to offer support but do not try and change me into someone else.

—

Sources

UK's National Autistic Society: *www.autism.org.uk.*

Stanton, Mike. *Learning to Live with High Functioning Autism: A Parent's Guide for Professionals.* London, England: Jessica Kingsley, 2000.

Stanton, Mike. *Convivir con el Autismo: Guia Para Padres Paidos.* Barcelona, Spain: Ediciones Paidos Iberica, 2003.

Willey, Liane Holliday. *Asperger Syndrome in Adolescence: Living With the Ups, the Downs and Things in Between.* London, England: Jessica Kingsley, 2003.

Action for Autism: *actionforautism.co.uk*

NAS First International Conference: www.autism.org.uk/news-and-events/nas-conferences/our-previous-conferences/international-conference-2005.aspx

Jardine, Cassandra. "I Wanted To Rip The Autism Out of Her." Interview with Liz, Lady Astor. *The Telegraph* (London, England). May 8, 2006. *www.telegraph.co.uk/health/main.jhtml?xml=/health/2006/05/08/hastor08. xml&sSheet=/health/2006/05/08/ixhmain.html*

Astor, Liz. *Loving Olivia: My Life with My Autistic Daughter.* London, England: Rodale International, 2006.

Open letter to CBS and Dr. Phil McGraw: *neurodiversity.com/weblog/article/73*

Autism Hub: *autism-hub.com*

Wobus, John. "Lorna Wing—Nonfiction." *Autism Resources. www.autism-resources.com/nonfictionauthors/LornaWing.html*

—

This essay was written in 2006 and was originally published at Action for Autism.

---

[1] The Honourable Elizabeth Constance Mackintosh married John Astor, 3rd Baron Astor of Hever, in 1990. Their younger child, Olivia, was born in 1992, and turned 18 in August 2010. Lady Astor published her memoir, Loving Olivia in 2006. In May 2006 the Telegraph published an interview with Lady Astor entitled "I Wanted to Rip the Autism Out of Her," from which these quotations are drawn.

What Now? Ten Tips for Families with a New Autism Diagnosis

Squillo

I'm sure the person who said hindsight is 20/20 didn't have a child with autism. (Actually, I'm sure he or she didn't have a child of any kind.) You're never finished being a parent: as the Jason Robards character said in the movie *Parenthood*, "You never get to spike the ball and do your touchdown dance." I have no idea if some of the things I've done will end up having helped or hindered my attempts to attain that Holy Grail of Parenthood: happy, healthy children.

Of course, this has nothing to do with autism, and everything to do with just being a parent, but there are challenges (and joys!) specific to parenting a child with autism.

I was asked to put together a list of things I wish I'd known when my son was first diagnosed. I have followed this request to the letter; what follows reflects my personal experiences and observations, and—more often—my own mistakes. My list includes both the emotional and the practical advice I received, and some I wish I'd received.

All the usual caveats apply: Your-Mileage-May-Vary, n=1, and so on. I'm sure other parents of children with autism have many more tidbits to add, and others will disagree with some of the items on offer here. I plead guilty to any sins of omission, commission, or offence; these are mine alone.

1.   Take a few days (at least) before making any important decisions.

The first thing you need to deal with is how you feel. Even if you think you're prepared for the diagnosis, you will have lots of emotions to process, and some of them may surprise you. I know I was blindsided by grief I never thought I'd feel—we'd known for years before the "official" diagnosis that our son was autistic—compounded by guilt for feeling it. There were a number of other emotions, too, some expected, some not, and this roiling sea of feeling sapped my reason for a short while. My rational brain knew this was normal, but that didn't obviate the need to let myself just float without resistance on that sea for a bit before I could start actively navigating.

2.   Try to plan some alone-time with your partner (if you have one) for a week or two after diagnosis.

If you're the talky type, you'll want to talk about your feelings. If not, you will have some practical issues to discuss (see items below). Either way, it's good if you can do it without the usual distractions and without your child listening in to your discussions.

3. Decide whom you're going to tell.

When my husband and I first realized our son had "issues," and with the dawning realization that these "issues" were most likely related to autism, my husband felt strongly that we should tell nobody who didn't absolutely have to know. I felt otherwise, so we hashed it out and came to an agreement. It was important because if either of us had simply assumed how the other felt, it might have fostered resentments (as assumptions often do), and we would have missed an opportunity to understand how each of us felt about our son's autism. My husband's feelings have changed over time, but I am glad I respected them at a time when he was dealing with his own emotions surrounding our son's diagnosis.

4. Don't focus (too much) on the future.

No parent, whether of an autistic or typically developing child, can help worrying about the future. It's especially easy to let these worries—Will my son live independently? Will my daughter ever speak?—niggle at the corners of your psyche, and they are especially persistent in the weeks just after diagnosis. Let those worries out to play, but learn to pack them away most of the time, or you'll have trouble focusing on the short-term goals that may actually affect the future.

Just as important, focusing too much on the future can prevent you from enjoying who your child is today and from celebrating his or her achievements. I think we all fall victim to this on occasion, but my observation is that those who are most concerned most often with "big picture" goals—"curing" the child's autism, for example—travel the hardest road.

5. Remember that your child is a child, not a project.

It sounds glib, I know, but it's a mistake I've made again and again. It's so easy for me to get caught up in the checklist—the next appointment, the next goal, the next letter to be written, the next battle to be fought—I sometimes forget that both my kids need me to be Just Mom as well as Warrior/CEO Mom.

Moreover, there are aspects of my son's autism that I sometimes enjoy because they are uniquely him—his habit of relating everything back to his obsession with boats and cephalopods, for example. While I do want to help him learn to ameliorate aspects of his behavior that cause problems for him, I have to be careful to remember that some of those things are not just "problems to be solved"—they are part and parcel of who he is. The next task, the next goal, will always be there, but his childhood will not, and I don't want to miss it.

6. Get a few binders and a three-ring hole-punch and decide on a single, accessible place to keep them.

You probably have a lot of paperwork related to your child already. There will be more—much more—and you will need to refer to it all at one time or another.

I started off keeping my son's records in separate hanging folders—one each for school, for medical issues, for evaluations, etc.—and it ended up a big, unruly mess because all those things were interrelated and I frequently needed to refer to something from each folder in the course of one task or meeting.

Save yourself time and hassle by keeping it all organized in one place from the very beginning. Binders are great because they are portable—you can bring them to meetings, and they're easy to grab in case of emergency. (We live in earthquake country, so I think *a lot* about portability.)

7. Keep a record of every interaction you have with schools, therapists, doctors, etc., regarding your child, even if it's just a casual discussion in a hallway. Make copies of every questionnaire you fill out.

Yes, it seems like overkill, but together these things will give you a more complete picture of your child's progress than a simple collection of official reports and test results. In our house, autism is a constant tide of leaps forward and steps backward, and sometimes even a casual comment by a teacher, for example, can help pinpoint the genesis of a problem or the catalyst for a burst of achievement.

8. Get familiar with laws that affect individuals with disabilities, especially those dealing with special education.

One of the biggest challenges for every single autism family I know is getting necessary services. I can almost guarantee that this will take up a disproportionate amount of your time and worry. Knowing what services your child is entitled to receive is up to you—nobody is likely to offer them unless you ask, and unfortunately, you may need to fight for them.

My husband is a federal attorney, and even he was at sea regarding this at first. In the United States, I have found the Wrightslaw website, www.wrightslaw.com, and their books very helpful.

9. Find a local support or advocacy group.

Even if you don't make friends through the group (I didn't), it is a good source of information on local resources—schools, camps, and professionals like pediatricians, dentists, and barbers—who are especially good with autistic kids.

One caveat: support groups—especially the online type—are often full of discussions of the latest miracle autism "treatments" and "cures" (scare-quotes intentional). As tempting as it may seem, don't get sucked in by these; the "treatments" will cost you time and money and may even be harmful, and getting involved in discussions about them will only waste your time.

In the beginning, you may feel guilty if you don't pursue every possible lead in hopes of helping your child, but try to let it go. There are too many for you to try them all, and the majority are useless at best. If you later decide you want to pursue any of them, they will still be there, and you'll have a better sense of what's likely to be helpful for your child.

10. Meet with a financial planner—preferably one with knowledge of special needs planning.

This is one area where "Don't focus on the future" doesn't apply. You need to make a financial plan for the near and possibly the distant future. This is a good idea for every family, but having a child with autism can add extra financial stress, and unless you are yourself a financial wizard, you will need professional guidance.

Even if you take my advice and stay away from DAN! doctors and others offering unproven therapies, having a child with autism can be expensive. Evaluations, therapies, special equipment, respite care, medications—chances are you'll need to pay out-of-pocket for something now or in the next few years.

You also need figure your child's unique needs into your basic estate planning. You may need to consider carrying extra disability or life insurance for yourself and your partner. You definitely need to think carefully about who may be able to care for your child in the event of your death—it might not be the same person/people you would choose to care for a typically developing child.

How Do People React When They Learn Your Child Has Special Needs?

Emily Willingham

What response do you get from people when you mention your child's difference or try to explain it to them? I can categorize our responses into three distinct groups.

From total strangers—and my mentions of autism in this context are rare— the response is pity. Clearly pity, and with it a lack of understanding of what I'm even talking about. And then, of course, I find myself struggling to clarify why pity simply isn't necessary, to get across with pith what a great person my son is, what a total joy it is to have a wonderful person like him in my life. It's rare that I bring up autism to strangers, although if I were savvier, I could use it as a way to enhance awareness and downgrade the pity response.

From casual acquaintances, such as parents of other children and periodically from others closer to me: "I don't like labels." "He seems like a pretty normal kid to me."

These responses set my teeth on edge. They speak to so many things: Diminishing my son's struggles. An accusation that we're magnifying his struggles, or worse, have sought and gotten the "diagnosis du jour" of autism for a child who's merely quirky. An implication that if we just left him alone without labels, he'd be just fine.

Of course, I have to forgive these responses. Sometimes, they're just well meaning, an effort to say, "Well, even with that difference, he's just a kid like other kids." Sometimes, it's exactly the implied criticism I think it is. But I must forgive. They know not of what they speak. How could they?

Invariably, these responses come from parents of neurotypical children. The fact is, they just don't get it. They never will. Sorry, but unless you've spent hours wondering why your child's anxiety leads to nonlinear, bizarre suicidal ideation at age three, you're not gonna get it. Unless you look at your nine-year-old child and marvel at how far he's come that he can say, "I'm going to go interact with that child over there," and wonder if it's the intensive therapies or your own efforts or his efforts or all of the above, you're not gonna get it. Unless you've spent days fending off perseveration over strawberry plants because you unwittingly drove by a plant nursery, you're not gonna get it.

Unless you still, every day and all day, remind your child that making those faces and noises in certain situations isn't gonna fly, you're not gonna get it. Unless you've spent every car ride listening to a symphony of self-regulating Bobby McFerrin sounds and echolalic bursts from the back seat, you're not gonna get it. Unless you've peeled your child off of every door frame associated with every new encounter involving new people just to get him in the room (or, if the meltdown's bad enough, out of it), you're not gonna get it.

And unless you've helplessly watched your child, for years, be unable to fend off even the most overt bullying and childish attacks on the playground because he either didn't detect them or has no idea what to do, you are not gonna get it. If your heart hasn't broken over watching the contrast between what your child doesn't get about human interaction and what other children do get, You. Are. Not. Gonna. Get. It.

Parents of neurotypical kids worry, I know. I just don't know what exactly they worry about. Their worries are not mine. Their triumphs and pleasures are not ours. I do not get them. They probably wouldn't understand the sheer breakthrough it would be for us one day to go to a playground and have one of our sons play with a strange child without seeing that child back away slowly, confused or bemused, or downright hostile.

They probably don't lie awake at night, wondering, hoping, considering whether or not there will be a person out there, the Just Right Person, who some day will appreciate their child's quirks and oddities and inability to remember to zip his pants or put his shirt on with the tag inside right along with his incredible sense of humor and beautiful mind. They likely don't stare into a void sometimes in which their child is lonely, ostracized, suicidal, and devastated as an adult, even as he sometimes was as a child thanks to the verbal—and sometimes physical—brutality of people who see him as an oversized, grimacing freak rather than as the complex, funny, brilliant, unpredictable, entertaining fellow he is. They may not submit themselves helplessly on a daily basis to the side of grace and positivity and hope in humanity and progress simply to keep functioning and moving forward and looking to the future.

So, because they do not get it, I must forgive them. I must forgive the skepticism, the inherent criticism of my parenting or my choices or our use of a "label." They're not gonna get it, and right along with that, they're missing out on so much of the happiness we have in our lives thanks to our complex, fascinating, joyful children. As with everything else, there are tradeoffs here.

And that takes me to response category three, the responses I get from other parents of special needs children and from professionals who work with them. It's always been, "You're a member of our club. We get it."

I've had parents of special needs kids pick up right away on our son's differences. We laugh over the funnier commonalities of behaviors our children share. We commiserate over the anxieties these differences can bring to us and to our children, anxieties ironically not often borne of our children themselves but of how others receive and perceive them.

I cannot recall a single instance of a professional therapist or a special needs parent who queried our son's autism or questioned whether or not it was real or shrugged off his "label." Why? Because they get it. They know how important that label can be as a key to the special needs toolbox. They know what it means for people to stare when your child flaps or says something odd and without volume or tone modulation. They know what it means for others to blow off your child as a brat or needing a spanking or as a willful bully or just requiring a firmer hand (things don't get firmer than they do around here, I can assure you.)

And for them, rather than having to be forgiving, I am simply thankful. You all know who you are. You're the ones who, like us...just get it.

Getting to Know Your New Neighborhood: Reaching Out and Building a Network

Susan Walton

It's important to realize that you cannot cope with this new element of your life alone. And you shouldn't try. There is help out there for you, for your child, and for your family, and you should take advantage of it. In addition to uncovering the services and agencies that offer assistance, you want to find and keep the friends and professionals who will sustain you. And conversely, you may need to minimize your exposure to the people, feelings, and obstacles that drag you down.

First and foremost, your best allies are other parents who have a child on the spectrum. You can find existing parent networks through local support groups, parent clubs, assistance agencies, and online autism parenting forums in Yahoo! or Google Groups. Joining those groups is a great way to get started.

You will also need to build a more personal network. You shouldn't try to learn everything by yourself; that would waste valuable time. Other people already know what you need to know. They know where to find the best speech therapists, which local preschools welcome special needs kids and have the most caring teachers, and how to get the best results with your caseworker. When you connect with local parents who can share that kind of information, chances are that you'll find they become a safety net of emotional support as well.

Putting Your Best Foot Forward

Developing your own network may mean overcoming a sense of personal shyness, which can be difficult. If you are reserved about making contact with people you don't know or feel reticent about impinging on other people's privacy, the first stage of building a network can be the hardest part. You have to reach out more than you might otherwise, asking sometimes personal questions, talking to people sitting beside you in waiting rooms, and cold-calling references. If that falls outside your usual personality style, steel yourself to do it for your child. If you are more comfortable communicating in writing, you can use email as often as possible, but there is no substitute for the kind of parent-to-parent conversations that often reveal more than you'll learn through correspondence or official channels.

Some of your best contacts can be the people sitting in waiting rooms with you. You already have something in common with them, and you know something about each other if you are reading outdated magazines together. Try to strike up a conversation and compare notes on the provider or clinic you are there to visit. You can get a feeling for the other person's opinions: Are they compatible with yours? Have they noticed things that you missed? Do you admire their apparent confidence; their ability to seem relaxed? This could be a sign that they have been getting services for their child longer than you have. They may have good information to share, so put aside that aging copy of *People* magazine and trade stories. Are they as new to their diagnosis as you are to yours? Then they will understand what you are going through better than anyone else on the planet. Don't unload all your emotions, but make a connection. Try to keep your tears in check and remind yourself that their pain may be as fresh as yours. You can help each other most if you use your time to talk rather than weep.

I have friends whom I met sitting in waiting rooms during the first weeks following my son's diagnosis. When we looked at each other back then, our eyes told our whole story. We were all sick at heart and desperately trying to make sense of the news and figure out what to do. And it is amazing how strong we look to each other now. When we run into each other or find time for a coffee date, we see entirely different people looking back. Even as we are sharing news about the latest round of problems in our lives, the difference is amazing. We are in control and things are moving forward every day. We see battle-scarred but victorious soldiers in each other. These are valuable friends indeed.

Building a strong personal network of smart and experienced parents means taking good care of the network over time. You need to keep your eye on being a friend as well as using your friends. You'll find that no one is as sympathetic to the problems of your world as another parent who has been there. But you cannot forget to listen, too. And when you discover a great therapist or a wonderful babysitter, share the wealth!

And again, as raw as your pain may be, try to keep it in check when you meet new people. All too often, it is clear which parents are collecting themselves and trying to move forward and which are so overcome with grief that they are not ready to participate. The kind of parents you most want to know will be reading signals and gravitating towards others who will be the most positive contacts for them. Try as best you can to be one of the ones who can offer help as well as accept it. Put your brave face on and save personal meltdowns for close friends and family.

The Art of Self-Protection

Your child's diagnosis may change your relationship with your existing friends, and it is something you cannot prepare for or prevent. Anyone who has been through a difficult time will tell you that they discovered who their friends were and just how much they could be counted on. This situation is no different. Some people are uncomfortable around bad news and "don't know what to say." Others want to take the easy road in life and prefer to spend their time with peers whose kids are easier playmates. These are people you can let go of easily.

There are also those who can be unintentionally insensitive to what you are going through. They may mean well, but they do not understand the depth of your pain. These are friendships you may need to put on hold and reexamine when you feel stronger. If it is too painful to be around a friend who constantly gripes about how little Jimmy won't pick up his toys or eat his vegetables (at a time when you are wishing your little one would just call you Mommy), don't put yourself through it. Friends who invariably cause pain can drag you down. Protect yourself and place friendships on hold if they are hurting your mental health. Your own peace of mind is important during this time. Your family needs you, and they need you at your strongest. You can and should avoid putting yourself in situations that erode your confidence or your ability to carry on. Later, when you are ready, you can reopen those doors or not, as you prefer.

Sometime during the first year after my son's diagnosis, I took stock and realized that there were two kinds of conversations going on all too frequently. They were weighing me down like rocks. With some friends I was able to redirect to new topics, but I also needed to prune my network to avoid people who could not stop repeating the same fruitless conversations over and over.

The first was the "Why?" conversation, and you may know it. Was it the vaccines? Was it a preservative in the vaccines? Is autism environmental, hereditary, geographical? Does it run in my family or my husband's? Is it because I had fertility treatments, drank from a bad water supply? And so on.

For a time, this topic was at the forefront of my mind as well, and I engaged in it with equal enthusiasm. But I began to see how circular it was. The fact is that at this time, no one knows why people develop autism. All of the time I spent discussing it and comparing my own variables with others was time wasted. Instead of feeling ventilated, my sense of frustration and agony only increased.

The other kind of conversation that I had to stop was the frequent reliving of the grief. When you get news of a lifelong disability like autism, most people traverse the traditional stages: Denial, Anger, Bargaining, Depression, and Acceptance. It is a loss, a very real loss, of the future you wanted for your child. But deciding how, with whom, and when to share those feelings is a different equation for people. I met some wonderful parents who simply could not carry on any other kind of conversation with the intensity they put into talking about how awful it was that this had happened to their family. I felt sympathetic, but it was all I could do to cope with my own pain. I began to shy away from weepy, angry, or depressed people who were focused only on their pain and their problems. I began to seek out parents who were either containing their feelings or moving past them. We developed bonds that allowed us to share our pain in more appropriate doses over time, and those bonds outlasted the freshness of the pain.

The pierce of my own wounds eased when I focused on "what next?" instead of "where did I go wrong?" or "why us?" Moving forward should become the most important item on your list, and for a time you may have to be a little ruthless in how you choose your company. Even though you may be lying in bed at night wondering how this happened to you (was it the genes from your husband's odd uncle or your pregnancy craving for corn dogs?), you will get past that. The bottom line is that it has happened. You need a group of close friends or family to talk to about your pain. Try not to make it a day-to-day obsession or to burden new acquaintances with it.

Collecting Your "A" Team

Aside from your personal friends, there is another core group of people that you will assemble over the next year, and they may differ from the kinds of people you've had in your life until now. But your team will be composed of people and professionals who will be important to your family's continuing contentment.

The Core Team

You will assemble a group of professionals to rely on for therapy and medical services. Each member will have a particular role to fill, and his or her knowledge will contribute to the well-being and education of your child. Generally speaking (and this may differ from child to child, just as specific needs will differ from child to child), a core team for a child on the spectrum will involve:

- Pediatrician. Your child's medical doctor.

- Child Psychologist. An autism expert who can make a diagnosis and recommendations for appropriate treatment.

- Speech Therapist. Also known as an SLP or speech and language pathologist, this person will help your child learn to understand and use words.

- Occupational Therapist. A therapist who uses creative activity to treat physical and sensory issues.

- In-Home Specialist. A therapist who works in the home (or sometimes at school) to develop positive behavior techniques and life skills for people with autism.

With time, and depending on your child's issues, you may add others, such as a neurologist, a developmental pediatrician, a physical therapist, a play therapist, specialized doctors or nutritionists, or junior therapists and aides.

As you begin setting up and carrying out service relationships with therapists, remember that these professionals may go on to become a vital part of your child's learning as time goes on. They have a unique combination of professional expertise, direct knowledge of your child, and a detached perspective that no one else can provide. Over time you will get a sense of which providers are caring and dedicated versus those who are less concerned. You may get to know a great many people before you settle in with a core team, and even then you'll find that changes happen as your needs, your school district requirements, and other people's lives shift around you.

Parents ask, "Will this ever calm down? Will I ever be able to just relax?" The answer is twofold: Yes, things will settle down as your child's needs become clearer and therefore easier to address. Your team will become more familiar to your family, and the schedule will settle in. But you will probably never find that you can "just relax" when it comes to managing a team. Circumstances continually change, and you'll always need to be involved to make sure your child's therapy adjusts as his or her needs develop over time.

Getting to the Know the Pros

Cultivate relationships with the professional people you'd like to have as trusted advisers. That doesn't mean you should rush the fences and try to create friendships with the professionals on your team, because that wouldn't be in your child's best interests. You want these people to be focused on your child in their professional capacities and to be able to advise you about his or her needs. Frankly, you don't want to know about their personal problems any more than they want to hear about yours. Maintaining appropriate boundaries can be challenging, especially in the early days when you need these people so much and they seem to understand what you are facing better than so many other people in your life. But it is important to maintain the professional aspect of the relationship to keep the services they provide at their most valuable.

With that in mind, assist as they develop a bond with your child and encourage them to care. For that to happen, you'll have to provide important input.

Respect and appropriate professional behavior top the list. When your life is in turmoil, it can seem natural for everyone around you to make allowances. But if that continues for long, it will impact every relationship negatively. Always remember that for professional people, their time is their livelihood. Treat it respectfully and be careful never to abuse it.

The difficult part of these new professional relationships that center on your child is finding balance between respecting the opinions of others even as you maintain the ability to assert your own opinions. It is critical to remember that you know your child best. But these professionals may know autism and therapy practices that are new or strange to you.

Children with autism will behave differently with different people. They also may behave differently in different settings and under different sets of expectations. While a therapist may know a particular aspect of your child's personality, you know many, entirely different sides of your child with a depth they cannot match. That makes you the most important expert on your team. You want to be treated as such and to behave that way, too. You should express your opinions and feel able to make decisions that contradict professional advice if you believe it is the best thing to do.

Tips For Building Strong Professional Relationships

Never be late for appointments. Always call if you are unavoidably detained. Always cancel if you cannot attend. These are golden, unbreakable rules.

If you need extra time to talk about your child, say so at the beginning of an appointment so they can end the appointment earlier. Don't monopolize the therapist at the end if your time is up.

Respect their opinions in conversation.

Let them know you value their work with your child.

Remember to report back when you see progress at home that you can connect with their work.

Support them by letting them know that you'd like to know about what they are doing and how you can carry over techniques at home. But be realistic about what you can do and don't overpromise.

When you assert your own opinion over professional advice, do it respectfully, explaining why you hold the opinion you do, and including appropriate members of your team in decisions whenever possible. The team is there to help and support your efforts to teach your child. Each of them is important, but any therapist that does not treat you with respect or fails to consider your opinions is not a team member you want to keep.

If you find that a therapist treats you with condescension, or devalues you as "just the parent," then you are probably not working with the right provider. How professionals interact with you is as important a factor in developing a successful relationship as how they relate to your child. Often parents try to work around bad chemistry, thinking, "Even though I think she's awful, my little boy loves her." But it is usually a matter of time before the aggravation outweighs the benefit. It can be frustrating to wait a long time to get in with a professional only to find the chemistry is terrible. But it happens. You'll have to decide whether you can continue to see the provider during the time it takes to find a replacement, or if you must discontinue the relationship right away. Take stock by asking yourself if your child is benefiting from the time spent. If the answer is no, it's easy, and you know your next move. If the answer is somewhere in between yes and no (he's doing all right, but not nearly as well as he could be), then factor in other issues like how the appointment works with your schedule, how far the office is from home, or how unpleasant it is for you to go. Tally it up as impartially as possible and make a call. And refer always to Rule One: No intervention at all is better than bad intervention.

As you meet therapists and discover your own personality preferences, watch your child's reactions too. Most kids have a "type" and respond well to a certain profile. Knowing that type will be hugely helpful as you look for providers and ask around for advice as to who will work well on your team. Watch to see: Does your child respond best to "big" personalities, people who are entertaining and silly and put on a show? Or is this kind of person scary and unpredictable for him? Does he prefer a calm, soothing person who makes him feel safe? Perhaps she tends to warm up to women more than men, or acknowledges the authority of older therapists but tends to ignore younger people. My son could tell a tentative or inexperienced therapist a mile away, and he tended to take wild advantage of the lack of confidence. I had to be careful to avoid tentative personalities in roles that required occasional firmness. These are observations that you should note as you are exposed to a variety of styles and personalities.

Your child is accustomed to you and your style, as well to as your partner and other home relationships that have figured largely in his or her life up to now. He or she may seek adults who relate in similar ways to help make sense of relationships as a whole. This tendency can help you to find people compatible with you both. But don't rule out a particular type without giving it a try. In general I found that my son responded best to big personalities, people who were fun and vivacious. It was a tremendous surprise when we met our best speech therapist, a quiet, composed woman who communicated calm in her tone and manner. Rather than being under stimulated or bored by her style, my son responded by matching her calm and paying attention to her every word. She stayed within his receptive language boundaries and never overwhelmed him. It was wonderful to see the inception of what became a long and successful relationship. We didn't go ahead and fill his days with calm, quiet therapists, but the time he spent with this speech therapist was unique and a welcome change.

Your Autism Advice Network

In addition to professionals, you also need to be building your "autism advice network," a group of friends and support people who have more knowledge than you do. It is hugely helpful to be able to bounce ideas and trade resources with these contacts. Your autism advice network may contain members of your core professional team, but often it does not. It may contain certain personal friends, but not always. The autism advice network should be specifically composed of people who know about special education or autism. Often as not, they have a child on the spectrum themselves. These are parents who are moving confidently in the world you are joining. They have been building and managing a team, and learning the autism ropes, longer than you have. Their expertise and advice will be critical. These are your waiting room pals, your Yahoo! and Google Groups list-mates, and other special education contacts you meet along the way.

Dealing with Agencies and Bureaucracy

Last but not least, you will find yourself dealing with a host of new bureaucrats. There will be agency employees, school district officials, and possibly social workers who control funding and entrance to programs for individuals with disabilities in your area. One issue that new parents cannot help but feel is the sudden change in the family's privacy. In order to gain access to the services and support your child requires, you have to interact with a variety of people about your child's needs and your family's circumstances. You are asked questions that seem personal and sometimes even rude. You are queried about the level of support you get from your extended family, the income you make, the way you live. I wish I could offer good advice for the emotional difficulty this can create. But it is unpleasant and no one likes it.

Listening to strangers talk about your child and his or her deficits dispassionately can also be awful. If the people involved are untrained or insensitive, it can take every ounce of patience to maintain a pleasant facade. Some of these situations require balance and extreme patience. It might be necessary to listen to a certain amount of such talk in meetings and to endure the burn when a disinterested voice enumerates your baby's difficulties. But if you feel participants have gone from dispassionate to disdainful, you don't need to continue to endure. You are not required to submit to cruelty, and anyone doling it out should be confronted, reported, or dismissed, as you see fit. If you meet with such a bureaucrat, temper your reaction by sleeping on things overnight. If you wake feeling all the more convinced that your family's feelings have been misused, write a letter to the person's supervisor and copy another higher-up supervisor if possible. Take whatever action seems appropriate and recover that dignity. Even though we are constantly asked to submit to a heartless system, sometimes the best thing you can do for your child and for yourself is to be strong and insist on compassionate treatment. Advocacy for your child means balance: knowing when to submit and when to speak up. Discretion can be the better part of valor, but dignity is non-negotiable.

Jumping through hoops is part of working the system in your child's favor. Most people want amicable relationships with the contacts they expect to deal with regularly. But reality can also be that the squeaky wheel gets the grease. Even though you want a pleasant relationship, that doesn't mean that you need to be nice to the point of pain. If your own ability to endure and be patient is leading you to lose out on services or wait indefinitely for answers, go ahead and lose your cool! Even though an agreeable relationship is on your priority list, it falls well below getting your child what he needs. If you have to make a choice between being liked and getting help for your child, I wouldn't hesitate to suggest sacrificing popularity.

A common tactic with agencies that are strapped for funding is to play the Delay Game. Not a fun game at all! But every day that they don't answer your phone call is another day they don't have to pay for service. Every confusing answer that leads to another round of phone calls buys them more time. Some parents will get wise to this trick and hold the agency's feet to the fire more quickly. Others become victimized by the tactic and are strung along for months before getting some of what they need. Be in the savvy group. Never end a phone conversation without asking when the person will get back to you with the information you need or with the next step. If they refuse to be specific, let them know you will call in a day or two to see how they are doing. The bottom line is that you may need to get pesky and go beyond persistence to get past barriers. But you can do it. It is for your child.

Identifying and Avoiding Autism Cults

Shannon Des Roches Rosa

A child's autism diagnosis can mess with parents' heads. Media portrayals of children with autism and their adult spectrum-mates dwell too frequently on negatives and challenges, so when parents are told that their child is autistic, they are usually incredibly upset.

It doesn't help when doctors lack the bedside manner to soften the emotional impact of their diagnoses or have no information about contemporary autism therapies and resources. When that happens, parents are both freaked out and flapping in the wind. Their child's doctor was supposed to give them answers and guidance but instead upended their lives and then shoved them out the door. No one can explain why they have a child with autism, and they know nothing *about* autism. They are emotionally reeling, angry with the medical establishment, and hungry for any information that will help their child.

Most parents start researching autism treatments and quickly become overwhelmed by competing approaches, therapies, and programs. There is no primary autism authority to direct them, so the parents' decision-making process becomes fueled by desperation. Their critical-thinking skills degrade as they are asked to decide between evidence-based approaches that take time and effort, and unsupported testimonials promising recovery, and even cures. And they're still looking for someone to blame, even as they search for answers.

They are perfect targets for autism cults.

According to ex-"Moonie" and cult expert Diane Benscoter, cults rewire the brain via viral mimetic infections while bypassing critical thinking. According to Ms. Benscoter, cults provide:

> Easy ideas to complex questions [which] are very appealing when you are emotionally vulnerable. Circular logic takes over, and becomes impenetrable...The most dangerous part is that [the cult mindset] creates Us & Them, Right & Wrong, Good & Evil. And it makes anything possible, anything rationalizable.

Autism cult members ignore the one current reality about autism—that in most cases, its cause is currently untraceable—and position themselves as autism's truth-speakers, as fonts of uncompromised autism knowledge. They inappropriately promote biomedical approaches for all autistic children and undermine public confidence in vaccines. They support their claims not through evidence, but with exceptions. They make scientists and critical thinkers rage with indignation. They aggressively denounce skeptics and foster a culture of righteous true believers. They rarely talk about support, respect, and love for their autistic children in the present and focus instead on how "broken" their children are, or on their theoretical future nonautistic kids.

I understand how tempting it is to trust people who offer an outlet for all that pent-up post-diagnosis fury, and who dangle visions of cured children in front of your eyes when others offer improvements only through painstaking behavioral, speech, occupational, and other therapies, or recommend noncomplacent acceptance and awareness. It might be a temporary relief to stop thinking and succumb to those promises of turning the autistic child you have into the neurotypical one you assumed you would get—but it would also be a betrayal, because few children are as vulnerable or in need of clear-headed advocacy as those with autism.

The best investment you can make in your autistic child's future is a commitment to intense scrutiny of treatment options. Does an approach make sense, or do you just really, really want to believe it will help? Are there real risks and only possible benefits? Do data and studies support it? If so, are they from independent sources or biased ones? New autism parents need to work past their fear and confusion and embrace their critical reasoning skills. (If you need a skeptical thinking refresher, do an online search for Michael Shermer's Baloney Detection kit, which lists 10 criteria for evaluating questionable claims.)

Parents also need to systematically track their child's therapies, behaviors, and health so that they have the data to back up any decisions. Gut feelings and impassioned anecdotes are not reliable indicators of progress, despite autism cult members' declarations.

I wish someone had given me and my husband this frank advice after our son's diagnosis and prevented us from becoming one of those frustrated, susceptible post-autism-diagnosis couples, had helped us avoiding falling in with a moderate autism cult, Defeat Autism Now!, or DAN!.

I consider DAN! an autism cult because they generally recommend putting autistic children through their customized, costly, and rarely insured diet, supplements, and alternative medicine wringer whether the child is a legitimate candidate or not (review tales of children helped by DAN!-type methods and you'll almost always encounter kids who are physically ill in addition to their autism diagnoses; as their physical symptoms improve, their autism symptoms diminish). Think of it this way: Would you send your child to a doctor known to prescribe chemotherapy every single time he or she even suspected cancer? My husband and I wanted to believe that DAN! methods would help cure our son, but they didn't. It was irresponsible for our doctor to say they would and unethical for him to continue recommending them when it became obvious that our son wasn't a responder.

We embarked on our son's DAN! journey around the same time we started our son's home applied behavioral analysis (ABA) therapy program. We saw improvements from ABA right away and I thought I saw them from DAN!, too, probably because ABA's slow and steady gains were not as alluring as the magical thinking of DAN! I became fully invested in the DAN! protocol and was such a true believer that I would choose DAN! appointments over those for speech or occupational therapies. I even walked into my pediatrician's office and self-righteously lectured him about DAN! theories.

Our one roadblock to going full-DAN! was chelation—using the drug DMSA to leach excess mercury from our son's body. (This was in 2004, before the autism/mercury poisoning/vaccine theory was thoroughly discredited.) We trusted our DAN! doctor when he said that mercury was exacerbating our son's autism and intended to chelate once we'd researched the matter thoroughly. But our research (and that of our relatives) revealed nasty side effects, and we started to waffle and doubt.

Then my father-in-law, a former doctor with a reverence for scientific methodologies, spoke up about his chelation concerns, and we became even more skeptical. The chelator behind the curtain was finally revealed after our DAN! doctor tested our son's mercury levels, said they were low, and told us it was because mercury was being stored in his fats and needed to be chelated out. My husband asked what would be recommended if our son's mercury levels had tested high and got the reply, "Chelation." The test results didn't matter; the DAN! doctor was always going to recommend chelation. We could no longer suspend our disbelief and rejected chelation outright.

We tried to remain true to the rest of the DAN! protocol but became increasingly discomfited by ceaseless recommendations for new supplements, expense, and the lack of even a placebo effect. When our son's cobra-like reflexes resulted in cookie-based "challenges" to his special wheat-free, dairy-free (GFCF) DAN! diet, our diligent ABA data showed the transgressions didn't affect his health or behavior, at all. I started to wonder if my son might not get the miracle cure we'd been promised. Then we had another crack in the DAN! armor: our ABA program supervisor spent four months tracking my son's DAN! supplements versus his behaviors and determined that illness was the only variable that affected our son noticeably. Not diet. Not supplements.

We started to realize that DAN! diet and supplements affected nothing except our bank account. We stopped seeing our DAN! doctor, gradually took our son off the GFCF diet, and eventually abandoned all but the nutritionally significant supplements.

I guess that makes us the recovered ones, not our son.

Families of children with new autism diagnoses can avoid cultish mistakes like ours if enough veteran parents reach out to them and encourage them to choose logic over hype. We can help parents of newly diagnosed children with autism make careful choices and maximize limited resources. We can prevent them from taking their kids on expensive and emotionally propelled journeys to nowhere.

To do this, we need to be outspoken in identifying crusaders for fringe autism interests, and those who ignore autistic voices yet claim to speak for all autism families. We need to be vigilant in calling out misinformation, ignorance, and potentially harmful advice. And we need to keep our virtual doors open and welcome mats out because most of the families who fall into autism cults will eventually lose their faith and start looking for answers anew. They'll need to know where to find them.

Two days after I wrote this essay, my son had one of the best language days in his life: full sentences, descriptions, new constructions—and lots of them. It was jaw-dropping, but even so I applied rational thinking and reminded myself that, despite his delays, my son will naturally continue to develop and expand his skills. Yet if I were still following the DAN! protocol, I would likely be freaking out, trying to figure out which supplement and dietary modification had brought about his remarkable change.

Be careful about falling for an autism cult; you might never trust your own judgment again.

—

A version of this essay was originally published at BlogHer.com.

Welcome to the Club

Jess at Diary of a Mom

My Dear Friend,

I am so sorry for your pain.

Don't worry; no one else sees it, I promise. To the rest of the world, you're fine. But when you've been there, you can't miss it.

I see it in your eyes. That awful, combustible mixture of heart-wrenching pain and abject fear. God, I remember the fear.

I see it in the weight of that invisible cloak that you wear. I remember the coarseness of its fabric on my skin. Like raw wool in the middle of the desert. You see, it was mine for a time.

I never would have wanted to pass it on to you, my love. I remember so well suffocating under the weight of it, struggling for breath, fighting to throw it off while wrapping myself in its awful warmth, clutching its worn edges for dear life.

I know it feels like it's permanent, fixed. But one day down the line you will wake up and find that you've left it next to the bed. Eventually, you'll hang it in the closet. You'll visit it now and then. You'll try it on for size. You'll run your fingers over the fabric and remember when you lived in it, when it was constant, when you couldn't take it off and leave it behind. But soon days will go by before you wear it again, then weeks, then months.

I know you are staring down what looks to be an impossibly steep learning curve. I know it looks like an immovable mountain. It is not. I know you don't believe me, but step-by-step you will climb until suddenly, without warning, you will look down. You will see how far you've come. You'll breathe. I promise. You might even be able to take in the view.

You will doubt yourself. You won't trust your instincts right away. You will be afraid that you don't have the capacity to be what your baby will need you to be. Worse, you'll think that you don't even know what she needs you to be. You do. I promise. You will.

When you became a mother, you held that tiny baby girl in your arms and in an instant, she filled your heart. You were overwhelmed with love. The kind of love you never expected. The kind that knocks the wind out of you. The kind of all-encompassing love that you think couldn't possibly leave room for any other. But it did.

When your son was born, you looked into those big eyes and he crawled right into your heart. He made room for himself, didn't he? He carved out a space all his own. Suddenly your heart was just bigger. And then again when your youngest was born. She made herself right at home there, too.

That's how it happens. When you need capacity, you find it. Your heart expands. It just does. It's elastic. I promise.

You are so much stronger than you think you are. Trust me. I know you. Hell, I am you.

You will find people in your life who get it and some that don't. You'll find some that want to get it and some that never will. You'll find a closeness with people you never thought you had anything in common with. You'll find comfort and relief with friends who speak your new language. You'll find your village.

You'll change. One day you'll notice a shift. You'll realize that certain words have dropped out of your lexicon. The ones you hadn't ever thought could be hurtful, like, "Dude, that's retarded." Never again. You won't laugh at vulnerability. You'll see the world through a lens of sensitivity. The people around you will notice. You'll change them, too.

You will learn to ask for help. You'll have to. It won't be easy. You'll forget sometimes. Life will remind you.

You will read more than you can process. You'll buy books that you can't handle reading. You'll feel guilty that they're sitting by the side of the bed unopened. Take small bites. The information isn't going anywhere. Let your heart heal. It will. Breathe. You can.

You will blame yourself. You'll think you missed signs you should have seen. You'll be convinced that you should have known. That somehow, you should have gotten help earlier. You couldn't have known. Don't let yourself live there for long.

You will dig deep and find reserves of energy you never would have believed you had. You will run on adrenaline and crash into dreamless sleep. But you will come through it. I swear, you will. You will find a rhythm.

You will neglect yourself. You will suddenly realize that you haven't stopped moving. You've missed the gym. You've taken care of everyone but you. You will forget how important it is to take care of yourself. Listen to me. If you hear nothing else, hear this. You must take care of yourself. You are no use to anyone unless you are healthy. I mean that holistically, my friend. Healthy. Nourished, rested, soul-fed. Your children deserve that example.

A friend will force you to take a walk. You will go outside. You will look at the sky. Follow the clouds upward. Try to find where they end. You'll need that. You'll need the air. You'll need to remember how small we all really are.

You will question your faith. Or find it. Maybe both.

You will never, ever take progress for granted. Every milestone met, no matter what the timing, will be cause for celebration. Every baby step will be a quantum leap. You will find the people who understand that. You will revel in their support and love and shared excitement.

You will encounter people who care for your child in ways that restore your faith in humanity. You will cherish the teachers and therapists and caregivers who see past your child's challenges and who truly understand her strengths. They will feel like family.

You will examine and re-examine every one of your own insecurities. You will recognize some of your child's challenges as your own. You will get to know yourself as you get to know your child. You will look to the tools you have used to mitigate your own challenges. You will share them. You will both be better for it.

You will come to understand that there are gifts in all of this. Tolerance, compassion, understanding. Precious, life-altering gifts.

You will worry about your other children. You will feel like you're not giving them enough time. You will find the time. Yes, you will. No, really. You will. You will discover that the time that means something to them is not big. It's not a trip to the circus. It doesn't involve planning. It's free. You will forget the dog-and-pony shows. Instead, you will find fifteen minutes before bed. You will close the door. You will sit on the floor. You'll play Barbie® with your daughter or LEGO® with your son. You'll talk. You'll listen. You'll listen some more. You'll start to believe they'll be okay. And they will. You will be a better parent for all of it.

You will find the tools that you need. You will take bits and pieces of different theories and practices. You'll talk to parents and doctors and therapists. You'll take something from each of them. You'll even find value in those you don't agree with at all. Sometimes the most value. From the scraps that you gather, you will start to build your child's quilt. A little of this, a little of that, a lot of love.

You will speak hesitantly at first, but you'll find your voice. You will come to see that no one knows your child better than you do. You will respectfully listen to the experts in each field. You will value their experience and their knowledge. But you will ultimately remember that while they are the experts in science, you are the expert in your child.

You will think you can't handle it. You will be wrong.

This is not an easy road, but its rewards are tremendous. Its joys are the very sweetest of life's nectar. You will drink them in and taste and smell and feel every last drop of them.

You will be okay.

You will help your sweet girl be far better than okay. You will show her boundless love. She will know that she is accepted and cherished and celebrated for every last morsel of who she is. She will know that her Mama is there at every turn. She will believe in herself as you believe in her. She will astound you. Over and over and over again. She will teach you far more than you teach her. She will fly.

You will be okay.

And I will be here for you. Every step of the way.

With love,

Jess

—

This essay was originally published at www.adiaryofamom.wordpress.com.

2 Practical Advice for Autism Parents

As parents, we strive to give our children the best life they can have, then support them as adults to help them reach their potential.

—Jennifer Byde Myers

"Autistic" or "Person With Autism?"

Jean Winegardner

When I write my column "Autism Unexpected," for Washington Times Communities, I use the words "person with autism" and "autistic person" pretty interchangeably. Every once in a while, I get a comment telling me I should use "person-first" language, meaning I shouldn't use the word "autistic" to describe a person.

Because I've heard this criticism more than once, I feel it necessary to tell you that I not only use the word "autistic" intentionally but also thoughtfully and with purpose.

The theory behind person-first language ("person with autism") is that it recognizes the person before the disability and stresses that there is more to a person than just autism. I asked my blog readers and my Twitter followers which they preferred, and the majority, mostly parents of children with autism, reported that they prefer the person-first terminology.

Person-first language is an easy philosophy to accept. It makes complete sense, and I find it to be a perfectly reasonable way of thought. However, I tend not to prefer it. The reasons for rejecting person-first are more complicated but, I believe, equally valid.

I use the adjective "autistic" for several reasons. I have taken my cues from many autistic adults who self-identify as autistic. For these individuals, autism is simply a part of them that cannot be separated from who they are. Autism is, in a way, a description of how their brains work, not something that has been added to their being. Without autism, they would not be the same person; therefore, it is not something they have but rather something they are.

Autistic adult and autism activist Jim Sinclair wrote a very clear, articulate essay about why he dislikes person-first language. This essay lays out why he identifies as an autistic person, and his reasons are very similar to mine.

I use "autistic" because I don't see autism as an affliction but rather as a character or physical trait (such as blond, nice, intelligent, or short) or as a major life characteristic (such as religion or race). Often, person-first language refers to a disease: "living with cancer," "a person with lupus," or "has AIDS." I think this type of language, while not necessarily wrong, doesn't work with autism in that it tends to pathologize the condition, which I do not see as a disease but rather a way of being.

My entire goal with my son is to raise him as a proud autistic person. He is what he is, and that is wonderful. I want to teach him that his autism is a part of him that gives him the gift of being able to think differently. It also gives him challenges, and he needs to learn how to compensate for those shortcomings. But I don't want him to think he has this extra thing that makes him less.

I do understand many people don't care to hear their children referred to as autistic. I respect that. When referring to other people's children—or other adults for whom I don't know their preference—I almost always use the phrase "person with autism." For my own son, or when referring to people in a group, as I've mentioned, I use them interchangeably. Once my son is old enough to have a preference, I will follow his lead and refer to him as he sees fit.

I personally subscribe to a live-and-let-live philosophy. While my beliefs lie with "autistic," I tend to use whichever phrasing works better in my sentence. I also see many people feel passionately about person-first terminology. I would like to let these people know that, when I use the term "autistic," I am not doing so with derision, nor am I making a comment on you, your child, or the people you know with autism.

I have a tremendous amount of respect for people with autism and their caregivers, and no matter what terminology I use, that will never change.

——

This essay originally appeared in Washington Times Communities' "Autism Unexpected."

Feeding Issues and Picky Eaters

Judy McCrary Koeppen M.S., CCC-SLP

Having your child diagnosed with autism can be overwhelming. Adding to an already challenging parenting experience is that children with autism are often very picky eaters or have eating issues—yet many of those children's parents aren't aware that they may face this struggle. Having your child refuse to eat any foods that are not white and soft in consistency can be maddening, but as a speech therapist and parent, I've found that having a clear understanding of why a child self-limits his or her diet goes far in helping your child cope.

Eating is a multisensory experience. Each mouthful brings the possibility of a variety of flavors, textures, and temperatures. A feeding specialist would break this down further:

- **Flavors** include sweet, sour, salty, spicy, bitter, and neutral.

- **Textures** include crunchy, chewy, soft, mixed, puree, thick liquids, and thin liquids.

- **Temperatures** include cold, room temperature, warm, and hot.

In addition, we experience food odors and often the way foods feel in our hands. Many children who are picky or problem eaters may have Sensory Processing Disorder (SPD). In her book *The Out of Sync Child: Recognizing and Coping With Sensory Processing Disorder*, Carol Stock Kranowitz, M.A., defines SPD:

> Sensory Processing Disorder is difficulty in the way the brain takes in, organizes and uses sensory information, causing a person to have problems interacting effectively in the everyday environment...SPD is an umbrella term covering several distinct disorders that affect how the child uses his senses.

As I see it, a child with SPD may be hypersensitive, hyposensitive, or a mixture of both. The hypersensitive child may experience flavors, textures, temperatures, and smells to a degree that is not perceived by most others, or he or she may under-experience them. The smell and texture of grilled chicken may elicit the same noxious sensory response as being stuck in a room with skunk stench; the message the body will send is, *"Get out of here!"* The hyposensitive child may seek out strong flavors and crunchy, hard textures to make up for experiences he or she is missing. This child may like spicy food, sour flavors (lemon, vinegar), and only crunchy foods.

Food choices are based on individual children's sensory experiences. Foods providing a favorable sensory experience will be selected over those that provide a noxious sensory experience. Because a child with SPD can have eating experiences that are altered and different from that of their parents, it can be very difficult to understand the child's preferences.

Children with autism can have SPD, but autism has its own factors that can contribute to picky eating. Children with autism are often uncomfortable with a change in routine. This preference for sameness can show up at mealtime as well. Children may want foods to be from the same container, the same brand, served on the same plate. So they may want a steady diet of a certain brand of chicken nuggets (no other brand), a certain brand of raspberry tea (only from a bottle with that logo), and a certain brand of vanilla yogurt (no other brand or flavor), served on the same plate.

Eating involves the integration of a variety of sensory experiences and is influenced by the "mealtime experience." So what is a "typical" eater and when is eating a problem?

The Continuum of Eating Type

A "typical eater" will usually:

- Eat a variety of foods
- Show interest in foods
- Tolerate the presence of new foods and try new food

A "picky eater" can:

- Have aversions to some foods, but still eat a variety
- Eat foods from each texture group and food group
- Tolerate the presence of new food
- Be willing to touch or try new foods

A "resistant" or "problem" eater will often:

- Eat fifteen to twenty foods or fewer
- Refuse one or more food groups (often preferring carbohydrates)
- Refuse one or more texture type (often preferring crunchy or soft foods, not both)
- Tantrum or melt down at meal times
- Prefer one flavor (often sweet or salty)
- Prefer strong flavors or bland flavors
- Prefer foods of the same color
- Prefer certain foods to always be the same brand.
- Gag when trying new foods
- Display anxiety over the presence of new foods on his or her plate, on the table, or even in the room
- Find the smell of certain foods to be noxious

A child who may become a problem eater often starts to refuse foods when parents introduce chunky baby food. The combination of a solid requiring chewing and puree (or liquid) that does not require chewing is often perceived as noxious. This can play out in a child refusing to eat vegetable soup of diced vegetables and broth but then eating the same soup when pureed. Many fresh fruits can present the same way. Citrus fruits, watermelon, ripe peaches, and pears consist of a solid and juice combination. These are also often refused. Children may have "food jags" where they will request and eat the same food at every meal. The problem with this is that often children will suddenly refuse this food. For a child with a severely limited diet, the elimination of a key diet item can be problematic.

What parents of problem eaters need to understand is that they did not create the feeding problem. Problem eating is the result of very real physical and neurological responses on the part of the child. Usually, the parent of a problem eater has continually offered their child a large variety of healthy foods. When given the choice of a food perceived as noxious or not eating at all, these children will choose not to eat. They would do so over consecutive meals if made to. Withholding food or physically forcing a child to eat is never a successful method to get them to eat. In her book *How to Get Your Kids to Eat...But Not Too Much*, Ellyn Satter defines the role of a "good parent" when feeding one's children:

> "Good parents are responsible for feeding their children...*Parents* and *professionals* working with children are responsible for preparing and providing a well balanced meal at an appropriate schedule and setting. The *child* is solely responsible for whether they eat and how much they eat."

What You Can Do

- Create the best schedule and setting for successful eating.
- Have meals and snacks at predictable times. A written or picture schedule can be helpful.
- Insist on eating and drinking at the table during snacks and meals.
- Offer water to drink between meals.
- *No grazing*. If children are allowed to eat throughout the day, they will not be able to regulate sensations of hunger and satiation. They may also snack on preferred foods during the day to fill themselves and eat fewer healthier foods at meal time.

- Rotate foods and when they are served. For example, if a child can predict always having a large glass of milk before bed, he or she will eat fewer foods offered earlier in the day.

- Mealtime should be a non-stressful experience for a child. Stress decreases appetite, and children will avoid mealtime if the they perceive it as a stressful time.

- Don't use dessert as reward, because doing so reinforces the idea of having to eat "bad food" to get "good food." Incorporate small amounts of dessert items into meals.

- It's okay to leave food.

- Mix food choices up. It is okay to have pancakes for dinner.

- If needed, post behavior rules (written or pictured) near the table. For example, no throwing food.

- Include preferred foods at every meal.

- Be a model. Eat with your children. Talk about the foods and their textures, flavors, smells, etc.

- Have children participate in meal planning and preparation as is developmentally appropriate. Include them in shopping, choosing foods, preparing and cooking foods, setting the table, serving food, etc.

- Let children choose the plates and cups they use at mealtimes.

- Redefine "success." Children are taking risks and showing progress when they do any of the following with new foods: smell, touch, poke with a fork, touch to lips, touch to chin, or lick. Even tolerating a new food in the same room or on the table is success. All of these activities are worthy of big praise. It is important to recognize these as signs of success, even though the child may have not actually taken a bite.

- PRAISE, PRAISE, PRAISE any participation in food-related experiences.

- Rethink what foods to offer.

The "Food Chaining" method for working with problem eaters looks at the individual child's eating habits. In their book *Food Chaining: The Proven 6-Step Plan to Stop Picky Eating, Solve Feeding Problems, and Expand Your Child's Diet,* Cheri Fraker, Mark Fishbein M.D., Sibyl Cox, and Laura Walbert offer a common-sense approach to dealing with problem eaters. In short, an analysis of a child's eating is done by looking at the characteristics of he or her preferred foods. Characteristics examined include: food groups, flavors, and textures. Foods that are highly similar to the preferred foods are selected to be introduced. I have had wonderful success in my practice using this approach.

An additional approach that has had excellent success is the Sequential Oral Sensory (SOS) feeding program created by Dr. Kay Toomey. This program integrates sensory, motor, oral, behavioral/learning, medical, and nutritional factors and approaches to comprehensively evaluate and manage children with feeding/growth problems. It is based on the "normal" developmental steps and skills of feeding. Information on this approach is available to professionals (and possibly parents) who attend SOS training.

What Else Can I Do?

- Consult your pediatrician and/or nutritionist with concerns regarding adequate growth, nutrition, and hydration.
- Continue to educate yourself about SPD and problem eaters.
- Seek out support from other parents of problem eaters.
- Incorporate developmentally appropriate food experiences and education into your child's day, such as songs about food ("Apples and Bananas") and children's books about food and eating.
- Play with plastic foods. Sort by food groups, create pretend balanced meals, and so on.
- Paint with food. Make potato or melon stamps to use with paint.
- Use carrot, celery, and other foods to paint with condiments.
- Avocado (or banana) can be cut up, peeled and squished to use as finger paint or "shaving cream."
- Load and dump toy trucks with various crackers or nuts. Talk about textures, colors, and smells.
- Create a picture by gluing dry foods on paper (crackers, dry roasted soy nuts, dried fruit, freeze dried fruit).
- Make necklaces of diced, pierced fresh, or dried fruits and veggies.
- Look at and experience foods in various forms: whole carrot with greens, peel the carrot, shred it, dice it, cook it, carrot juice, freeze-dried carrots (also works with apples, peaches).

Professional Help

Quite often, parents need to seek out professional help for their children. When pursuing an evaluation and treatment, it is important to find a feeding specialist who has experience with problem eaters. Some speech language pathologists and occupational therapists have specialized instruction in feeding problems or problem eaters. Ask to have a phone consultation with a therapist to gain information about the approach he or she uses. While the use of one-to-one reinforcement for eating a new food (for example a bite of non-preferred saltine cracker earns a bite of preferred fish cracker) can be acceptable, forcing a child to eat is never acceptable. These therapy services can be expensive, and it is reasonable to ask a therapist about his or her approach, training, and experience with problem eaters.

References

Ernsperger, Lori, and Tania Stegen-Hanson. *Just Take a Bite: Easy, Effective Answers to Food Aversions and Eating Challenges!* Arlington: Future Horizons, 2004.

Ernsperger, Lori, and Tania Stegen-Hanson. *Finicky Eaters: What to Do When Kids Won't Eat.* Arlington: Future Horizons, 2005

Fraker, Cheri, Mark Fishbein M.D., and Sibyl Cox. *Food Chaining: The Proven 6-Step Plan to Stop Picky Eating, Solve Feeding Problems, and Expand Your Child's Diet.* New York: Marlow and Company, 2007.

Kranowitz, Carol Stock, M.A). *The Out-of-Sync Child: Recognizing and Coping with Sensory Processing Disorder.* New York: Penguin, 2005.

Morris, Suzanne Evans, and Marsha Dunn Klein. *Pre-Feeding Skills: A Comprehensive Resource for Mealtime Development.* Texas: Pro-ed, 2000.

Piette, Linda. *Just Two More Bites! Helping Picky Eaters Say Yes to Food.* New York: Crown Publishers, 2006.

Satter, Ellyn. *How to Get Your Kids to Eat...But Not Too Much.* New York: Bull Publishing, 1987.

Websites
Roon, Erin, M.A. "Picky Eater or Problem Feeder?" March 31, 2008. *www.buzzle.com/articles/picky-eater-or-problem-feeder.html*

www.sensory-processing-disorder.com/picky-eaters.html

The Sequential Oral Sensory (SOS) feeding program. *www.educationresourcesinc.com/index.cfm?event=CourseDetails&CategoryID=11&CourseID=116*

Mealtime Challenges and the Autism Spectrum. Marsha Dunn Klein, M.Ed., OTR/L. Mealtime Connections, LLD, 2009. *www.mealtimeconnections.com*

Children's Books
Brown, Marc (1997). *D.W. the Picky Eater.*

Elhert, Lois (1996). *Eating the Alphabet.*

Fleming, Denise (1996). *Lunch.*

Tenzyk, Judy (2009). *Mommy What Do Carrots Do? A Children's Book on Food.*

Sensory Seekers and Sensory Avoiders

Hartley Steiner

For our purposes here, I am going to list sensory-seeking and sensory-avoiding behaviors to paint a more accurate picture of what sensory-based behaviors look like. You can consider these as "symptoms" or a "checklist," but my real goal in listing them is to help parents and caregivers recognize the sensory challenges for the children in their lives. In addition, I hope to paint a more specific picture of the kinds of behaviors that sensory seekers exhibit.

I completely ignored the first person who suggested Gabriel had Sensory Processing Disorder (SPD). I even made fun of her; how stupid was she to suggest my son had sensory issues? My kid wasn't one of those children who covered his ears at every little noise; nope, not my kid. My kid was fine with loud noises, loved water, mud, hot salsa, and was not afraid of anything—okay, besides bees. I had a child who would climb to the tippity-top of a play structure—and stand on top of it. No, my kid was not at all averse to sensory stimuli—as a matter of fact, he couldn't get enough. I didn't understand how that could be a sensory processing problem.

When I finally gave in to our psychologist, an embarrassing full year later, and read the book *The Out of Sync Child,* it became much clearer that my son did indeed have SPD and was continually seeking input. I had no idea that SPD included sensory seekers. I thought that all children with sensory issues were avoiders; I couldn't have been more wrong.

There are two types of people with sensory issues: *Avoiders,* who seek to escape sensory input, and *Seekers,* who cannot get enough noise, touch, texture, and other sensory inputs. But I think many people still share my initial misconception. It can be easier to understand kids who avoid input—too much noise, too much touch, too much texture—than to understand kids who can't get *enough.*

Avoiders tend to get labeled as "fussy," "sensitive," "picky," or "spoiled." Seekers are often considered "behavior problems," "hyperactive," "difficult," "stubborn," "coddled." Many of us parents have been blamed, told our kids need more discipline, or that they are "in need of a good spanking."

These are not complete lists, but they're a starting point:

Here are some things you might notice about a sensory seeker:

- Spins
- Climbs too high
- Climbs everything
- Crashes into things (people, furniture, walls)
- Mouths/licks inedible things (furniture, toys, body)
- Chews inedible things (clothing)
- Eats excessively
- Constantly wrestles with siblings
- Touches everything
- Plays with food
- Eats messily
- Overstuffs their mouth
- Eats spicy/hot foods
- Under-responds to pain ("shakes it off" quickly)
- Dumps out toy bins just to look at everything
- Engages in excessive sensory play (mud, water, soap, etc.)
- Jumps
- Pushes
- Runs barefoot
- Chews on his or her toothbrush
- Does not sit still at his or her desk
- Falls out of his or her chair for no apparent reason
- Seeks loud noises (turns up TV, battery toys against ears, vacuum)
- Fails to monitor his or her own volume (you constantly say, "Stop yelling!")
- Smells everything, even bad smells

Sensory avoiders are probably what comes to mind when people think of a child with sensory issues: the child with his hands over his ears. But there is more to it than that. These children can have sensory challenges with even the basics in life: eating, dressing, bathing. The sensations from day-to-day living can interrupt an avoider child's functioning and make it nearly impossible for him or her to learn or socialize appropriately.

Here are some things you might notice about a sensory avoider:

- Is a picky eater (prefers one texture or basic flavors)
- Covers ears at noise (hates vacuum, blender, hand dryers)
- Avoids touch (not a "huggy" or "cuddly" kid)
- Hates tags/seams in clothing
- Won't wear shoes (or prefers only one shoe type)
- Avoids messy activities (mud, sand)
- Avoids art activities like painting or Play-Doh®
- Walks on toes
- Doesn't engage in playground activities (climbing, swinging, etc.)
- Hates a wet/dirty diaper/underwear
- Dislikes having people too close
- Refuses to take a bath/shower or play in the sprinkler
- Hates water on his or her face
- Hates/refuses to brush his or her teeth
- Complains about smell
- Complains that normal light is too bright (wanting to wear sunglasses)
- Over-responsive to pain (everything hurts!)
- Avoids/refuses stickers/fake tattoos

Although most kids tend to fall primarily on one side or the other, many kids have experiences in both avoiding and seeking. And there are more examples of both avoider and seeker behaviors on the Red Flags for SPD checklist (*www.spdfoundation.net/redflags.html*). If your child is not diagnosed with SPD but has many of these behaviors, please seek a good occupational therapist trained in sensory integration techniques to consult with your family.

Sensory issues are on a continuum: some kids avoid nearly all sensory stimuli, and some kids seek excessive amounts of sensory stimuli. And many kids do a combination of both, depending on their "arousal" level; it is a constant balancing act to get the input just right. My son Gabriel is primarily a seeker yet often gets overstimulated and requires some down time to regroup to be "calm and organized."

Gabriel will climb anything, eat anything (with hot sauce added), loves deep pressure input, and can spin and spin forever. But at the end of a school day, he becomes an avoider—he is already exhausted and melts down at the smallest sound from his brothers—even a normal speaking voice can be a problem. His body just can't handle more input, and my usually "sensory-seeking" kid is yelling at his brothers to "*shut up!*" while pressing hands against his ears so hard you would think we were blaring an air horn at him.

The solution for Gabriel is simple: he needs less input to bring himself back to neutral. But the sensory challenges for each child are different; hence, the solution for each child is different. What *is* constant is the balancing act of trying to control the amount, intensity, and duration of sensory input coming into his or her body. This is no easy task for a child (or a parent).

Understanding the significant differences between seekers and avoiders can help not just parents who are trying to raise a child with sensory issues, but all caregivers—teachers, coaches, babysitters, and daycare providers. Increased understanding of sensory-seeking and sensory-avoiding behaviors allows everyone to better understand our kids.

When Medication Is the Right Choice

Jennifer Byde Myers

Jack is asleep in my bed right now. He wandered in while I was folding clothes; I pulled back the covers and asked if he wanted to snuggle. He's nonverbal, but he made a happy sound I know is a yes, and from across the room he leapt in, buried his head under the pillows, and fell back asleep as I returned to my unmatched socks.

It's hard to believe that he's the same boy who as a three-year-old didn't sleep for fifty-two days. *Fifty-two days* where he didn't rest longer than twenty or thirty minutes in a row, and no more than one to two hours in a twenty-four-hour period—screaming and thrashing the entire time between conking out. It's an example—the worst one—of what we call "episodes," what appeared to be pain from unknown source, and it happened every five to six weeks for nine to eleven days straight. "Episodes" meant severe agitation, self-injurious behavior, and complete inability to respond to any request; he was uncomfortable in his own skin. Without sleep we all turned gray and haggard.

We've come a long way at our house. Jack has grown and learned and changed, and we've all developed better coping skills.

We also found the right medications.

Jack's first diagnosis was benign congenital hypotonia, which we eventually got upped to cerebral palsy (ataxia). In those early years, most people—teachers, family, and therapists—focused more on his physical disability than any behavioral or academic issues, so the flapping, the avoiding eye contact, the spinning plates and tapping forks—the autism diagnosis—came later.

Along the way, Jack had multiple evaluations, including brain scans (MRIs), examinations of his cerebrospinal fluid, and genetic screens. Other than an early test that showed "delayed myelination"—his nerves weren't growing conductive sheaths on schedule—the tests were inconclusive. The results didn't give us much guidance as to how to help Jack make the most of his gifts and minimize his challenges, and we were all at a loss as to how to help Jack through his episodes. We suffered. He suffered more. We tried changing his diet, his sleep schedule, his curtains. We tried over-the-counter remedies, pain relievers.

Jack started kindergarten in the fall of 2005, a few months before he turned five. It wasn't our idea, but our school district's, and it wasn't a particularly successful transition from his preschool/early intervention setting. We thought he wasn't ready since he wasn't able do some simple precursors to a successful placement, like walk from classroom to library to lunchroom without dropping to the ground. He couldn't ride the school bus without trying to get out of his seat belt and wander the bus. He couldn't engage in classroom activities like circle time without bouncing up to pace around the classroom. But it was more than not being ready for kindergarten. We came to realize that these were internally driven behaviors, ones he could not control, not even with a 1:1 aide.

Ironically, I think the idea of seeking medication for our son came out of my reading a magazine article discussing the over-medication of America's youth. As I read the descriptions of ADD and ADHD, it was a checklist of so many of my son's behaviors.

Eventually, considering his difficulty at school and at home, we decided to consider psychoactive medications to help Jack. And as much as we believe in science, in the power of medicine, it still wasn't an easy decision for us as a family. One of the things that made the decision difficult for me was the judgments I heard all the time, everywhere, about the use of these medications for children. I can't do much about radio and talk show guests—I've learned to pretty much ignore them anyway—but it was hard to ignore the harshest critics: other moms, some in my social circle, especially those with kids on the spectrum.

Some of these moms believe in the "toxins cause autism" myth. Or if they skipped over that argument, they might call parents who turn to medications "lazy," choosing to define my son's adverse neurochemistry and the resulting behaviors as being the fault of non-parenting or bad parenting. And of course, I've been questioned for "putting all those drugs" in my child.

As a culture, we are generally okay medicating other medical issues children face, aside from those who have a religious reason for not seeking medical intervention. If my child had diabetes, you certainly wouldn't tell me to deny the kid insulin. You might even suggest I have an insulin pump implanted under my child's skin to have a more regulated drip of the necessary drug. Why would a parent be so quick to take care of diabetes but not want to try a potentially life-altering drug a with a half-life of two to four hours? It is out of the child's system by the next day! You could know in two hours if your child feels better, can concentrate, can sit in class, or can go out to dinner. If the child is verbal, a parent could know in an afternoon how to improve their child's life because your child could *tell* you that they felt better, calmer, and more able to focus on classwork.

My husband and I began the discussion together, and then included our extended family of psychologists, scientists, plus a social worker and an elementary school teacher. With their contributions and our own research, my husband and I were ready for our first step: consulting with our pediatrician.

She agreed that our son might benefit from pharmacological intervention. While she has guided our family through many harrowing turns, she was also willing to refer us to doctors and specialists with greater expertise in certain aspects of our son's health, which we appreciated. In this case, she made an excellent recommendation to a child psychiatrist with a tremendous amount of experience in prescribing psychoactive medications for complex children. Because our son is nonverbal, it was very important to me that we get a doctor with a lot of pediatric experience; I didn't want a doctor for adults doing any more guessing than necessary.

We like this psychiatrist. He has a great knowledge of pharmaceuticals and explained at length the differences between the various medications and their side effects. In addition to drawing on his clinical experience, he gave us guidance from the research literature, with just a touch of the anecdotal.

The right doctor can make all the difference with our kids, just like the right teacher can make a class successful. It took some experimentation to get the medication timing and dosage right, so in the beginning, the psychiatrist made himself available for phone consultations. He recommended our son start with a stimulant medication commonly used in treating ADHD and try it in a short-acting, low dose. It was wonderful to be able do a short trial (three days, in different environments) to see if this type of drug could help Jack manage some of his symptoms.

Once we knew that this class of drugs would work, we looked for the best way to give Jack the appropriate dose that would last the course of the day. We placed him on the medication for one month and visited the doctor again. After describing the changes in his behavior, we tried adjusting the dose downward, to see if we could get the same results with a lower dose of the drug.

I think we have figured out the right dose for Jack. Our psychiatrist was very specific, "You should not see a zombie. You should not see a flat child. It should be your child, with your child's personality, who is able to focus on the teacher a bit longer, able to sit still long enough to complete assignments. Children who look like they are drugged are being prescribed too much." Once we got the prescription nailed down, we visited the psychiatrist every six months to ensure that we did not need to make adjustments.

My son, with medication, is more available. Jack is able to be present in the classroom, follow some directions, and learn, and he can also sit nicely enough to eat meals at a table. He can even manage to use a fork (preloaded by us). The second day he was on his medication, we were able to take him to brunch, in public, at a restaurant—an activity we had given up on. He was not drugged-out or a zombie at the table. Instead, he was a smiling boy who was able to sit for nearly an hour, eating with his extended family, without stimming out of control, grabbing the tablecloth off the table, or spinning plates. We already had a limited number of activities that were successful for our multigenerational family, and if eating had been taken away from that list, it would have reduced his interaction with grandparents dramatically. This might seem silly, but our family—well, one thing we actually do together is, we eat. It's something everyone can do. It makes us feel safe.

This wasn't the end of the medication story for my son; it rarely is for psychoactive medications. Children grow, the dosages need to be adjusted, some medications lose efficacy over time. This is the norm and where many people get discouraged. And though I knew that this might happen, it was still surprising a year later when we saw behavior changes, and it took me at least a week to figure out why it was happening.

We started having very rough afternoons. Jack couldn't sit for dinner, couldn't be in small room with his sister without kicking her, and couldn't follow any type of direction. We also saw tears and temper tantrums—he was nearly beside himself every afternoon, throwing his body to the ground.

Basically, the extended release was wearing off as he got home from school. It was the perfect storm: Jack had an expectation of how he feels all day, and it was gone. I had an expectation of how many directions he can follow, and he couldn't follow any. I was tired from being me all day, and, of course, we have "the Four o'clocks" at our house like so many families do. So we gave Jack an additional dose of a shorter-release form of the same medication in the afternoon. He quickly gained control of his emotions and his body until bedtime. Phew.

On a new medication, a year later, my son was still happy, available to learn in school, with less stim behavior. He went to sleep-away camp. He went on road trips. He played gently with his baby sister.

Later, in consultation with the psychiatrist, we added a second daily medication. Our son was having bouts of inconsolable crying and agitation, which sometimes added to his sleep issues. The psychiatrist suggested an anti-depressant, which has smoothed out the agitation and reduced the crying jags. Again we made adjustments, increasing over the course of a year, and more recently decreasing the dose to see how he responded. And although we went back to that original dose, we will try again in another year and will continue to evaluate each medication to make sure he is never on more or less than he needs.

There's a third medication we use as needed, for migraines. At some point, we all put it together that Jack might be having terrible headaches. I have migraines, as do several people in our family, on both sides. We added an anti-migraine medication to be used when his behavior indicates he may be experiencing a migraine, or when we thought a migraine was imminent, based on his behavior. The medication has made a huge difference for my son and for our whole family. And those "episodes" of days and days without sleep are now gone, or at least drastically diminished—as long as we get him his migraine meds as soon as we see the symptoms that had always been there along with the thrashing and restlessness: light avoidance, pressing his head into the pillow, lack of appetite.

Our life—his life—has been made so much better because of medications. He can function, we can do things as a family, travel on planes, visit other families' homes. Still, every time I open the cupboard and see the little brown bottles, I have mixed feelings. I feel a little shame, somehow my emotions clouded by all the times I've heard people malign parents who put children on psychoactive meds. I also feel a little pride, because my husband and I didn't just buy into underinformed declarations like, "that's the way it is with autism," but worked with our son's treatment team to get medications that have changed his life for the better. Mostly, I feel relief that my child is happier, more present, and ultimately more included since he began taking medications a few years ago.

As parents, we strive to give our children the best life they can have, then support them as adults to help them reach their potential. These medications don't "fix" Jack or alleviate all of his frustrations or remove all of the barriers his body or society has put before him, but they give him a better chance to participate, perhaps a little boost to help level the playing field. And these drugs are not one-size-fits-all; my son's autism is different from that of his classmates, and he'll be different when he is a teenager, and when he's an adult. Choosing a doctor, finding the right medications— I know it's not a one-time outlay of emotion and time. It will be a life-long affair but one that will be worth every minute of research if it makes his life a little easier, a little richer.

These medications allow him to have access to more information, more environments, and more relationships so he can do what we all want to do: learn and grow and love.

Outings, Travel, and Autism

Shannon Des Roches Rosa

We are adamant about taking Leo on as many excursions as we can, to stores, movies, restaurants, parks, and other destinations—including holiday visits with relatives. He is an able-bodied and energetic boy, and he likes a good adventure as long as we respect the limits of his tolerance. Also, we want Leo to be a boy-about-town so he gets used to being part of our community, and our community gets used to him.

Outings and trips aren't always easy. But I have no intention of leaving Leo home when we might succeed. I do not care if other people think he behaves strangely or makes funny noises; as long as he is not harming or interrupting anyone, we carry on with heads raised, meeting strangers' stares with confident and unapologetic smiles that I will admit to having practiced in the bathroom mirror.

Here are some of the tactics that make excursions with Leo, and hopefully some of his friends, a bit easier.

Go Early, Go Off-Season

We arrive at popular local destinations like aquariums, science centers, and amusement parks right when the doors open, and we go elsewhere during summer. We do this to avoid crowds. People with autism don't always do well in mobs, especially if they are bolters who like to run away and disappear into throngs, cannot tolerate crowd noise and jostling, need extra time to navigate, have gear that requires extra space, or—like Leo—just take up a lot of room.

Plan Ahead

If you're worried about a new excursion, try searching the knowledgeable souls on autism and special needs parenting email lists (including lists for your destination) or social media spaces. Tell people what your child's needs are and ask after positive experiences. You should get some good suggestions. Some museums and science centers have special events or extra hours or will even arrange special tours for visitors with special needs.

Be Open to Failure

Success to me means going out on top. When Leo shows signs of stress beyond that which can be cajoled or negotiated with special-occasion treats, it's time to go—my son does not deserve to be someone else's cautionary horror show. I am okay with leaving theaters mid-movie if need be—we can always come back later and try again.

Leo once had a spectacular meltdown at Costco. I had all three kids with me, it was the late afternoon witching hour, we took too long because I needed to buy too many items, and the checkout people were passing out balloons that Leo's baby sister wanted but I couldn't accommodate. She started crying, which has always been a trigger for her brother. Leo went ballistic: hitting, screaming, stomping. I'm not sure how we made it back to the car.

And we went back the next week and everything was fine. Because of our spectacular failure, I had learned what not to do.

Take Advantage of Anything That Will Make Your Outing Easier

If you don't already have a disabled parking placard (rear-view mirror hanger to use as needed) and you think you might ever need one, get it. I haven't turned in our signed application, but there have been a few times when we've had to do an emergency extraction of a howling thrashing boy, and it wasn't really safe for us to haul him across a parking lot. I really should get that placard, as should you. I know you won't abuse it.

Lots of places such as Disneyland have special passes for kids with autism or other special needs. Call ahead to find out what your destination can do for you. I am often pleasantly surprised by existing accommodations.

Have an Escape Plan

Park as close to your destination as possible. Disabled parking and parking in general can be limited at popular destinations, which is one more reason to arrive early.

If you're going with a group, consider taking two cars. It's nice if everyone doesn't have to leave when one child is ready to go.

Scope Out Quiet Areas for Recharging

Whenever we arrive at a place for more than the shortest of visits, it is critical for my son to have some downtime so he can mentally recalibrate and we can stay longer. Scoping out such places is always a high priority.

ID Your Kids

Few things frighten me more than the thought of my nonconversational boy getting away from me and being found by unequipped strangers. So, I got Leo a med-alert bracelet from Oneida Medical Jewelry. He hated the bracelet at first, but as he's a battle-picker, he soon tolerated it (this will not be the case for all kids, especially those with sensory issues). He outgrew it rather quickly, so I recommend a secondary backup solution like Safety Tats for backup ID.

I also tend to dress Leo in bright colors so I can spot him more easily should he dive into a crowd.

Distractions and Treats

We always bring along activities so Leo will have something to do if our outing involves downtime, as it does when eating at a restaurant or staying with relatives for the holidays. His current first choice for independent play is his iPad, but we also keep an activity-filled backpack in the car—where it stays, so the activities remain special and thoroughly engaging.

If You're Going to Fly, Know Your Rights

I never pass up an opportunity to cite my favorite section of the U.S. Department of Transportation's official policy of Nondiscrimination on the Basis of Disability in Air Travel:

SUBPART C—REQUIREMENTS CONCERNING SERVICES
382.31 Refusal of transportation.

> *(a) Unless specifically permitted by a provision of this part, a carrier shall not refuse to provide transportation to a qualified individual with a disability on the basis of his or her disability.*

> *(b) A carrier shall not refuse to provide transportation to a qualified individual with a disability solely because the person's disability results in appearance or involuntary behavior that may offend, annoy, or inconvenience crewmembers or other passengers.*

Being Around Excursioning Kids with Autism

I recently told the very nice salesperson at a destination gift shop that we'd arrived early because Leo couldn't tolerate crowds. Her perk turned to pity, and she looked at me like I'd said we'd accidentally run over a kitten. If my eyes had been daggers, she would now be perforated.

If you need to, remind people around you that kids with autism are still kids. That they might not look or act like stereotypical, regular kids, but that no one should assume they need different treatment. I love it when people talk to Leo like they would any other child and understand that if they need to modify their approach, I'll let them know.

Good luck, and happy trails!

———

A version of this essay was originally published at BlogHer.com

Preventing Meltdowns:
Outsmarting the Explosive Behavior of Individuals
with Autism Spectrum Disorders

Judy Endow, MSW

Meltdown behavior is quite common for those with Autism Spectrum Disorders (ASDs). And indeed, the most frequently asked question by parents and educators is "What do I do when my child has meltdowns?"

When the meltdown is occurring, the best reaction is to ensure the safety of all concerned. Know that explosive behavior is not planned but instead is most often caused by subtle and perplexing triggers. When the behavior happens, everyone in its path feels pain, especially the child.

Stages of Explosive Behavior

So, what exactly is explosive behavior? In my book *Outsmarting Explosive Behavior: A Visual System of Support and Intervention for Individuals with Autism Spectrum Disorders* (Endow, 2009), explosive behavior is defined as having four distinct stages, followed by a clearly defined recovery period. In addition, the physiological fight/flight mechanism is triggered immediately prior to the explosion.

In this model, the four stages of explosive behavior are the same for every person experiencing explosive behavior and are depicted by four train cars called Starting Out, Picking Up Steam, Point of No Return, and Explosion. The idea is to try to prevent the train cars from hooking up because when they do, we have a runaway train that ends in Explosion.

Working backwards, Explosion is the stage where the meltdown behavior is evident. Immediately prior to this is the Point of No Return, which is exactly what it implies—there is no going back from the meltdown because this stage is where the fight/flight response is triggered. The pupils dilate, and breathing and heart rates increase. Physiologically, our bodies respond as if our very lives are at stake, and we automatically behave accordingly: we fight for our lives. It is entirely impossible to reason with anyone in this survival mode. As soon as you see the child's identified Point of No Return behavior you can know the Explosion is coming and need to do your best to quickly create and maintain a safe environment.

The place to address explosive behavior is prior to when it occurs. In the Starting Out phase, whispers of behaviors are evident. The Picking Up Steam phase is just that—the whispers become louder. Though you can learn to successfully intervene at these stages, the most effective way to manage explosive behavior is proactively, before the whispers even start.

Strategies to Prevent Meltdowns Before They Start

An individual mix of three major supports and interventions is usually most effective in preventing the first stage of meltdown behavior from starting. These three major supports include proactive use of a sensory diet to maintain optimal sensory regulation, visual supports, and managing emotions that are too big (Endow, 2010).

People with ASD usually do not have sensory systems that automatically regulate; instead, they must discover how to keep themselves regulated. This is most often accomplished by employing a sensory diet. A sensory diet for a person with autism is like insulin for a person with diabetes. It is easy to understand that a person with diabetes has a pancreas that is unable to regulate insulin effectively. We can measure blood sugar and know the exact state of affairs, and from there figure out how much insulin the person needs.

Sensory Diet: Unfortunately, medical science does not allow us to take a blood sample to measure sensory dysregulation. However, we can figure out and employ a sensory diet to prevent dysregulation, and just like insulin prevents serious consequences for a diabetic, a sensory diet prevents serious troubles for an individual with ASD. As an adult with autism, I spend time every day on sensory integration activities in order to be able to function well in my everyday life. A sensory diet employed proactively goes a long way in preventing the Starting Out stage of explosive behavior from ever occurring (Brack, 2004).

Visual Supports: Another crucial area of support to put in place proactively is that of visual supports. As an Autistic, I can tell you that the saying, "A picture is worth a thousand words," is the monumental truth. Although each person with ASD has a unique experience, processing written and spoken words is not considered by most of us to be our "first language." For me, the meaning I get from spoken words can drop out entirely when I am under stress, my sensory system is dysregulated, or my felt emotions are too big. Visual supports can be anything that shows rather than tells. Visual schedules are very commonly used successfully with many individuals with ASD. Having a clear way to show beginnings and endings to the activities depicted on the visual schedule can support smooth transitions, thus keeping a meltdown at bay. For maximum effectiveness, put visual supports in place proactively rather than waiting until behavior unravels to pull them out.

Managing Felt Emotions: A third area in which many with ASD need proactive support is in managing felt emotions. Most often, felt feelings are way too big for the situation. An example in my life is when I discover the grocery store is out of a specific item; I get a visceral reaction very similar to the horror I felt when first hearing about the 9/11 tragedy. I know cognitively the two events have no comparison, yet my visceral reaction is present, and I need to consciously bring my too-big feelings down to something more workable in the immediate situation. Managing felt emotions does not come automatically but can be learned over time with systematic instruction and visual supports such as The Incredible Five-Point Scale (Buron & Curtis, 2004).

The good news is that explosive behavior can be positively impacted. With proactive supports, explosive behavior can be outsmarted so individuals with ASD can move on to living purposeful and self-fulfilling lives.

References

Brack, J.C. *Learn to Move, Move to Learn! Sensorimotor Early Childhood Activity Themes*. Shawnee Mission, Kansas: Autism Asperger Publishing Company, 2004.

Buron, K.D., and M. Curtis. *The Incredible 5-Point Scale.* Shawnee Mission, Kansas: Autism Asperger Publishing Company, 2004.

Endow, J. *Outsmarting Explosive Behavior: A Visual System of Support and Intervention for Individuals with Autism Spectrum Disorders.* Shawnee Mission, Kansas: Autism Asperger Publishing Company, 2009.

Endow, J. *Practical Strategies for Stabilizing Students With Classic Autism: Getting to Go.* Shawnee Mission, Kansas: Autism Asperger Publishing Company, 2010.

—

First printed on *Education.com* with permission of the Autism Society: *www.education.com/reference/article/explosive-behavior-asperger-syndrome*

www.asperger.net

www.makinglemonadestore.com

Does Your Child with Autism Have a Daily Record?

Shannon Des Roches Rosa

There are so many factors that can influence or illustrate how our children with autism are wearing their own skin, including but not limited to: health, toileting, aggressive and/or self-injurious behaviors, sleep patterns, medications, language usage, diet, and school performance.

We've used an online spreadsheet to successfully track important factors for my son Leo for the past several years. A daily record of Leo's important variables helps track and explain underlying patterns if and when things go awry—or go well. Because Leo's record is online (we use a free spreadsheet service), it can be shared with his entire school and home program team, as well as with interested family and friends. Once a daily record has been set up, it takes only a few minutes each day to fill it out.

Leo's online daily record has been an invaluable tool for information sharing amongst Leo's family, teachers, and the rest of his team, and also for providing fast, hard evidence of how well he learns and how much progress he's made— especially helpful when I start fretting that things aren't going so well for him.

Below are the factors we track for Leo, with examples. I try to keep entries brief as that helps facilitate data analysis. (We also include his weight at the beginning of the month, the medication and vitamins he takes daily, as well as a list of the foods he typically eats.)

	Notes
HEALTH	Runny Nose
TOILETING	Accidents: 1 (slept in, wet bed)
SLEEP	Up at 7, to bed at 10 PM
DIET (CHANGES FROM NORM)	French bread, tried bite of hamburger
MEDICATION	Claritin, Tylenol meltaways for his toothache
LANGUAGE	"Time to go swimming!" "I'm all done bath. Nice dry towel."

BEHAVIOR	0 aggressive (towards others) 1 SIB (self-injurious behavior - slapped head when denied ice cream)
SCHOOL NOTES	I fill this out using daily communication email from his teacher(s)
ADDITIONAL NOTES	Additional factors that may influence Leo's behavior, e.g., "Spring Break" "Dad on business trip"

Tracking helps us back up our anecdotal observations: "Yes, he has had more self-injurious behaviors this week. He developed a runny nose on the second day of the behaviors, so possibly there is sinus involvement. The behaviors disappeared three days later, along with the runny nose."

Tracking helps us make better long-term behavioral analyses as well. When I enter an IEP meeting and ask for extra behaviorist support during winter months, I am backed up by several years' worth of data about Leo's increase in aggressive and self-injurious behaviors during that time of year.

I heartily recommend setting up a daily record, if you haven't already.

Adolescence

Laura Shumaker

I was walking and venting with my friend Cathy after a rough day. My son Matthew, who has autism, had been sent home from school for knocking over one of his classmates at recess.

"She was wearing a yellow shirt!" he wailed in defense. "Yellow looks bad."

"You think you've got problems now," said my friend Cathy, whose son was also autistic. "Just wait until he goes though puberty!" Cathy's son was now eleven. "Let me tell you, it's not pretty."

"Matthew is just eleven now," I said," and so far I haven't had any problems."

"Eleven! That's when it hits!" she chuckled.

I just didn't want to hear it. I had decided long ago not to be concerned with issues I didn't have to deal with in the present. I had so much to worry about as it was.

"I think Matthew is going to be a late bloomer," I said, "He's still a little boy. Besides, I heard that sometimes people with autism actually calm down during adolescence."

Cathy laughed out loud. "You are so funny!" she said. "Thank God for your sense of humor. It's the only thing that will get you through."

I laughed weakly in return.

Maybe I just dreamed that puberty calms our kids down.

The following Sunday, our family went to church. Matthew usually went to Sunday school with a teen volunteer, but today was "Family Worship Sunday," when the children remained with the adults throughout the service.

Our family usually stayed home from church on "Family Worship Sunday" because it was a challenge for Matthew to sit still for a full hour. He'd stretch his arms over his head and lean back lazily. A pencil and a pad of paper were always on hand to occupy him when he got squirmy, but he often got so excited by what he was drawing that he would squeal and laugh. Our congregation had known Matthew since toddlerhood, and those who knew him were tolerant of him, but I couldn't blame them for snickering and frowning from time to time when he disrupted their religious concentration with his outbursts.

The five of us took our seats, and I studied the order of worship.

"Oh good," I told my husband, Peter, "it's Communion Sunday. We can sneak out after communion if Matthew gets restless."

In our church, Communion is served while parishioners sit in the pews. Deacons circulate large silver trays of bread and thimble-sized glasses of grape juice.

But when it came time for Communion, the deacons didn't march to the front of the church with the trays.

"Today," said our pastor, "we are going to try something new. We will celebrate Communion through the practice of intinction. We'd like to invite you to come forward and partake of the elements and then return to your seat."

Peter rolled his eyes.

"Maybe you should just sit here with Matthew," he whispered.

"*No!*" Matthew yelled, "I want to be like everyone else! I want to get the bread and juice!"

"Shhhh," I whispered. "That's fine. Just be a good boy."

"I will!" he yelled back, drawing stares.

We were sitting at the back of the church, so we had to wait a while for our turn.

A deep throaty and unfamiliar laugh erupted from Matthew, and when I shushed him again, I noticed it. At first I thought he must have stuck the pencil in his pants to cause the fabric to strain so dangerously.

"Matthew, take the pencil out of your pants," I whispered.

Matthew's brown eyes found mine.

"It's not a pencil," he replied, grinning broadly.

Peter had just stood up obliviously and was heading down the aisle with Matthew's younger brothers, Andy and John.

"Matthew," I whispered desperately. "We have to stay here..." but it was too late. He stood up—I couldn't believe my eyes—and started to walk down the aisle.

"Matthew, you need to stand right next to me." I looked down as we walked. Now what I had first thought looked like a pencil more closely resembled a flagpole.

God? Please help me. Please let Matthew be invisible just for a few minutes.

The best I could do was walk forward, avoiding all eye contact, with a straight face. When Matthew and I got to the altar, I glanced at him again.

It was still there. He still had that goofy grin.

Matthew darted ahead of me and took a piece of bread, dipped it into the grape juice, and snickered his way back to the pew. I could just hear Peter saying later, "Oh, I'm sure no one noticed," and I would tell him "Oh, yes they did, and what the *hell*."

"Shall we sneak out?" I asked Peter once we were all seated after Communion.

"Matthew seems to be doing fine," was his answer, and I thought about what Cathy had said earlier that week.

I realized my parenting life was entering a new phase.

———

Puberty is a confusing time for parents and children alike. Parents of neurotypical children tend to wait until it is absolutely necessary to talk to their children about the changes that are going on with their bodies (and minds!), but when you are the parent of a child with autism, it's best to be a few steps ahead to prepare your sensory-sensitive child for what lies ahead:

- Ask your child's pediatrician or developmental specialist talk to your child about puberty candidly. The impact of the message depends on the messenger!

- Be open to questions about puberty, no matter how awkwardly or honestly they are expressed.

- Answer questions in a soothing tone and keep your sense of humor. Just last week, Matthew, who is now twenty-four, asked me, "Who pulled me out of you?"

- Children with autism are well known for masturbating in public. (And who can blame them?) Repeat after me. Respond calmly, do not escalate. "Oops, sweetheart, that's okay only in your room with the door shut."

Brace yourself. There will be incidents. I was once standing in line at Whole Foods when a police officer called to report that Matthew was, shall I say, acting inappropriately in public. If you are prepared for incidents like this, you can go into problem-solving mode rather than hysterical mode.

Remember: Puberty does not go on forever. And everything gets just a little bit easier as our children age.

When You're Gone:
Practical Planning for Your Child's Future

Shannon Des Roches Rosa

A lot of us parents like to put our hands over our ears and shout *la la la la la* when asked to think about formulating a life care plan, because that means we're envisioning the future of our children with special needs without us at their sides. But denial and avoidance do us and our children a disservice. The time to think about planning for our children's future is now—the earlier we start, the more comprehensive our planning will be. And the steps involved are both more involved yet less daunting than you may think.

This summary is based on a presentation by Nick Homer (a Special Care Planner from MassMutual's general agency in San Jose, California, Miceli Financial Partners Wealth Management and Insurance Services), on Financial Planning and Your Child's Future. While the following information is critical, it is not official advice but rather a primer on how to get started and what to look for. Once you're ready to take action, you should consult with professional special needs financial planners and with attorneys and lawyers who specialize in special needs trusts.

What Is a Life Care Plan?

A life care plan takes into consideration the life, needs, and goals of people with special needs. It's about taking care of an individual with a disability after the parents are gone and ensuring quality of life for that individual and his or her remaining family in all areas of life. The goal is to create a flexible roadmap for the person in question's life: if any new therapies, medications, government benefits, etc., emerge, the plan needs to be able to adapt.

Misconceptions About Planning for Your Child's Future

It's not affordable.

Many special needs financial planning agencies do not charge fees for preliminary consults and advice. Just talking with a professional can be very helpful.

Someone will help financially.

People who are waiting for a benefactor will put their faith in grandparents who say, "Don't worry about it, we have money, property, business, we'll take care of your child." So people don't plan for the unexpected, like a parent with stroke or Alzheimer's who then needs to direct their assets towards their own care. If that happens and you haven't done planning for your child because you were waiting on grandma or grandpa, you've lost a lot of time.

Trust accounts are only for the wealthy.

Anyone who owns property or has assets can set up a living trust that avoids probate and allows your assets to be passed onto your heirs.

Everything will be taken care of in the will.

A will is an important legal asset, but it says only what will happen to your assets at death, who will be the guardian of your children, and who will be the custodian of your money (guardian and custodian are not always the same person).

Siblings will provide care.

Sometimes parents leave everything to a typically developing sibling, assuming he or she will take care of a sister or brother with special needs. But what if the sibling isn't financially savvy or falls in with someone who's not financially savvy? Or gets divorced, and the ex takes half of the money intended for the sibling with a disability?

Components of a Life Care Plan

- Life care plan vision
- Letter of intent
- Guardian/conservator
- Financial and support services
- Special needs trusts

Ten Comprehensive Life Care Planning Steps

(Money is only part of it!)

1.   Address Primary Issues

- What will my child do for schooling?
- Are we working on a diagnosis?
- Conservatorship—lining up benefits like MediCal. What about family issues: Do we have family in the area, do we have family members who "get it"?
- Communication is important throughout the process. Discussions between legal professionals, parents, doctors, etc.., will make the planning process easier so mistakes can be avoided.

2.   Create a Life Care Plan Vision

This means what you see happening with your child as he or she learns and grows. Some people assume their child will live with them forever. Others know that it may not be possible due to increasing behavioral challenges, strength, and size.

3. Choosing Guardians/Conservators

Often spouses have different ideas. Planners can help you prepare for best and worst possible outcomes (what if your designated custodian or guardian marries a loser who doesn't understand your kid?).

4. Identifying Financial Resources

Whatever cash or other money/assets you may have, such as 401Ks, government benefits, inheritances, etc., compared to your monthly and annual costs that will recur after you die.

5. You Have to Plan for Your Own Retirement, Too!

The best thing you can do for your kids is to plan to be personally financially secure in the future.

6. Letter of Intent: The Personal Side to the Plan

- Tells the caregiver how to step in, parent, and take care of the child.
- Talks about what your child is like, what the caregivers will need to know, what the child's quirks and routines are, what soothes him or her, doctors, medications, therapies, allergies.
- It's not a legal, binding document, but it sets a precedent and will hold up in court.
- It's a living document and will change. Recommend that it gets updated with each IEP.
- Many people keep Letters of Intent on flash drives (some medical jewelry now includes flash drives or other storage devices).

7. Will

This is a legal document that establishes who takes care of kids and who watches over the money. But it will not avoid probate, it will go in front of the judge, and it will be public information. It goes along with the trust.

8. Special Needs Trust

- Special needs trusts are designed to ensure that adult children with disabilities never get disqualified from government benefits.
- The trust needs to be stand-alone from any other living trust you may have.
- The trust is irrevocable in your child's name once funded. But the trust owns the assets, not the child.
- You really need to go to someone who has designed one.
- It doesn't have anything in it—it will be funded upon your death.

- What are the criteria for establishing that a child qualifies for a special needs trust? Diagnosis is not required. All that needs to happen is for the parent to draw up the special needs trust with lawyers.

- Your other children can be beneficiaries as well, or a charity if there's any surplus.

- You can gift to the trust.

- Why a trust? If child has more than $2,000 in his or her own name, the child does not qualify for government benefits, and the government will seize assets and withhold benefits until that money is spent down.

9. Whole Family Meeting

Once you've gone through the planning process, you want to have a whole-family meeting.

Send out a letter to relatives who might designate your child as a beneficiary, saying, "We're not asking for anything, but if you don't set this up the right way, it'll screw things up for our child's future."

Also make sure guardians *know* they're going to be guardians.

- Recommended: naming a corporate trustee to handle all the financial aspects, investments, cash management, bill paying, and not the actual caretaking.

- Caretaking can be a separate legal role (this is where the Letter of Intent comes in).

10. Review Life Care Plan Periodically.

Life changes. Life happens.

One option for finding a certified Special Care Planner like Nick Homer is to visit www.massmutual.com/specialcare. Thinking Person's Guide to Autism neither endorses nor is supported by Miceli Financial Partners, Nick Homer, or MassMutual.

—

A version of this essay was originally published at BlogHer.com.

Autism and Toilet Training: Never Give Up Hope

Shannon Des Roches Rosa

My clearest memory of an autism professional's fail happened when I was told that if Leo, then aged five, wasn't toilet trained by the time he was six, he would likely never achieve self-sufficiency. Yet in the four years since that proclamation, our boy has completely mastered every aspect of toileting. Sure, he has occasional accidents, but so do plenty of neurotypical boys his age. That autism expert can, on matters toileting-related, kiss my ass.

We were lucky; we had my son's longtime, staggeringly competent behaviorist leading my son's home therapy program and countering the expert's declaration. She held my hand when I sobbed that Leo would never be toilet trained because that autism expert told me so. She reassured me that, in her considerable experience, kids like Leo can and do become toilet trained—but they need rigorous support and a lot of patience. Sometimes years of patience.

Leo's behaviorist's practical outlook for toilet training, our patience, and Leo's hard work have paid off. Let me tell you how we all went about achieving total toileting domination.

We readjusted our expectations, as we have for so many aspects of Leo's development since his autism diagnosis—an accepting rather than pessimistic attitude. We knew that since Leo has developmental delays, many of his milestones are stretched out or delayed as well. We set realistic goals for Leo and toileting: gradual successes while anticipating occasional regressions.

First, we looked for signs that Leo was ready to toilet train. These signs were more subtle for him than for neurotypical children because Leo is not conversational. At the beginning of his toilet training, he did not notify us when he needed to use the bathroom. So we looked for physical signs and initiated his toileting proceedings when he stopped tolerating wet or dirty pull-ups.

Then we set up in-home boot camp. Telling him why he needed to use the toilet didn't really register, so we would wait until we thought he needed to go (usually an hour since the last time he went), then walk him over to the toilet and help him situate his naked bottom atop it. While he sat on his throne, we would let him watch a favorite video until he produced—that way he could see for himself why using the toilet was a good idea, and so much less icky than using pull-ups. And every time he produced, we gave him huge positive reinforcers: M&Ms, goldfish crackers, hugs, cheers—sometimes all four.

His home Applied Behavior Analysis (ABA) team backed us up not just with the toileting but also with its peripheral aspects—of which there are so many, and which because there are so many can be overwhelming for kids like Leo who need extra time and support to process sequences. Like wiping (and checking for effective wiping); pulling up underwear first, then pants; and washing hands (multiple steps). We encouraged him via reinforcers with his post-toileting routine as well.

Once he started using the toilet reliably and compliantly, we took him out of pull-ups during mellow at-home times and during his home ABA therapy sessions. He still wore pull-ups in the car, about town, at school, and at night. Then, when he started demonstrating that he could stay clean and dry for two to three hours and was regularly letting us know when he needed to use the toilet (that magic spontaneous phrase, "Go to the potty!"), we gradually reduced pull-up use until he wore underwear all day long. This transition took several months, during which time we tapered off his reinforcers as well.

When he was under stress and had regressions, we would ramp the reinforcer system back up, so as to reboot his motivation. To those worried that their children will become completely reinforcer-dependent, I will note that: (1) we've always been able to successfully fade out reinforcers, i.e., gradually stop using them, and (2) what do you think causes more stress for you and your child: cleaning up after a toileting accident or giving your kid a small treat for toileting successes?

The final frontier for Leo was wearing underwear at night. And I have to be honest, I never considered this milestone a guarantee. Leo had a two-year stretch between the time he started strutting around in underwear all day long and the time he became reliably dry at night. But eventually, he was waking up dry almost every morning, and we knew it was time.

It hasn't been breezy for Leo or for us, living this pull-up–free lifestyle. Leo really protested changing his nighttime routine and giving up pull-ups—we had to wait an extra 10 days to begin Operation Bedtime Underwear because Leo knew exactly how many pull-ups were left in his drawer and that he would be using one every night—there was no donning of the bedtime underwear until all his pull-ups were gone. But he did make the change eventually. And I think that the extra laundry is worth both the money we're saving on pull-ups and the dramatic demonstration of Leo's ongoing ability to master new skills. As with all matters autism and development related, it's important to remain open to success.

3 Caregiving and Autism

The big lesson in life is that you can't control things, and you have to be open to what life brings you.

—Kristen Neff, Ph.D.

On Autism and Self-Compassion

Kristin Neff, Ph.D.

My field of study is self-compassion; it's what I do all my research on. One of the things that this practice has given me is that I'm really okay with being my honest, authentic self.

It's not that I like people judging me. It was kind of hurtful when some people really went after us because of the [Horse Boy] movie featuring my family; they said that we made it all up, that we're in it for the money—and people who didn't know me were making all these assumptions about my character. It was strange; I never thought I'd be in that position.

But in terms of the stuff that is true about me, I'm really okay with it. I'm also okay with admitting my flaws and my shortcomings and that it's okay to be imperfect. In my book [on self-compassion], I actually go into some quite personal details about my life because I feel that if you're going to tell a story honestly and you're going to affect people, if you then make it a picture-perfect, Ozzie and Harriet–type thing, it's not real life.

Self-compassion made a huge difference in raising Rowan [my son with autism]. Both my husband Rupert and I are committed to self-compassion. We really made sure we had compassion for how difficult it was to be Rowan's parents. We gave each other breaks, nights off.

I think a lot of autism parents are so in problem-solving mode, and they're so focused on helping their kid that it's hard to admit the grief because you feel, "I love my kid so much—how can I admit how difficult, and how painful, and how depressing it is sometimes?" And I think that you have to acknowledge those painful feelings, and that actually allows you to love your child even more. I don't think autism parents do that nearly enough—or any parents, for that matter. But especially the autism parents. You have to acknowledge the grief.

When Rowan was first diagnosed, I went to a local Autism Society of America meeting, and everyone was kind of happy and talking about this and that. I said, "Look, I am struggling with an intense amount of grief right now," and then they all helped and supported me.

So it can be really hard, like one time when Rowan had a bad day, and for an hour he was in such distress, and there was nothing we could do. I made him a little replacement toy wheel [for his train], and I was so clever and I was so proud of myself—and it would *not* do. It's very frustrating and hard. Sometimes. And then sometimes it's beautiful and glorious, and he's the best kid in the entire world—and he is! But it's all of it. It's the whole—spectrum.

It's not the positive instead of the negative; it's both. As Kahlil Gibran says, "The deeper that sorrow carves into your being, the more joy you can contain." And I think there is really some aspect to that with autism. The amount of sorrow and frustration and grief is intense, but it matures you. And then you have the joy and you have the good things, and that's more intense. I think it's a growth-learning-opening experience, every bit as much—or more, actually—for the parents than the kids. And that's beautiful, and it's difficult. It's certainly an interesting path to go down, isn't it?

I think autism breaks open your heart. The big lesson in life is that you can't control things and you have to be open to what life brings you. You can bang your head against the wall of reality as much as you want and it won't help. Autism forces you to accept what you don't want. That is the whole lesson with Buddhism and a lot of spiritual traditions; it's all about surrendering to this greater unfolding and not trying to control things. Autism parents are forced to learn that lesson, and that's a really good lesson to learn.

A Single Mom's View of Autism Divorce Rates

Estée Klar

I have always found the idea of blaming the autistic child for the deterioration of marriage unfair to autistic people. Yet, when my own marriage ended, I couldn't help but wonder if any of those ideas behind the eighty percent divorce rates and autism might in some way be true.

A single mom of an autistic child for several years now, I've seen that when relationships fall apart, we begin by looking outside ourselves for the external causes to blame. No matter what the circumstance, illness, disability, and death are the certainties of a full life. We make vows for better or for worse, even if most of us want the "better." Frequent divorce seems to reflect the advent of the restart button—an impatient, quickly gratified culture with many options at our fingertips, and a waning attention span. It's perhaps an unforgiving view about what as I see as the *marriage du jour*—the one that bypasses commitment. Even so, two people who come together with the best of intentions (or delusions) sometimes cannot endure the stress when faced with life's many challenges. This has nothing to do with autism.

Consider some of our flippant views about marriage and commitment against the last decade of autism in the media. The media and many in the medical field created an environment of fascination and fear about autism. Most parents relate to the panic we felt on the day of the official autism diagnosis. We heard and read that we had a six-year window in which to cure our children. That is, we were told that if our children didn't talk and lose those autism behaviors by the age of six, our children were doomed to be autistic for the rest of their lives. With such pressure, as individuals and couples, we can be extremely challenged. Coping with stress and even grief is different for all people. Press restart?

It shouldn't come as a surprise, then, that autism is frequently blamed by some autism charities, and in the media, for divorce. When we blame something else other than ourselves, such as perpetuating the notion that autism is to blame, the innocent autistic child is targeted. This creates reasons to research autism in order to eradicate it. As a result, it is one more reason added to an exhaustive list of why we must cure and change the autistic child as quickly as possible. Instead of considering that *all* children are a test—that in fact, all of life is one big test—we yet again *blame the autism.*

In comparison to other disabilities like dyslexia, Down syndrome and deafness, public policy makers and educators still struggle to understand autism. We are just beginning to learn about the accommodations autistic people need in order to contribute as autistic people (as opposed to having to change in order to become normal for normal sake—this no longer happens with many of the other disabilities). There is more stress when parents have to fight to get kids into schools, obtain financial support, and acquire respite help, augmentative communication devices, and social skills. In later years, we seek appropriate housing accommodations, vocational training, access to community colleges and universities with aides, and supports that allow our adult children to continue to learn and contribute. The list is longer for some families dealing with medical issues or extreme behavioral issues. By default, we've become activists and advocates by no choice of our own.

It can be an exhausting introduction in the first few years following a diagnosis, for the support, guidance, and understanding are scarce. Autism still requires a lot of reading, research, funding, management, and self-inquiry. As life evolves and our children mature, we move beyond that "crisis" phase. We have read and learned, and we learn to love and accept our children as they are. We even learn to accept the prejudice and discrimination that becomes a part of our children's lives and we feel and live with it too. We work tediously and patiently, hoping that attitudes will change, services will become better, and our children will be included in all facets of society.

We hope that our partners will continue the journey along with us. I say this because it's fairly typical that there is one parent doing more of the advocacy, work, and research than the other as part of the division of labor. This of course is not always the case, but for the sake of argument and statistics, it is usually the mother who takes on the bulk of such work.

Mothers are especially blamed because it is expected that we are supposed to be better caregivers. "If only the child was 'normal,' then the mother would be able to attend to her husband more often," is but one of the comments I heard during my separation—speeding me through a time warp to 1950. Blaming the mother for the failed marriage is an old idea—we're either cold-as-ice Bettelheim-Refrigerator-Mothers, or we are terrible wives.

If the learning curve about autism is not shared, the divide can start there. Or it can start when the child doesn't run up to Daddy when he walks through the door at the end of the day. The mother feels guilty that she has done something wrong. Maybe dad feels rejected. Is this the cause for divorce? Or is it that the spouses already do not have effective communication and commitment in place? Is one partner less committed to the marriage to begin with? Maybe someone read that autism causes divorce and the message deteriorates the confidence and strength we actually need in our relationships? These are but some of the questions that need to be asked prior to assuming that autism is the reason for higher divorce rates.

Single parenting of autistic children is a topic that needs a lot of discussion, according to my Facebook and blog readers. The single mothers I've spoken with claim that all their time is dedicated to autism—from management to finding subsidy, services, and respite, and dealing with the schools. There are single mothers struggling and in need. I suggest that *these* are the caregivers who should be at the top of the list for such financial and respite support—not only do children need it, but parents do as well. This of course also applies to single dads. When single, extra time is committed in order to accomplish the tasks that were once shared. Lack of understanding and support, unlike other disabilities, does affect the shape and nature of our lives. It doesn't necessarily make it worse. It can, in fact, make it richer, even if it's challenging.

It's ironic that, even though so many women of *typical* children get caught up in their motherhood roles, that mothers of autistic children get blamed for failed marriages because we get so involved in our "autistic" children's lives. In the beginning when I wrote reams about autism on my blog, I was criticized for being too involved one moment, only to receive another message from another source that I needed to do *more* for my autistic son.

Children have been vulnerable targets for generations. Add the stigma around autism and disability, and the autistic child is spotlighted in this divorce speculation. Instead of studying the ingredients of successful marriages and families with autistic people in them such as attitude, family communication, and compatibility, the purported correlation between higher divorce rates in autistic families simply bypasses these considerations.

A 2010 study debunks the incorrect 80 percent divorce rate and some of the assumptions that accompany that myth. Dr. Bruce Freedman of the Kennedy Krieger Institute found that a child's autism "had no effect on the family structure." In fact, he found that 64 percent of children with autism belong to a family with two married biological or adoptive parents compared to 65 percent of children who do not have ASD. Freedman's study acknowledges that parenting an autistic child may be more stressful and it may put pressure on the marriage, which he found in past studies.

Yet Freedman's teams analysis of a 2007 National Survey of Children's Health data showed that other factors can contribute to divorce, "such as having a child with particularly challenging behaviors with and *without* autism." [emphasis mine]. For some families, the challenges of parenting a child with special needs may indeed result in straining the marriage to the breaking point."

Freedman wishes to conduct more longitudinal studies to find out how relationships can survive such stressors and what factors may enable the successful marriage. Alison Singer, founder of the Autism Science Foundation, agrees that it would be helpful to find the "net stress reducers" for families, noting also that the 80 percent divorce rate myth may have added to our stress as parents and marriage partners.

It might help to add here that Canadian researcher Lonnie Zwaigenbaum in his paper "A Qualitative Investigation of Changes in the Belief Systems of Families of Children With Autism or Down Syndrome" (*Child: Care, Health and Development*, 2006, 32: 353-369) concluded that having autistic and Down syndrome children in a family resulted in a reconstruction of values, expectations, and actually added to a sense of overall happiness and joy. His team noted that most families believed that their children added to their quality of life in that the way in which they regarded their lives were improved. I will concur. Having an autistic child, even with the challenges, has made me more patient and appreciative. My son Adam has been the most profound teacher in helping me see not only to see the realities of life, but to live them to the best possible degree. While I was married he brought me joy. When I became separated, he reminded me, when I needed it the most, of my values, commitment, and the importance of a healthy attitude.

Still, after grappling with the divorce rate myth immediately after separation (which, by the way, only made me feel worse), I thought it really important to discover why so many people believe that families with autistic and other special needs children are more vulnerable to divorce. I also became interested in the underlying fears that may prohibit some people from believing that future relationships for autistic children are possible. Again, as I walk in their shoes, I know that parents are afraid of new potential partners being interested in a relationship where there is an autistic child. Parents believe they are not attractive as prospective partners. We also worry about whether our children will be safe and accepted. When people believe that autistic people are incapable of affection, or violent (among many of the generalities), it is easy to see why there is concern.

One of the reasons why we believe divorce and relationships are so complicated is that *we believe* we suffer more because we perceive that we devote much more time to the autistic child than the neurotypical child. We forget to consider the issues belonging to typical children that can also strain marriages. In my current relationship, I overheard my partner claiming how much more delightful my son is compared to some of the typical children he's encountered. The reality is, children are children and the outcome of them *all* is uncertain.

Yes, autistic children, and their parents, need more support in a world that doesn't value them as they are. I also see this changing. I see more acceptance as the years pass. I have more understanding and patience for others who have not been in this as long as I have, and that really does make things a little easier. A change in attitude has effected a lot of positivity in our lives. I've always viewed my son Adam as a joy in my life and I've seen him become a joy in the lives of others. The time I devote to him is worth it.

Overall, though, divorce is not easy, whether you have an autistic child or not. Though my life has taken more turns than I expected, I have learned to accept them and to make a life for Adam and myself that fits us. We must fashion our uncommon arrangements, whatever they may be, and forget the traditions, systems, and beliefs that can influence the way we function and even make us sick. We must create our own ways through life to find contentment.

If you want to be married or in any kind of committed arrangement, and you have autistic children, perhaps my best piece of advice is to just stop listening to the messages about how hard life is with autistic children, or how you are supposed to be married or be a family in the first place. Don't let anyone tell you how to be a family or that your autistic child must be normal to be valued. If you have remained together, lovely. Keep looking to each other, and cry, laugh and grow together.

I hope you continue to live…happily ever after.

On the Verge of a Meltdown

Prather Harrell

No, not my autistic five-year-old son—I'm the one on the verge of a meltdown!

It was one of those days where I could not seem to make anyone happy. Jonah, my five-year-old, had been having a bad summer all along. I can't say that I blame him. Here we go changing his schedule around from KinderPrep (ABA/habilitation) in the mornings and public preschool in the afternoons with a few therapies sprinkled in between, to therapies in the morning and KinderPrep in the afternoon and no more Mrs. Marsha period (his preschool teacher—Jonah completed preschool this spring and will be headed to Kindergarten this fall). The teachers changed, the students changed, some of his therapists changed—we flipped his entire schedule around, and no one ever consulted him about it. I guess I'd be pretty pissed, too, if somebody started messing with the calendar in my Blackberry and just expected me to go with the flow. Much like my son, I don't always handle change very well.

I was simply trying to get out the door to drop off Jonah to physical therapy, and none of my three boys were cooperating. My seven-year-old son Julien was acting like my two-year-old son, whining about having to eat pancakes instead of cereal; my two-year-old son Jace (who started his terrible twos at eight months) was being his typical demanding self and didn't want to eat at all; and all the while Jonah was screaming at the top of his lungs about having been asked to brush his teeth. My husband was at work, and I was at my wits' end.

Jonah's behaviors had reached an all-time high this summer with screaming and tantrums at every request we made of him. It was as if I had two toddlers all summer long. I had been as patient as I could possibly be, and I just didn't have any patience left. I told Julien to straighten up and finish his pancakes or once we got back he wouldn't be able to watch any TV, all day long. I turned on Thomas the Tank Engine to distract Jace for a few minutes so I could deal with Jonah and finish getting him ready to go. Jonah was beginning to get very angry and yelled, "I don't want to brush my teeth!" I just looked at him. For the fourth time he pleaded, "I wanna play computer!" and for the fourth time I said, "First, you have to brush your teeth and finished get dressed and then you can play PBS Kids."

All Jonah heard was the word "first," and he started to lose it. He paid no attention to the rest of that sentence as he purposely got louder to drown out my denial of his request instead of actually hearing what I was saying to him. He continued to scream and whine, and it was like nails on a chalkboard—I couldn't take it anymore! I grabbed Jonah by the arm firmly and yelled, *"Jonah, if you don't stop screaming right now, you are going on time out, again!"*

He'd already been put on time out once that morning, by his dad. We always allow the kids to feel what they're feeling and try to validate how they're feeling, but we give them two choices: feel bad (cry, scream, or whine if they need to) alone in their rooms, or stay amongst the family, calm and pleasant. If they need time to themselves, that's fine and when they feel better (and only when they've managed to compose themselves and can stop the crying and screaming in front of the rest of the family), they can come out and join the rest of us.

Jonah persisted in protesting so I marched him into his room and told him, "You can come out when you're *all done screaming!*" I had to say it loudly so he could hear me—at this point it had become a contest as to who could yell louder. Then he proceeded to do what he always does, which was to scream *as loudly as he possibly could for as long as he could*, through the bedroom door, until he grew hoarse and voiceless.

It was glaringly obvious that this separation technique was not working well at all. It simply stressed him out, stressed me out, and no doubt bothered Julien and Jace, too, as they stared, helpless and scared, in the corner of the kitchen. My eyes welled with tears as I felt defeated and thought to myself, "God, there has got to be an easier way…"

In that moment, I decided to step into my bedroom where I could be alone and collect myself before I fell apart. I spent a couple minutes beating myself up for handling the situation all wrong. I shouldn't have yelled. I shouldn't have put him on time out again—it clearly wasn't changing his behavior. Was this autistic behavior or was he just being a testy five-year-old? I should've taken it easy on him. I shouldn't discipline the autistic tantrums, just the five-year-old tantrums. Which ones are which? I should have given him more warning before I asked him to switch from a preferred activity (playing on the computer) to a non-preferred activity (brushing his teeth). I should never have let him play on the computer before getting ready for therapy in the first place. I should have never taken down his picture schedule. The list went on.

Then something told me to just stop. I took several deep breaths and said a quick prayer for God to grant me strength, patience, and clarity, and then returned to the kitchen. Just as I was walking out of my bedroom, Jonah was walking out of his.

He looked at me with very sad puppy dog eyes and said tearfully, "I'm all done screaming, Mommy."

I replied, "And what else do you need to say?"

He responded, "I'm sorry Mommy," with a quivering bottom lip.

I kneeled down eye-level to him and responded, "You make Mommy very sad when you scream and cry. But I get very happy when you use your words! Show me your happy face." He proceeded to force a smile.

I said, "I love you. Do you feel better now?"

He said, "Yes."

We hugged and then I said, "Me too! Now go brush your teeth."

He complied. And that's when it hit me: look at how far he's come! Even in the midst of the tantrum drama, he verbalized his protests, knew how to say he was done crying, and is about 60% able to brush his teeth on his own. Wow! I shouldn't be beating myself up, I should be patting myself on the back, in awe of all of the hurdles we've jumped and mountains we've climbed.

I should also note that, unfortunately, I'm not excused from the hardships of motherhood and parenthood just because I have a special needs child. The rules don't change. There are going to be good days, great days, bad days, and horrible days. My kids will take everything out of me, a lot of which will go unappreciated and unnoticed. And yet I will continue to give them everything I've got, and then some. I will face some parenting mishaps and mistakes. I'm going to lose my patience at times, I'm not always going to choose the best form of discipline, and despite my best efforts my kids will not always comply with my rules and requests.

Time out may not be the most effective method of discipline in every case, especially for a child with autism, but I also have to remain cognizant of the standard I'm setting for all of my children. The rules of the house don't change for Jonah, and he is neither exempt nor excluded from anything we do (no matter how difficult it can be for him at times). It might take a bit longer to implement, and we may have to adjust the technique, but the rules for Jonah are the same for Julien as they are for Jace. There are no free passes!

When my beautiful young princes become adults in society, they will be neither exempt nor excused from following the rules of society just because they (two of them) have special needs. They'd be lucky if anyone even bothered to ask them if there are any special circumstances that need to be taken into consideration before a decision is made that may impact their futures. And since I am raising African-American men, this is of huge concern to me—the rules of society are especially strict for these young men. I have to make certain that Jonah and his brothers know without question that rules are there for a reason, and if they aren't followed, there will be a consequence for their actions, whether they like it or not.

For any parent out there on the verge of a meltdown, it's okay! Just remember to take a lot of deep breaths and honor the space you're in. If you're tired, lie down. If you're stressed, take your own timeout. If it's a good day, pat yourself on the back! And most important, take it easy on yourself and put the "beat myself up" bat down. As a matter of fact, it would be best to take it out with the trash!

When a Single Mother of a Special Needs Child Is Suddenly Ill

Asperger Ninja

As parents, we always worry if our children get sick. That's part of our job. We are prepared before they are even born, having been told countless stories by our parents, friends who have children, and sometimes, complete strangers who are more than happy to spin tales of their children's maladies.

But no one ever truly prepares you for when you get sick. There is no chapter in the Parent Handbook on how to prevent illness or be ready when you need to be taken care of. That's usually not an option. Moms, dads, and caregivers are known for working when under the weather, but there may come a time when you have to actually go to the hospital. In most incidents, one parent will take care of the child (or children) while the other parent is ill. But what if you don't have that choice?

I'm a single mother of my son, Nathan, who has Asperger syndrome. When I was married and a trip to the ER was necessary, my husband did the honors and took care of our child while I convalesced. I had been lucky, with no major illnesses for several years. Until one came quite out of nowhere.

It was July 2009. I was working for our local ARC in their summer camp. I remember getting into a minor fender bender on July 12th, which was a Sunday. I am a very good driver, so this really threw me for a loop. I recall feeling a little fuzzy in the head before the accident, so I wondered if maybe I was tired.

The next week, on Wednesday, I started getting some lower GI problems. It was hot that summer, and our rooms at the camp had no air conditioning, so this did not surprise me. I am sensitive to high temperatures, so my body normally reacts this way. I knew to keep hydrated and not worry if I was not eating.

By Saturday, my symptoms had increased significantly. I was eating next to nothing. I tried to keep water in my system, but it wouldn't stay. My skin started to tighten around my hands and my feet, a sign of dehydration. I checked my temperature, but I showed no signs of fever, which would indicate infection. I couldn't sleep at night, as I was making almost hourly trips to the bathroom.

Monday rolled around and I was barely conscious at camp. It was a really hot day, I was in the lunchroom, and I truly wanted to pass out—but our kids had autism, ADHD, and bipolar disorder, and it probably wasn't a good idea for them to experience me in that state.

My co-counselor said, "Amy, you look awful."

I said, "Yeah, I feel pretty awful."

He said, "You should go to the hospital."

Then it hit me. Who would take care of Nathan? Who would get him? Who would be able to explain to him what happened, without his getting upset? That thought was too much for me to handle, so I asked my co-counselor to get me a popsicle from the kitchen. I promised if I didn't perk up after eating two popsicles that I would go to the hospital—secretly hoping I wouldn't have to go.

I rallied enough to make it through that day and to go to work on Tuesday, the 21st. I still was feeling lousy, but had a lot more energy than before, which I took as a sign that maybe I was finally past this illness.

Later that night, around 11 p.m., I was woken up from a sound sleep by the most intense abdominal pain I had ever experienced. It felt like someone had taken a knife and had split my stomach open and the contents were burning my insides. I was terrified.

I went through my mental list of people I could call. Nathan's father was over seventy miles away, as were his grandfather and grandmother. Both of my sisters were quite far from where we live. I thought of my best friend, J.T., who only lived ten miles away. I was worried that I would wake him up, but I was also starting to panic, as I needed to know someone was going to take care of Nathan.

I called 911, trying not to cry while I was talking to them. Then I called J.T., who told me it was very okay to call him at 11:45 p.m. with an emergency. He said he would meet us at the hospital in 30 minutes. I can't even describe how much relief that gave me, knowing that Nathan would be with someone he knew and felt comfortable with.

The ambulance arrived, and they were wonderful with both of us. Nathan was so brave; he held my hand as I was wincing in pain. I kept my face as calm as possible, so that he didn't know how much distress I was truly having. Ten minutes after we arrived, J.T. showed up and I just started weeping. Tears fell down my face as he hugged me and said, "Its okay, Amy. I'm here."

I discovered that I had been exposed to freshwater bacteria (by drinking water from a system with older pipes). My doctor proudly announced that he had never heard of it and had to Google it. I took two days to recuperate, in and out of feeling tired and nauseous. They gave me

Ciprofloxacin, a strong antibiotic with the side effect of sun sensitivity. I spent two weeks sympathizing with vampires, feeling like my flesh was burning off during daylight hours.

This experience was one I definitely do not want to repeat. I think if I had been a bit more proactive and had gone to my doctor earlier, even without signs of infection, he would have treated me and I wouldn't have had to go to the ER. I think as parents we neglect ourselves and focus all of our energies on our children, which is very common. However, if we do not take care of ourselves, we are not the only ones we put in jeopardy.

Parents of children with special needs have to go above and beyond what is necessary to ensure our good health and well-being. Since my ambulance trip, I have made sure to have more than one person I can call if there is an emergency. I have also taken better care of myself, so that I will minimize the possibility of a repeat performance. I learned my lesson in the hardest way but have taken steps to ensure that I will be more prepared if it ever (hopefully never!) happens again.

All Showers Lead to Australia

Hartley Steiner

"Do you want to go to Australia with me?" My husband asked casually while I stood at the stove cooking the taco meat for dinner the other night. Such a ridiculous question didn't warrant an actual verbal response, so I just looked at him out of the corner of my eye and gave a sarcastic smirk. He smiled and said, "I am being serious. If you and I both start working on it now, we could find someone to take care of the kids for a few days and you could come with me to Australia in June." He really was serious. And you know what, I wanted to go!

It isn't going to surprise anyone to find out that spending a week away from our kids is something we have never done—heck, we haven't even made it 48 hours away from our kids in the last seven years. Seven years.

Normally, when I get asked by friends or relatives about traveling for an extended period of time, I always say my dream is to "be away from my kids long enough to miss them." And it is true. The kind of stress I am under every single day as a special needs parent is not the kind that dissolves with a twenty-minute shower. Not even close. And I spent years using that excuse to justify not spending any time taking care of myself.

But that changed about a year ago.

The light bulb went on when I stepped on the scale last spring—and well— let's just say that instead of displaying a number, it actually said, "One at a time, please." That was the first sign I had stopped making time for myself.

The other signs were equally disturbing: I was eating horribly (what my kids left behind, or fast food drive-through), wasn't getting any exercise (chasing Matt should make me thin, but no such luck), hadn't been to the doctor in years, never mind the dentist, and was down to having my hair cut two times per year at best, no matter how awful it looked. I would never accept those things for my kids, so why was it okay for me?

I realized then that respite time had more to do with how I was treating myself—that taking the twenty-minute shower was symbolic of self value and, more important, a steppingstone on the way to Australia. (Okay, so I didn't actually know the whole Australia thing then, but I knew it was a stepping stone towards something.)

I made a commitment to treat myself better. To treat myself, my health, my body, my mind, all of my needs, as if they were as important as my son's needs.

The irony is that if we have special kids, we sometimes convince ourselves that taking care of our own personal needs is a luxury. It's not a luxury. A Mercedes-Benz is a luxury. A Rolex is a luxury. One-thousand-thread-count sheets are a luxury. Taking a shower, spending time with our spouses, or even going out with our friends is not my definition of a "luxury."

The well-kept secret here is that we can *choose* to take care of ourselves and our kids.

I started my new self-care campaign by committing to getting myself a shower, if not every day, hopefully every other day. Do you think that was easy? *Not even close.*

My choices were either A) wake before my kids like my husband does, by getting up and into the shower before six in the morning, or B) find a way to distract my youngest son Matthew while the older boys were at school and jump in then.

Now, I am not a morning person, and I don't drink coffee because I can't stand hot beverages, so that ruled out option A pretty quickly (I may just be the only SAHM on the planet who doesn't sip a latté every morning, but thus far, Starbucks hasn't seen a dime of my money).

This left me choosing option B, which requires a great deal more creativity and even a tinge of daring on my part. Matthew, as much as I love that small child, is a mess waiting to happen. Which means, no matter how well laid my plans are, no matter what awesome "new" show I have recorded for him, no matter how many bribes he has in front of him, he will be nowhere near the spot I left him when I get done with my shower.

But I am willing to take that risk.

And when I get out of the shower, wrap a towel around my head, and run through the house in my underwear surveying the damage he did in mere minutes, I remind myself that it was worth it. Because I am worth it.

But showering was only part of the plan.

After I had showering under my belt, I began to feel better about myself—dare I say even less stressed, and that feeling was addictive.

Soon I turned my new self-care addiction into going out for dinner with my girlfriends, attending more support group meetings, occasional trips to the gym, going to the doctor, getting my hair cut, replacing ten-year-old clothes with new ones, and going on dates with my husband. I even painted my own nails at night when the boys were asleep.

It was a change of attitude really: a change of perception about me and about my life. It wasn't (and isn't) about just being away from my children, or doing frivolous things, but rather about allowing me to see myself as more than just a stay-at-home-mom or a special needs parent. Those are only part of who I am.

Taking time out to take care of my needs allowed me to remember that I am a whole person, not just one label or another.

I spend a great deal of time talking about my family on my blog and in my real life because I love them and they are truly the focus of my life every day. But they aren't the sum of who I am. I am much more. I love to laugh, can bake amazing desserts (cheesecake and lemon pound cake are my favorites), still listen to rap music, enjoy photography, and have been infatuated with the ocean since I was nine years old and decided to become a marine biologist despite getting decompression sickness and going through hyperbaric treatment after scuba diving in Hawaii when I was fourteen. I bet you didn't know those things about me, right? Truthfully, I'd begun to forget about them myself.

The bottom line here is this: it is okay that I want to go to Australia.

Two years ago, there was no way I would've been able to admit that and honor that I needed time for myself and that it would be okay to leave the kids for a week (although I have yet to master the logistics involved). I know now that taking time for myself and for my marriage will make me a better person, wife, and mother.

And I have proof of it in my daily life—in the way I am able to be with my kids and honor their challenges. In the way I am able to see my husband and support his dreams. And in the twenty pounds I've lost without so much as being on a diet this last year. Turns out, taking care of your own needs is a good idea—and it is never too late to start.

Now, I know all of you are not going to read this and run off to Australia— but my hope is that you do run off to the shower because as you now know, all showers lead to Australia.

4 Therapies and Service Providers

You will have to make decisions between learning components that appear academic, social skills that are cognitive, language-dependent, and functional skills like toileting that are tied to motor development. Many children do better if more time is focused on fewer expectations.

—Barbara H. Boucher

What a Great Speech-Language Pathologist Can Do for Your Child with Autism

Jordan S. Sadler, M.S., CCC-SLP

When your child is diagnosed with autism, one of the first professionals you will need on your child's team is a high-quality speech-language pathologist (SLP). This is because challenges in communicating and relating are core features of the diagnosis, and improvement in this area will make a tremendous difference in a child's—and family's—life. For many children with autism spectrum disorders (ASDs), the SLP is the cornerstone of the therapeutic team.

A speech-language pathologist may also be referred to as a "speech therapist" or the more descriptive "communication therapist." Whatever the title, parents will want to be sure their child's therapist is licensed by the state and certified by the American Speech-Language-Hearing Association. Furthermore, be sure to work with a practitioner who has extensive training and experience in the field of autism, and don't be afraid to ask the therapist specifically about the areas that you feel are of greatest concern for your child. All SLPs are trained in helping children communicate better, but finding a therapist who also specializes in helping a child form and maintain positive relationships with others will be highly beneficial.

An SLP provides a great many services for a child with autism and his or her family, including the critical element of parent education. It is part of the speech-language pathologist's job to ensure that parents understand the diagnosis of ASD and how it affects their individual child's social, receptive, and expressive communication.

Look for an SLP who has the ability to point out a child's strengths and explain how she will help the parents build on those strengths to overcome challenges. One of the most valuable things an SLP can do is to observe the child in a variety of environments and focus on the best moments: the ones when the child is attentive and engaged in joyful interaction, at the "top of her game." If time is spent evaluating the characteristics of those moments—noting that the child was in a swing with her body supported and that her father was at eye level using lots of facial expression and affect, for example—we will have found strategies that will allow us to immediately increase and then expand upon those moments throughout the child's day. Not all speech therapists know to do this, but if parents find someone who does, the work is going to be so much more meaningful and will have better results.

The SLP is also in a unique position to evaluate and explain how a child is communicating, assessing everything from eye gaze, gestures, intonation, and movement to sounds, words, and complex sentences and interaction with peers. To a speech-language pathologist, nonverbal communication should be at least as important as verbal language—especially at first—and is often where the best SLP will start with your child with autism, even if the child uses verbal language at times.

In other words, when we work with children, we start with developing communication first in order to solidify the foundation for a child. It can be frustrating at times, even for the SLP, to back up and teach foundational skills to a child who has some verbal language already, but in the long run the communication benefits are enormous if we take our time and fill in any missing skills. Not doing so is akin to building a house without a foundation; a child's team might be able to help build a beautiful first floor with all kinds of impressive details such as pronouns and multiword sentences, but if the foundation of eye gaze, multiple circles of reciprocal interaction, and meaningful gestures (to name a few) are missing, the house will crumble at the second or third floor because it will most assuredly not be sturdy. The child won't be able to use those higher-level skills with others in a meaningful way if basic interactive skills are not yet in place. This is true for children who rely on verbal language as well as those who use an augmentative and alternative communication (AAC) such as the Picture Exchange Communication System (PECS) or a voice output speech device.

Once the fundamentals are firm, an SLP works on a wide variety of language goals, depending on the child's needs. Typical goals in the area of language comprehension are following directions, understanding concepts, and answering various types of questions. The speech therapist may also work on expressive language skills with your child as she learns to use pronouns, put multiple words together, and tell a story with correct narrative formation.

If needed, a speech-language pathologist will also work with a child on speech sound production, or articulation skills. Some children with autism have apraxia of speech, which is an oral motor planning disorder that causes them to have trouble pronouncing words, especially as they become longer or are in sentences. (Quite often these are children who have general motor planning difficulties in their bodies, which would be diagnosed by an Occupational Therapist (OT). Sometimes apraxia or challenges with oral sensitivities also cause feeding difficulties. If a child is having any trouble with feeding, caregivers will want to find an SLP who is also trained in this area. A speech therapist can work with the child individually or in a feeding group with peers to make this work more fun and social.

In the field of autism, a well-trained speech-language pathologist will have a solid understanding of pediatric social–emotional development to support the child's emotions around communication with others and to help him or her learn to identify, express, and grade her emotions appropriately. The SLP will need to fully understand and help parents interpret the child's sensory profile to respond to behaviors accurately. For example, it is critical that caregivers and professionals recognize sensory-seeking behaviors and help the child self-advocate for movement breaks, something to chew on, or a few minutes in a quiet space when needed to soothe herself. Understanding each child's unique sensory profile is best accomplished with the help of the child's OT.

Work on early social–emotional development is critical for many reasons. First of all, a child must be in a regulated state (and have some strategies to achieve this state at her disposal) to learn. Just as an adult wouldn't be expected to learn a new skill while distracted by horrible airplane turbulence or when exhausted, a child can't learn new skills when in an over-aroused or under-aroused state. Second, an SLP will teach a child early social-emotional development to help him or her with peer interaction. Many SLPs facilitate social groups to work on skills within the natural context of peer play and conversation, depending on the child's age and skill level. Here a child learns to take the perspective of other people, stay with a group both physically and cognitively, and play cooperatively, among other things.

In the school setting, a speech-language pathologist might be found working on a child's goals in the classroom setting. This may include presenting higher-level linguistic concepts such as synonyms, antonyms, and multiple meaning words, teaching students how to organize and write a paper, or helping a child prepare for an oral presentation. The school SLP should also be monitoring the child's social-emotional development, ensuring positive social interactions in group work, during lunch, and on the playground.

Finally, the potential role of the speech-language pathologist within the child's family should not be underestimated. Beyond the early task of education about autism and its impact on a child, the SLP can facilitate improvement of the family dynamics around communication and play by incorporating various family members into therapy. Caregivers should also feel comfortable sharing communication and behavioral challenges going on at home with their SLP in order to problem-solve together.

All of this is a big job for one therapist. The speech-language pathologist is able to work productively on so many aspects of a child's development when she is supported by parents and other therapists who actively participate and communicate about the child's changing profile of strengths and needs on a regular basis. A good speech-language pathologist pathologist will make a significant difference in your child's life.

What Is Applied Behavior Analysis, and Why You Want a Behavior Analyst on Your Child's Team

Michelle Hecht, M.A., BCBA

When it comes to helping children with autism to achieve their learning goals and to become participating, contributing, and independent members of society, intensive Applied Behavior Analysis, or ABA, is currently the educational treatment approach with the strongest scientific support. So, what is applied behavior analysis, and why should you have a behavior analyst on your child's team?

What is Applied Behavior Analysis?

Behavior analysis is the scientific approach to understanding how environment affects behavior. These days it is generally accepted that behavior is impacted greatly by both biological and environmental factors. Professional and academic fields as diverse as education and advertising examine how various aspects of the environment affect human behavior, to promote their respective knowledge bases and goals. Behavior analysis stands out among these fields as a science. It relies on the same tools as other sciences: clear definitions, objective measurement, controlled experimentation, data analysis, and replication. Applied behavior analysis utilizes these tools in order to bring about important changes in the behavior of individual clients. A behavior analyst then is a scientist–practitioner who can help your child to achieve his or her own goals and potential.

What does a behavior analyst do?

A behavior analyst is an expert observer, and his or her focus is behavior of the individual. Your behavior analyst will directly observe your child's behavior in a variety of environments to develop an accurate picture of his or her current learning strengths and needs. The behavior analyst will objectively define the behaviors he or she is observing so that everyone on the team can also observe and reliably agree on what they are seeing. The behavior analyst will clarify murky terms such as "share" into more precise descriptions, like "put a toy in someone's hand." Such clear, objective information provides you with an accurate baseline of your child's current skills and performance and permits ongoing evaluation as to the effectiveness of therapies and treatments. This is essential for you to make sound decisions about your child's treatment.

Your behavior analyst is also skilled at experimentation. She selects procedures to address your child's various learning goals and then designs mini-experiments to determine the effects of these procedures on your child's behaviors. When it comes to which treatments to use, she is well-positioned to select interventions that are likely to work with your child.

Her treatment toolkit is uniquely stocked with interventions supported by the latest scientific research and anchored in the durable principles of behavior analysis. One example is video modeling, in which video clips are used to prompt a child to perform a new behavior, such as putting on a jacket. Another is prompt fading, in which the assistance provided to a child while acquiring a new skill is systematically reduced to promote independent use of the skill and to prevent dependence on adult assistance. Your behavior analyst will train instructors, family members, and others to implement the selected procedures so that your child will use his new skills across the many people and places in his life. He or she will oversee data analysis on how your child's behavior is responding to the various treatments to ensure they are working for your child and will recommend program modifications based on the data.

In summary, a behavior analyst will help you to clearly define the strengths and learning needs of your child. He or she will address those needs using research-based methodologies and will guide your child's program based on performance data to maximize his or her progress and development.

Why do I want a behavior analyst on my child's team?

Because your child is a unique individual. If your child has been diagnosed with autism, then a professional has determined that your child is experiencing significant challenges in the three general areas: language, social communication, and restricted interests/repetitive behaviors. Yet, while all children with autism show some challenges in each of these diagnostic areas, the similarities among children end there. One child may speak somewhat typically but be unable to engage in a two-way conversation, while another may not speak at all; one child may repeat all of the bus routes in town, while another may play only with a single Thomas the Tank Engine by rolling it along the edge of a table. In other words, children with autism all share similar diagnostic features, but they are very different from one another. Behavior analysts are well suited to this predicament; by definition, behavior analysis examines the behavior of the individual. A behavior analyst applies knowledge of autism treatments to his or her understanding of how these challenges manifest distinctly for your child. Of importance, the behavior analyst addresses these challenges by building on your child's personal strengths and motivations.

Every opportunity should be a learning opportunity. We know that early intervention works. A majority of young children with autism respond well to early intensive ABA intervention, and earlier gains can magnify subsequent learning opportunities and later progress. As a parent, you want to maximize your child's time spent engaged in learning that is working to address the autism symptoms and further develop his or her strengths. This means selecting the most effective and efficient treatments for your child— a daunting task, given the explosion of Internet and other material directed at parents of children with autism: the tempting promises of cures, simple fixes, and attractively packaged therapies.

When recommending and selecting procedures to use, your behavior analyst begins with those documented in the scientific behavior analytic literature, ideally with individuals who are similar in age and diagnosis to your child. There are now hundreds of scientific studies documenting the effectiveness of various behavior analytic procedures for children with autism. The behavior analyst narrows the selection based on individual variables related to your child's profile, such as prerequisite skills, child and parent preferences, and ease of implementation. Examples of well-researched, effective ABA procedures include prompting, fading, shaping, chaining, and differential reinforcement.

Some of the more celebrated ABA approaches, such as pivotal response treatments and discrete trial training, are actually complex combinations of individual procedures. Uniquely, all applied behavior analytical procedures are based on the original behavior analytic principles—the science of behavior—which have been established for more than fifty years.

Your behavior analyst will not only ensure that your child's time is being spent engaged in evidence-based therapies, but he or she will also supervise the collection of data to ensure that these therapies are actually working. If your child is not progressing with specific treatments, the behavior analyst will recommend modifications.

If you are interested in pursuing non-behavior analytic treatments, a behavior analyst can assist you in evaluating the quality of evidence available for these treatments so that you can make informed decisions about how to maximize your child's progress and avoid ineffective and possibly harmful treatments. (All parents of children with new autism diagnoses should read Gina Green's chapter, "Evaluating Claims About Treatments for Autism," in Catherine Maurice's book *Behavioral Interventions for Young Children with Autism*.)

Your behavior analyst will not make promises. ABA does not come in a glamorous package. It is smart, hard, effective work.

Behavior analysts like to talk about pivotal behaviors, and so should you— we all need to focus on pivotal behaviors. They lead to desirable changes in the environment, which then lead to more and more complex pivotal behaviors, and then further positive environmental changes—an upward spiral of skill growth and a resulting increase in life opportunities.

Let's look at the ability to make a choice as an example of a pivotal behavior. For a young child with autism, making a choice may begin as simply choosing between two visible selections. This generally results in a positive change for him—he might get to participate in an activity he or she has selected, rather than one chosen by someone else. When our actions have preferred outcomes, we tend to repeat them. So, this child will likely continue to make choices—perhaps initially from two visible options, and later when presented with a few verbal options, and perhaps in the more distant future when discussing together with the family, "What should we do this weekend?"

The significance of learning this basic skill of choosing between two selections is pivotal because it can naturally lead to further vocabulary growth and independent choice-making behavior. As a society we greatly value being able to make choices for ourselves, and we often consider our options and ability to make choices as a quality-of-life indicator. So, too, will your child be happier and less likely to use problem behaviors when there are opportunities to make choices in life and when he or she has the skills to take advantage of those opportunities.

A behavior analyst will guide your child's program towards such pivotal behaviors, which maximize the kind of learning that leads to further learning and a greater quality of life for your child.

How do I find a qualified behavior analyst?

The first place to look is the Behavior Analysis Certification Board (BACB), where a list of board-certified behavior analysts (BCBAs) in your area can be found. A BCBA is qualified, at a minimum, with master's-level coursework in behavior analysis, supervised practice as a behavior analyst, and a passing score on a board-certifying exam. BCBAs have master's degrees in behavior analysis or related fields (e.g., special education or psychology), and BCBA-Ds have doctorates. In addition to the above initial qualifications, BCBAs are obliged to document their engagement in ongoing professional development activities such as conferences, workshops, and coursework. BCBAs must also adhere to the Behavior Analysis Guidelines for Ethical Conduct. Thus, a BCBA is accountable to the communities he or she serves via the Behavior Analysis Certification Board.

This is not to imply that practitioners without a BCBA are not skilled or qualified. There are expert behavior analysts who have had years of training and experience who are not board certified. And board certification does not guarantee that a behavior analyst is good or is a good match for your child.

Beyond the above minimum competencies, seek a behavior analyst with at least a few years of experience in working with young children with autism and with current knowledge of the autism research literature. Finally, as with all professionals on your child's team, find someone with whom you feel comfortable—a good match.

—

Resources

Websites
Cambridge Center for Behavioral Studies: *www.behavior.org*

Introductory article about autism: *www.behavior.org/resource.php?id=299*

Applied Behavior Analysis For Autism:
www.behavior.org/resource.php?id=300

Behavior Analysis Certification Board: *www.bacb.com*

National Autism Center's National Standards Project:
www.nationalautismcenter.org/index.php

Professional Research Journals
Journal of Applied Behavior Analysis (JABA)

Analysis of Verbal Behavior

Journal of Autism and Developmental Disorders

Books
Maurice, Catherine, ed. *Behavioral Interventions for Young Children with Autism: A Manual for Parents and Professionals.* Austin: Texas, ProEd, 1996.

DIR®/Floortime™: An Introduction

Sara Chapman M.A.

Navigating the world of autism is no easy task for parents, particularly with so much information—and misinformation—currently available. Parents spend hours searching for what is best for their child, understandably so, often confused or uncertain about what will truly help their child learn, develop, and grow into a warm, independent, and emotionally connected individual.

The DIR®/ Floortime™ model provides a framework for helping parents better understand their child and to re-establish those early connections that once seemed lost or unattainable. It is about finding the "gleam in the eye" and falling in love with your child all over again, no matter what your child's challenges might be. In turn, this will lead to healthy foundations for social, emotional, and intellectual development.

What is the DIR® Model?

The DIR® Model, or Developmental, Individual-Differences, Relationship-based Model, is an interdisciplinary framework for assessment and intervention developed by Drs. Stanley Greenspan and Serena Wieder. It is used to guide parents and professionals in designing a program tailored to each child's unique strengths and challenges to support developmental progress. The primary goals of the model are to help children:

• Better relate with warmth and intimacy to the important people in their lives

• Communicate more meaningfully, using words and gestures, through back-and-forth interactions

• Become more independent, abstract thinkers and problem-solvers

The "D." The "D," or Developmental, refers to the developmental levels based on typical emotional development. These six stages of early development include:

Self-Regulation and Interest in the World. A child needs to be able to process sensory information (i.e., sights, sounds, tastes, smells, and touch) while remaining calm in order to pay attention to you.

Engagement. A child begins to relate with warmth and smiles and prefers interacting with you over inanimate objects. You become your child's favorite toy.

Two-way Communication. Your child begins to engage in increasingly complex back-and-forth exchanges with you that begin nonverbally and later incorporate more and more language. Your child is becoming more purposeful and intentional. A continuous flow of affectively meaningful interactions is crucial at any phase of development. The first three levels are the foundation for all learning.

Shared Social Problem-solving. Your child begins to see that you can help him or her in solving problems. He or she will sequence several steps to achieve a desired goal, such as pulling you by the hand to the refrigerator, gesturing to open the door, and pointing to a juice container.

Creating Symbols and Using Words and Ideas. Your child begins using words or pictures to communicate meaningfully. He or she is beginning to use symbols to convey feelings or ideas.

Emotional Thinking. Your child begins to connect ideas logically and respond to various wh- questions. This is the basis for more abstract, creative, and reflective thinking necessary for higher levels of learning.

The "I." The "I," or Individual Differences, addresses the way in which a child takes in and processes information through their senses (sights, sounds, tastes, smells, touch) and also includes motor planning and sequencing, proprioception, vestibular processing, and visual-spatial processing. We each have unique, biologically based differences that make us who we are as individuals, and these differences affect how we process information and interact with others. For example, if you are sensitive to sounds, you might prefer to keep the television or music low in the house and avoid concerts or noisy restaurants. As adults, we can compensate for these differences and make choices based on our individual needs. Children, particularly children with special needs, often do not have this level of awareness or a way to communicate it.

Sensory processing challenges can have a significant impact on a child's ability to participate and function in daily routines and activities. A child's cues may be subtle, making it difficult for caregivers to read them, leading them to a misinterpretation of the intent, causing the child to disengage or even melt down. Once we learn more about a child's overall pattern, we can adjust the environment and interactions accordingly. For an under-reactive child, we can increase our "affect"—emotions, reflected in our tone of voice, facial expressions, body language, and pace—to wake up the child's sluggish sensory system. Affect is key to the learning process and gives meaning to our experiences. For the over-reactive child, we can slow down and create predictable patterns to help the child feel more calm and regulated.

The goal is to help the child stay regulated through affectively meaningful interactions, and to do so we have to understand a child's sensory processing differences. It allows us to begin developing a deeper picture of why a child might exhibit a particular behavior, such as why a child might wave his hands in front of his face. He may feel so overwhelmed by increased sensory input that he cannot process adequately, so waves his fingers in front of his eyes to tune it all out. We have to address the root cause or we will see behaviors continue to resurface or shift to new behaviors. Think of putting a small bandage on a larger injury. It simply won't work.

Considering a child's individual differences is a critical component of the DIR® Model. It allows us to gain a better understanding of a child's sensory system and the role that processing differences play in how a child relates to others and his or her environment. Families can learn how to work with their child's sensory processing challenges through affective interactions, ultimately leading to stronger connections and relationships.

The "R." The "R" represents the learning relationships that enable a child to develop. Parents are the first relationships for a child, and therefore are the driving force in the DIR® Model. You learn to play an active role within your child's team, but this doesn't mean that you have to become your child's therapist. With an interdisciplinary approach, your child will most likely work with a team that might include an occupational therapist, speech and language pathologist, an educator, a mental health provider, a physical therapist, and others. With the support of this team, you will learn to engage your child in new ways, and the mutual joy will become infectious.

What is Floortime™?

Floortime™ is often used synonymously with DIR®, though it is just one part of the comprehensive framework. It is a specific technique of engaging your child by following his or her lead for twenty- to thirty-minute periods that can occur during any activity, such as play time, bath time, driving in the car, etc. During Floortime, the child is engaged around his or her interests and encouraged to take initiative and direct the play. The caregiver's primary goal is to keep the interaction going as long as possible and avoid taking over.

For children with more significant challenges, it may feel difficult at first to find something your child gravitates towards, but there is always something that will spark a child's interest. You can always start with imitating what your child is doing and also make every action meaningful (i.e., if your child walks away, take that as an indication that it is your turn!). Your affect and pacing will help keep your child engaged, but keep in mind individual differences and how you might need to alter your interactions to support these differences.

How Do I Get Started?

The best way to truly learn and apply the DIR® Model with your child is to connect with a DIR®-trained professional who can assess your child and support you in developing a home- or school-based program that will meet your child's individualized needs and work in coordination with other service providers. DIR® professionals come from a wide range of disciplines, including educators, mental health providers, occupational and physical therapists, and speech and language pathologists. They receive intensive and comprehensive training in the DIR®/ Floortime™ Model.

To find someone in your area who can guide and support you in this process, check www.icdl.com and search for DIR® Professionals by state. The network of DIR® professionals is wide, but if you cannot locate someone in your area, many professionals work with families by reviewing and providing feedback on videotaped sessions.

You can read more about the DIR® Model, including a number of articles to get you started, on the Interdisciplinary Council for Developmental and Learning Disorders site at *www.icdl.com.*

Remember, the best way to begin is to acknowledge where your child is now and build from there. Meet your child at his or her level and use your affect to keep your child engaged. Focus on having fun with each other at first. If you are having fun, so will your child, and when he or she is having fun, learning is happening. Be animated, use lots of gestures, and keep the interactions flowing!

—

Resources

Greenspan, S.I., and S. Wieder. *Engaging Autism: The Floortime Approach to Helping Children Relate, Communicate and Think.* New York: Perseus Books, 1996.

Greenspan, S.I., and S. Wieder. *The Child with Special Needs: Encouraging Intellectual and Emotional Growth.* New York: Perseus Books, 1997.

Interdisciplinary Council on Developmental and Learning Disorders: *www.icdl.com*

The Floortime Repository (sign-up required): *www.floortimerepository.com*

What to Ask of an Occupational Therapist

Barbara H. Boucher, OT, Ph.D., PT

My identity as an occupational therapist (OT) runs as deep as my sense of being an adult. I begin on a personal note because if you have trouble discerning a person's face or need concrete affirmation of my being, you might imagine me to have three heads: As a naive undergraduate, I learned at the feet of Jean Ayers' generation of occupational therapists. For reasons that are most easily characterized as my professional "developmental" trajectory, I became a physical therapist, also. A complete psychological profile of me might read that I received a great deal of reinforcement in an academic setting. From my Ph.D. in Human Development and Family Sciences, I claim the title of Child Development Specialist.

If the words "occupational therapy" are new to you and accompanied your child's diagnosis, you are not alone in struggling to understand what "OT" means. Just last week my cousin asked me if occupational therapists assist people in finding a job. Yes, well, if you mean helping a person through the eleventybillion steps, tasks, and activities necessary to obtain a job!

In my own words: OT is therapy for learning to do, renew or revive those daily activities we do in everyday life.

For those activities that cannot be revived, OTs are specialists for adapting the home, person, or activity for participation in that activity again.

To get a more personal or individual benefit from the OT treating your child, I offer several request-suggestions for your child's therapist. These might appear to be different phrasings of the same questions, but I am intentionally giving you several verbal options in order to generate understanding between you and the therapist. There is no "magic" in good communication (with apologies to speech therapists), but the results can be magically effective for your child.

First request-suggestion: Please show me how to help my child live comfortably in our home with our family.

This broad request can open up a slew of techniques for helping you emotionally adjust to your child's diagnosis and give you options to choose from or try. Assuming your therapist is sensitive to your responses, if you are overwhelmed, he or she will adjust the slew to one suggestion at a time. I also expect your therapist to give you the opportunity to prioritize your concerns—to say which issue you would like to address first.

Along with the semantically strange name for this therapy, you are also learning the meaning of a whole new vocabulary to describe your child's particular responses to sensations. Response to sensations and using sensations as techniques are often misunderstood as curative of the behaviors commonly seen in children with spectrum diagnoses.

I am intentionally suggesting this request first to dispel the thought of OT as curative or medicinal. Therapy is distinctly different from medicine in that it is a process—many repeated actions over time that effect a change. And OT and PT are often "dosed" in a medicinal manner—as though thirty minutes, two times a week will effectively decrease problematic behaviors. But therapy is not curative so much as able to make life more livable.

Sensory dysfunction, or, rather, dysfunctional response to sensations, can accompany cognitive and social learning delays. Problems, issues, neural dysfunction evidenced by extreme responses to sensations are parallel to cognitive and social development, not the sole impediment preventing cognitive and social development. (Similarly, seizures are common in children with autism spectrum diagnoses. Uncontrolled seizures impede learning.) The behaviors that indicate sensory dysfunction can impede learning and need to be managed. An occupational therapist can help you manage your child's sensory dysfunction. (Alternatively, medicine is the primary means for controlling seizures.)

Dysfunctional response to sensation can mask learning potential, but careful and effective sensory management will reveal a child's potential on the intelligence spectrum. Indeed, many children have sensory proclivities that do not land them on the autism spectrum. If your child is on a different developmental trajectory, an OT can help you guide your child's growth and development toward a more independent (functional) life by meeting his or her innate potential. Home is the place to begin this guidance, and I urge you to invest your energy there first before you charge the school with your rights booklet in your raised fist.

Second request-suggestion: Please help us create a sensory diet for our child.

The analogy of a sensory "diet" is apt for the kind of lifestyle habits needed for managing sensory dysfunction. Food is necessary in life. Diets are individual to tastes—so many foods, so many ways to cook and serve them! I support the sensory diet concept—"a carefully designed, personalized activity plan that provides the sensory input a person needs to stay focused and organized throughout the day,"—but it can be difficult for parents to implement. Some have difficulty reading the daily nuances that indicate a child's need for a different "snack," and are best helped by following therapist-prescribed protocols (a diet).

By asking an OT for a sensory diet, you acknowledge and understand that your child's responses to sensation are interrupting your family life, and you want help to make changes to improve your family's life. Be open to the idea that you will (by extension) be receiving services from the OT. Treating the family "by extension" is consistent with OT theory and philosophy—the patient/child is seen as functioning within a context or "ecology" and not in a separate clinic setting.

Third request-suggestion: Please explain the services maze available for my child.

With this request, you are asking for a map and a compass into the jungle of acronyms and costs associated with your child's diagnosis. Some of this information is mandated (the rights booklet). However, unless you use a machete to cut your own path, you will be at the mercy of eleventybillion "mosquitoes."

Different and overlapping regulation layers exist for employers, licensing, schools/special education, insurance, Medicaid, and medical care. Each layer might touch (bite) your child's (your) life. Some of those regulations are particular to your state, and some apply to the entire country but are implemented in a seemingly individual manner—as with the "I" in IEP (Individualized Education Program), and IDEA (Individuals With Disabilities Education Act).

Commonalities between family experiences abound, so it is good to find other families with children with an autism diagnosis—add the words "support" and "advocacy" to your list of desirable jungle plants. Expect your OT to guide you to the sweetness of not feeling alone by showing you where to find other families "flowering" with autism.

If an OT shows you to the thorny "I'm-not-allowed-to-tell-you" bush, consider that a red flag. If you can, rephrase your request. Some information is not allowed to be passed between the therapist and a caregiver, responsible person, patient, or child. If you are able, seek out as much information as you can yourself via the Internet or a library before asking your OT.

Fourth request-suggestion: Please show me how to help my child progress in school.

This request logically follows the previous three requests. Before you armor yourself with rights and expectations for IEP battle, be sure you know your child really well. I have met parents who have been led to believe that a one-on-one aide with inclusion is the Holy Grail of success for a child in public school. Expect an OT to help you see the (many) steps needed for your child to be more independent in public school. OTs are philosophically primed to understand process—or how-to-get-there.

Knowing your child really well—as in how she responds to different sensations and the many methods of helping her manage her responses—

will help you interact with her teacher(s). However, this information is not necessarily the point of an IEP meeting—the P in IEP stands for plan or program, but not the lesson plan. Knowing your child really well, you can bring suggestions for possible next achievements in school (goals) to the IEP meeting. I recommend you focus on the annual goals and enlist the help of an OT determine those goals.

Fifth request-suggestion: Please show me how to help my child prepare for life after public school.

Whether your child is recently diagnosed or you are the veteran of years of special education meetings, looking towards the future can be painful. Lean on your OT and calculate his or her services into the long view for your child.

Using the example of independent toileting, ask your child's OT to project the next step in independence toward that goal. Ask her to give you every method to help your child achieve that step—to incorporate repetition at school. As I once suggested: What if there was only one goal on your child's IEP and that was independence in toileting? What if everything in your child's education was directed at independence in toileting? Once free of dependence in such a personal and typical activity of daily living, your child would be free to learn so much more. It would be like, well, having well-managed sensory responses. And once achieved, toileting would not be an issue for the rest of your child's life. Just imagine.

I am not suggesting a single-goal IEP because I think every child can learn in more than one domain at a time. At the same time, there is a relationship between rate of learning and what should go on the IEP. You will have to make decisions between learning components that appear academic, social skills that are cognitive and language-dependent, and functional skills like toileting that are tied to motor development. Many children do better if more time is focused on fewer expectations. Since occupational therapists have a holistic mindset, you should mine the brain of your OT to make IEP decisions for your child that will lead to a good quality of life after school.

Throughout my whole career, I have met the patient/client where they are and sought to nudge them forward or in their own self-determined direction. I truly believe in empowering people to grow beyond the time they spend with me. Expect the same from your child's OT, and you will get a return on the value of every cent you invest in him or her.

Autism Service Dogs

Sarah Low

In the Fall of 2003, my mother sent me an article from the *Vancouver Sun* newspaper. It was about an organization in Canada that was training dogs specifically for young autistic children. I was fascinated and excited—Josh was five at the time, and I had already been thinking about whether a dog could be of some help to him.

National Service Dogs in Canada (NSD) was responding to a need they discovered quite by accident. They had been in the business of training assistance dogs for adults with other types of disabilities. Then they received a desperate plea from the mother of a young autistic boy, asking if they could train a dog to help her keep her son safe. This little boy was a "runner"; he would get out of their house at all hours of the day or night and take off. His family was at a loss.

The NSD trainers weren't sure what they could do, but after talking with the family in depth, they came up with a training plan they thought might work. It involved the dog working with the child and an adult handler as a three-member team. The child would be tethered to the dog using a special belt attachment, and the adult would be the one managing the dog on a leash. They worked on this new system with the family, and the result was an amazing success. Not only did the tethering system have the obvious benefit of keeping the boy safe, but also a bond developed between this child and the dog that no one expected.

NSD began receiving more and more requests from parents of autistic children. There was clearly a need in our community; they'd seen real success with the program they'd developed, so from that point on, they chose to focus entirely on training and placing service dogs with autistic children.

Working dogs are new to the autism world. Working dogs for children are new to the entire service dog industry. Fewer than ten years ago, working dogs were only trained/placed with individuals considered old enough to handle the dog on their own—the minimum age I found while doing my own research at the time was sixteen, and for most organizations it was eighteen. And no one was training dogs for people with autism. Well, almost no one. There was NSD. In my later research, I found that there were one or two other organizations in the United States also working on programs for children on the spectrum, but at the time of my initial searching, NSD was all that I could find.

My son is not and was not ever a classic "runner." He did have a tendency to wander, though, and had on a few occasions either left or tried to leave the house. Taking him anywhere in public was a struggle—he would wander off if I didn't have him by the hand, but he didn't want to be held on to and would always fight to get free. This was always frightening in places like parking lots or anywhere his pulling away from me could possibly put him in danger.

The other benefit I hoped a dog could provide was simply to be a calming influence for Josh, who was prone to some pretty horrific tantrums. Josh is and always has been a very sensory-seeking child. I thought that a dog, with its fur, warmth, and constant presence, might just help Josh feel less stressed, give him an anchor, something he could count on always being there without placing demands on him. The testimonials from families who already had dogs were amazing. Of course, all of our children are different, and you really don't know how your child will respond to having a service animal and what, if any, relationship might develop until you actually have one.

With that in mind and after a great deal of discussion with Josh's dad, I started down the road to get a dog for Josh. It took three years. It was a long and often frustrating process that for us also involved changing organizations mid-course.

One of the questions—and it is a big, important question regarding a service or assistance dog—is "How much does it cost?" Depending on the organization, it will cost anywhere from around $8,000 to upwards of $15,000. Before you stop reading because those numbers just stabbed you in the heart, here is the rub: this is not a "fee" for the dog. All of the organizations that train service animals are 501(c)3 entities, and they cannot ask you to "pay" for the receipt of a dog. What they want is for you to fundraise for them. It's a lot of legal semantics, because yes, you send them money, you get a dog. But the money is considered and deemed a charitable donation to the organization. You get a dog because you were accepted to their program.

It's a fine line, and I know of only two exceptions. The first is Canine Companions for Independence—who were not training dogs for autistic children when we were going through the process but do now. They do not require any financial commitment from you at all. Despite being new to providing dogs for autism assistance, they are certainly not new to the service dog industry. Their application process is much longer and more involved than any of the others, and I would imagine that because there is no financial obligation of any sort that it is much, much harder to be approved for a dog from them—and I could not tell you what their waiting list is like. They have been training many different types of assistance dogs since 1975.

The second exception is NSD. While they do ask you to fundraise to reach a certain donation amount, you will receive your dog regardless of whether or not you reach that set goal. All of the other organizations ask for and require the donation requirement be met prior to receiving your dog.

So the other big question, "How long will it take to get a dog?" depends primarily upon which organization you work with and how long it takes you to meet the fundraising requirements. If you are fortunate to have the means to make the donation yourselves, then you will have your dog much faster than if you have to fundraise, though with NSD your place on the wait list is your place, regardless of meeting your goal quickly or not. Most of the larger organizations have programs in place to assist you in the fundraising process, so there is usually a lot of help and guidance available.

We started out with NSD, but after about two years on their wait list and facing what would likely have been another year, I was impatient. I started searching for alternatives and found one in 4 Paws for Ability. They are an Ohio-based organization that had been training dogs to work specifically with children with all sorts of different disabilities, and autism was now one of them. Because they did not rely on a breeding program for the dogs that they trained (unlike NSD and several other groups), they were able to speed up the process somewhat. They also set you up for training once you meet your donation requirement. 4 Paws uses donated dogs, rescued dogs, and some that they have bred for their programs. All of their dogs are temperament-tested before being placed into a training program. There are pros and cons to this that I will address later.

I had NSD take us off their list, then set to work with 4 Paws. With any of the organizations, a training session is required. They vary in length a little, but you should count on anywhere from one to two weeks where you will have to travel to their location to train with your new dog. This includes your child, since you will be working as a team. Most of the training is for the adult that will be the dog's primary handler, though, so make sure if you decide that a dog is right for your child, you have the ability to travel with at least one other adult who can be with your child during the times they are not involved in the training sessions. Keep in mind, the cost of your travel and related expenses will be up to you. Also remember that the journey home will include your dog, so if you are traveling by air, you will need to talk with the airlines ahead of time.

Our journey was a complicated one, and we ended up coming home from our first scheduled training early, without a dog. There had been communication issues and some misinformation between the 4 Paws staff and myself, as well as a situation that arose during training that we were unable to resolve. Due to some of the issues, I was not sure I wanted to continue with them, but after some discussion with their director, I chose to keep working with them to get my son his dog. We went back a few months later for another training session with a different dog and came home with Buddy, my son's autism assistance dog.

Buddy was a rescue dog, a Katrina refugee if his story is to be believed—he had come to 4 Paws with very little information about his past. No one even really knows what kind of dog he is, though everyone seems to have a theory. We have decided he is a Catahoula Leopard dog, though probably not a pure-bred one.

Having Buddy has made a big difference for us. Josh does not mind being tethered to him and seems to appreciate the freedom to move about on his own somewhat without anyone having to hold on to him physically. It has kept him safe and easily managed, from places like the grocery store, to very expensive furniture stores that would otherwise have been a nightmare, to Disneyland. Our first trip to Disneyland was before we got Buddy, and though it was fun, it was somewhat difficult having to keep Josh in a stroller all the time. We have been twice with Buddy, and both times were much better: I knew Josh was safe, never had to worry about his taking off and getting lost in the crowd, and he didn't have someone hanging on to him and had enough freedom to move around on his own— my son was happy.

Buddy was trained in tracking as well as obedience work, so if Josh ever did wander off, we should be able to find him very quickly. Josh does not wander so much any more, so though tracking was one of the things we practiced extensively in training, it's a skill that I doubt we'll ever have to have Buddy use. It is still important for many families, though.

Josh has not developed a "special" bond with Buddy that any of us can discern, so we have not seen related benefits, such as the dog being sensitive to Josh's needs—but it does seem that Josh is more content to do whatever it is we are doing when he is tethered to the dog and not being held by the hand. It can make an enormous difference.

Also, and this is one of the biggest benefits aside from safety, Buddy is a wonderful ambassador. When out in public with Josh before we had Buddy, most of the attention he got would be negative. When he is with Buddy, it's all positive. People come up to ask me questions now instead of simply staring at us, and I use the opportunity to do a little educating. This is of particular importance for kids who are higher functioning and taking their dogs to school, as it really helps build relationships with the other children and even staff. Instead of seeing a child who is "different" that they might not want to approach, the kids see the dog, and naturally want to know all about it—it's an ice-breaker that almost always promotes positive interactions.

A service or assistance dog is not for everyone, so I encourage you to think very, very carefully about your decision. Dogs in general require a lot of care and on-going maintenance; dogs that are specially trained to work require even more. And having a child or children on the autism spectrum is itself a ton of work, so just remember that while potentially being of great benefit, a service dog will add to your workload. Having a service animal requires much more of you when traveling, for example.

You should also determine whether you feel a therapy or companion dog would be better for your family; they are not the same as service/assistance animals. A therapy/companion dog is still trained specifically for certain behaviors; however, they are not trained or certified to be in public places with you. My experience is with the service/assistance dogs, but I would imagine a therapy dog would involve less expense overall. It really depends on what your needs are.

Look at your candidate organizations as closely as possible because there are a lot of considerations. Ask as many questions as you can and then make the best choice for your family.

Some organizations will send their trainers to you to spend time helping you after you get home from your initial training, which I believe is invaluable. But not all of them do this.

Some use dogs only from their own breeding programs, ensuring the breeds and temperaments that are necessary for these dogs to work as they do.

Some will use rescued dogs or donated dogs, and even though they have all been temperament-tested and trained, you never know what that dog has been through in the past. This is a concern with Buddy right now.

Only one of the organizations currently trains the dogs to track, if that is a skill you would like them to have.

You have to decide what your priorities are, look at all of your options, and go from there.

All of the organizations have satisfied and very happy families that can tell you how great their experiences were, so read the testimonials. Just keep in mind not everything always goes smoothly. If I had it to do over again knowing all that I do now, there are some things I would do differently, but I would still want a dog for Josh. In the end, if you believe a service dog could help your family/child, it will be worth what it takes to get there.

Organizations that train dogs for people on the autism spectrum:

Canine Companions for Independence:
www.cci.org/site/c.cdKGIRNqEmG/b.4010977/k.C959/About_Us.htm

Autism Service Dogs of America: *www.autismservicedogsofamerica.com*

Wilderwood Service Dogs: *www.autism.wilderwood.org*

Compassionate Paws: *www.compassionatepaws.org*

Highland Canine Training: *www.autismassistancedog.com/index.htm*

North Star Dogs: *www.northstardogs.com*

National Service Dogs: *www.nsd.on.ca*

4 Paws for Ability: *www.4pawsforability.org*

An Open Letter to Special Needs Professionals

Pia Prenevost

Hello?

New teacher, or therapist, or doctor? Is that you?

Oh hello...

I just wanted to chat with you a second. To caution you. Or warn you.

Please, tread carefully.

You see, what you might not realize as you look at me, talk to me, tell me your opinions, our options, our lack of options, and your predictions of our outcomes is that; well...you see that heart?

The slightly broken, definitely bruised one?

Yeah, that's my heart.

My slightly-broken, definitely bruised heart.

Now, I realize that as you look at me you might see...a confident parent...or an angry parent...or a happy-go-lucky parent...

You might think that I understand everything...or nothing...or that I have all the experience in the world because I have done this before or that I know the rules...or that I don't know the rules and that is for the best...

You might believe...that I am high maintenance...or overreacting...or maybe neurotic...or disengaged and uninterested...or that I don't really care...or maybe I care too much...

But regardless of what you see, what you think, or what you believe, this is what you should know:

I am broken-hearted. And it doesn't matter if it is the first day or a century later. It doesn't matter where in the "grief cycle" I might be. It doesn't matter if the wounds are healed, or healing, or fresh and new. This heart is bruised. Slightly broken. Different than it once was and will ever be again. And when you speak, or don't speak, in judgment or not, my heart is out there.

Some of "us" parents...the "special" ones...can be a pain in the ass. I know that. We know that. But we are fighting a fight we never planned to fight, and it doesn't end. We don't get to clock out at the end of the day. We don't get a vacation. We live it, everyday. We are fighting without knowing how to fight, and we depend so much on you to help us. We have been disappointed, by you or others like you. And we are disappointed in ourselves. We are your harshest critics. We are our own harshest critics, too. We are genuinely fearful, and driven, and absolutely devoted. And we also know, we need you. So please, be careful with us. Because as hard and tough as we may look outwardly, our hearts are fragile things.

Why I Can't Breathe Tonight

Anonymous Special Needs Professional

Recently I read a post on *Thinking Person's Guide to Autism* by a parent, Pia Prenevost. It was called "An Open Letter to Special Needs Professionals..." The title made me feel a bit guarded at first (as a special needs professional), because my experience is that "an open letter" usually warns that a negative letter of the "Oh, no, you di'n't" variety, is coming. But that was incorrect because in reality the author had written a lovely, heartfelt post about the vulnerability a parent of a child with special needs feels. I encourage you to read it; it's beautiful. Here's an excerpt:

> I am broken-hearted. And it doesn't matter if it is the first day or a century later. It doesn't matter where in the "grief cycle" I might be. It doesn't matter if the wounds are healed, or healing, or fresh and new. This heart is bruised. Slightly broken. Different than it once was and will ever be again. And when you speak, or don't speak, in judgment or not, my heart is out there.

I appreciated the beauty and truth of her words. I will share it with parents I work with, happily. And at the same time, it made me feel a bit hopeless as a professional, like there is really nothing I can do or say that might help a parent, even though I'm certain that wasn't the intent.

Later I came to find out that some teachers and therapists had commented on the post in anger. I read their responses with interest because what they were writing had precious little to do with anything Ms. Prenevost had actually written; instead, they had responded with their own raw emotion. It was as if they were arguing a completely different post or person, but their emotions were just as high.

Reading those comments from a few professionals left me short of breath. I have felt on the verge of a panic attack for the past two hours, and I've never had a panic attack. I couldn't concentrate on reading with my kids, or putting them to bed, I was so preoccupied.

Why? Where am I? I am, in my mind, back in a long-ago job, which was in a small, well-regarded public school district. A place where I was respected among my colleagues but clearly believed to be an idiot until proven capable to parents, assumed to know far less than my counterparts in private practice. Having come from a private practice job, I had suddenly been demoted to second-class citizen among my clients' parents because I was working in the schools. I can still see their suspicious expressions at my first Open House. It was an astonishing experience, and I never forget it when I walk into a public school meeting as a private therapist. Some therapists are better than others, whether they are in public school or private practice. "You get what you pay for" does not always apply.

Ninety-five percent of the parents I worked with were wonderful, once I had proved myself to them, and that didn't take long. I knew what I was doing. It didn't matter how significant their child's needs were, most of them were partners with us, their child's team. We were a very strong team. They were considerate, polite, and respectful. So were we. That didn't mean we always agreed, but we had the good relationship required to work things out when we didn't see eye-to-eye.

But the other five percent? Well, tonight I'd say I suffered some trauma at the hands of that five percent, because more than ten years later I am short of breath just thinking about them.

My colleagues and I were treated very badly. Certain of those parents visited me in bad dreams for as long as five years after I left that job. I was scoffed at in meetings by special education attorneys and expensive "experts" (put in quotes because the one who appeared most frequently was later discredited) flown in from across the country (the school district having been required to pay airfare and hotel bills for these visits on behalf of families). My clinical insights were dismissed by that small group of parents because to acknowledge that the school team had any insight whatsoever would weaken the "case."

The stress that was caused by a few families affected a great many of us: therapists, teacher, principal, administrators. It was out of hand and inappropriate. The kids didn't benefit; after all, their parents and special educators were at odds and all adults in their lives were under a lot of stress. I lost sleep. Our work suffered. Good teachers left, and I left. After only three years. Just thinking about it all these years later raises my blood pressure. This is not such an unusual story. I was in an excellent school district.

High turnover in special education? Good people who can make it on their own, fleeing? Yep.

Sure, I could—usually do—blame my leaving on lack of administrative support. On high caseloads and insane amounts of paperwork and more than fifty 20-page IEPs per year. On never, ever, even for a minute, feeling like I was doing enough for anyone, or like there was enough funding for me to do my job appropriately. On sitting in a meeting and being grilled by frequently snarky attorneys who were audio taping us while my supervisor sat by not backing me up, pretending she didn't hear the argument while she filled out the IEP paperwork, because she was sick to death of the whole thing and for once the attention wasn't on her. Often we were left hanging in the breeze.

I don't usually admit to myself that the paranoid, fight-at-all-cost behaviors and lack of faith of a very small group of parents also drove me out. Because I love parents; I work well with parents. I *am* a parent. I *get* a lot of it. I'd rather pretend that it's only those bad therapists, the ones who are really incompetent, who get driven out. But they both did me in, the fighting parents and the unsupportive administration, and I left the public domain. I'm going to go out on a limb and suggest that I'd have ended up one of those angry commenters anonymously spewing frustration in the wrong places had I stayed in a broken system much longer.

I have read two fascinating essays written by parents I respect greatly, about their initial misinterpretation of their children's teachers. Robert Rummel-Hudson wrote a post called "Mea Culpa" on his blog *Fighting Monsters With Rubber Swords*, to the teacher he believes he initially misjudged. And another excellent writer, Kim Leaird, who writes at *Autism Twins*, wrote "Hello, Doom! Welcome Back to School" about the conclusions she leapt to—and then discovered she might be able to let go of a little bit—with her son's new special education teacher.

I appreciated that both of these parents shared publicly the emotional roller coaster of a new school year and having to adjust to new professionals, and were willing to honestly share their realizations that maybe things are going to be okay at school after all. Parents have to advocate for their children, and I know as well as anyone that many programs and professionals aren't up to speed. It's extremely frustrating for us all. But when parents come in armed and ready for things to be wrong and for professionals to be incompetent, the professionals are demeaned on day one and left to play defense in a game no one taught them in college and that no one will win.

Parents of kids with special needs are allowed to share their horror stories about professionals with each other, and they do. Professionals are named and, sometimes, vilified. Sometimes this is warranted; sometimes it is not. But either way, it gives parents a web of support when they share their stories in person, on blogs, on Twitter. This support is important and, I believe, ultimately a very good thing.

Therapists and other professionals may have co-workers they can go to for support, but rarely is there an opportunity to truly give each other the type of support they need to share their own horror stories. Professionals can't write, blog, or tweet about these situations from our point of view in any real sense, or even (legally) talk to our spouses about them. Try explaining one of those contentious IEP meetings to your spouse without using anyone's names or sharing any actual information. We end up with a lot of pent-up frustration when we don't have a supportive administrator and time to deal with our emotions. It's more isolating than you'd think. We too need support.

That's what I heard in the comments that appeared to many to be "off base" in Ms. Prenevost's post. They weren't responding to her words, not really; they were responding to her raw emotion with their own. If, when I worked in public schools, a parent had implored us to excuse them for being our "harshest critics," I might have wanted to explode, too. But I doubt that Ms. Prenevost herself is her school staff's harshest critic because she sounds too self-aware to treat people the way the harshest critics actually do treat professionals. I may have felt bitter back then that I could not write such a letter, imploring greater understanding, too, without getting myself, and my school district, in trouble. I get it.

We professionals may not physically take your children home with us, but in a lot of ways we take them—and their parents—home emotionally, every day and (apparently, in my case) years later. Both the joys and the stresses of the job affect our personal lives and our own family's lives. As the new school year begins, I implore parents and professionals alike, on behalf of those who work in public schools, to please make an effort to give each other the benefit of the doubt, some support, a little credit, and as much gratitude as we can possibly muster.

5 Causation Theories and Dubious Therapies

We already know genetics contributes strongly to autism. The question is, what else, if anything, does?

And that's not an easy question to answer—if it can be answered at all. Certainly, there won't be an answer that a single, sensational headline can encapsulate.

—Emily Willingham

When a Mom Says Something Works:
The GFCF Diet

JoyMama

My daughter Joy loves Baby Einstein videos and has found them mesmerizing since infancy. I've heard them so often that I practically know them by heart, including the promotional material at the end of the episodes. In one of the self-advertising sequences, Julie Aigner-Clark, creator of Baby Einstein, is heard to exclaim, "As moms, we're all looking for help…and if a mom tells you, 'Try this, it works,' you automatically try it if you're a mom!"

She wasn't talking about alternative therapies for autism. But as the mother of a child on the autism spectrum, I hear the echoes.

One place I heard such reverberations was in a 2010 *Time* magazine article on Jenny McCarthy and autism.[1] Actress and former Playboy Playmate Jenny McCarthy, whose son was diagnosed with autism in 2005, had become the celebrity-mom face of the unproven-therapies-for-autism movement. The article's author somewhat wryly notes, "…it is hard to find a controversial, novel, or alternative treatment that McCarthy doesn't say has some merit." The article sums up McCarthy's autism treatment advice in these words: "Try everything," says McCarthy, "Hope is the only thing that will get us up in the morning."

The second part of McCarthy's statement resonates with me. Not the first part.

I had an extraordinary opportunity in early 2010 to examine controversial "try-everything" therapies, as part of the MCH-LEND program, which stands for Maternal and Child Health Leadership Education in Neurodevelopmental Disabilities.[2] This interdisciplinary leadership training program at select universities offers graduate students and family members the chance to engage with clinical and advocacy and public health issues around developmental disability, and to develop leadership skills to bring to bear in their professions and communities. One of our LEND seminar assignments involved small-group presentations on alternative therapies, for autism and beyond.

My group consisted of a nutritionist/mom, a psychology graduate student, and me (librarian/mom). We were assigned to examine the gluten-free, casein-free (GFCF) diet for autism. The point of the assignment was to become familiar with the claims of the intervention and learn how to evaluate non-standard therapies in general. We were to examine a substantial list of questions[3] for our presentation, including:

- What exactly is the claim made by this intervention? For whom is it intended?
- Is the claim consistent with current knowledge, i.e., does the rationale for its claimed effectiveness make sense in terms of already-existing scientific knowledge?
- What is the evidence base for this intervention?
- Have results been described in peer-reviewed journals, or only the lay press?
- Are there any known risks for using this therapy?
- Are there position statements issued by any professional organizations regarding this therapy?
- Are there conflicts of interest for those evaluating the claims?
- How widely used is the intervention?
- How much does it cost in time, energy, and money for families?
- What is the attraction for families to try this therapy?

Here's what we found: The gluten-free, casein-free diet is an elimination diet. To be eliminated from the menu are gluten, a protein found in grains (wheat, barley, rye, and some oats), and casein, a protein found in animal milk. Elimination diets have been around for a long time, and in general they rest on a sound premise: if you are sensitive or allergic to something in your diet, stop eating it! The gluten-free diet is the one best approach for celiac disease, and if you have a demonstrated sensitivity or allergy to milk, dairy-free is the way to go. They are not easy regimens to follow, but in those situations, elimination diets are known to be effective.

The "alternative" part of this therapy is the claim that GFCF can cure or ameliorate autism spectrum disorder (ASD)—in up to 90% of cases, according to the organization Talk About Curing Autism (TACA). The controversial underlying theory is this: People with ASDs are said have a predisposition to a gastrointestinal condition known as "leaky gut" or "autistic enterocolitis." The condition is supposedly triggered by an environmental insult—some say vaccines, some suspect other sources of toxicity. When the condition is triggered, the hypothesis goes, you wind up with an incomplete breakdown of gluten and casein, which escape through the leaky gut. The protein molecules/polypeptides travel through the bloodstream and attach to opiate receptors in the brain, leading to autism or magnifying the symptoms of autism.

According to this scenario, if you remove the gluten and the casein from the diet, the gut will heal, the opiate reaction is halted, and the autistic symptoms are alleviated—generally in a couple of months of strict adherence to the diet, sometimes taking up to a year.

GFCF is not an easy diet to follow, especially since people on the autism spectrum may already be eating a self-restricted range of foods. The diet requires constant vigilance on the part of parents, such as careful ingredient checking and diet balancing and making sure that gluten and casein don't slip in from unexpected sources: a playmate's cracker snagged from the floor, a bit of standard Play-Doh®, etc. Pre-fab GFCF foods can be very expensive. If you want to do the diet less expensively, you'll spend a lot of time in preparing foods from scratch. Recipe-sharing online can ease that burden; there's even a webpage from TACA that outlines how to do the GFCF diet on food stamps.

There have been related scientific studies from a number of angles: measuring opioid peptides in the urine, measuring intestinal permeability, studying the behavioral outcomes of people with ASD who go on the diet. In all of those areas, research is relatively thin on the ground, and the results are not definitive. There are even conflicting studies as to whether people with autism have more GI issues in general than people without, though we do know that GI issues that occur in typically developing folks do occur in folks with autism as well. One 2006 study found GI issues in 70% of their study group with autism, much higher than in their nonautistic comparison group;[4] another published in 2009 found little difference other than in GI issues that have behavioral sources (constipation and food selectivity).[5]

In a happy circumstance for our presentation, a consensus paper[6] came out in *Pediatrics*, a high-profile peer-reviewed journal, right at the start of the semester. A whole slew of GI experts had gotten together, weighed existing evidence, made consensus statements regarding GI issues and ASD, and recommended a lot of new research. Here are several of the consensus statements most pertinent to GFCF (there were twenty-three statements in all):

- Individuals with ASDs who present with gastrointestinal symptoms warrant a thorough evaluation, as would be undertaken for individuals without ASDs who have the same symptoms or signs.

- The prevalence of gastrointestinal abnormalities in individuals with ASDs is incompletely understood.

- The existence of a gastrointestinal disturbance specific to persons with ASDs (e.g., "autistic enterocolitis") has not been established.

- Available research data do not support the use of a casein-free diet, a gluten-free diet, or combined gluten-free, casein-free (GFCF) diet as a primary treatment for individuals with ASDs.

Of interest, this consensus paper received some acclaim from both skeptics and proponents of the GFCF diet as a treatment for autism. Skeptics said (and I paraphrase immensely), "Look, here it is in black and white—current research data do not recommend this treatment!" Proponents said, "Look at all this research they're recommending—we're finally being taken seriously!"

This kind of recommended research does not happen overnight. One pilot study of the GFCF diet for autism at the University of Rochester, approved as a clinical trial since 2004, announced results in the spring of 2010.[7] A group of children with autism were put on a carefully controlled GFCF diet. After four weeks, half of the group received "challenge snacks" containing gluten and casein, while the other half received GFCF snacks. Neither the families nor the evaluators knew which children received which snacks. After three sets of challenge snacks across twelve weeks, the results showed no difference between the challenge-snack children and those who remained strictly GFCF. In the words of Susan Hyman, the lead researcher on the study, "It would have been wonderful for children with autism and their families if we found that the GFCF diet could really help, but this small study didn't show significant benefits."

A previous pilot study published in 2006[8] took a different approach, putting only half the participants on the diet but providing all foods for both groups, such that the participants and parents did not know whether or not they were GFCF. The study did not find any significant effects on either behavior or urinary peptide levels. However—and here's the really interesting bit—the parental reports and the researcher reports differed markedly. Parents thought they were seeing improvements that the researchers could not document. And nine of the families decided to keep going with the GFCF diet even when they were told that the researchers' observations didn't support it.

To me, this screams "placebo effect." People see what they want to see. No wonder the claims of "try this, it works!" are so high. I'm sure the parents in the study truly believed that they were seeing benefits that the researchers didn't catch. But that's one of the core reasons that we need science to help us distinguish between real effects and rose-colored glasses. As physicist Richard Feynman described the scientific endeavor, "The first principle is that you must not fool yourself—and you are the easiest person to fool."

My husband and I have not tried the GFCF diet with our Baby-Einstein-loving daughter because we have not seen anything that would make us suspect a dietary sensitivity if she weren't on the autism spectrum.

Many, many families are trying it, however. This therapy seems extremely attractive to parents, and I think there are a number of reasons. There are powerful testimonies out there, and high-profile proponents, from Jenny McCarthy to the autistic author and animal scientist Temple Grandin (who takes a much more nuanced approach than McCarthy). The diet has a reputation of harmlessness, though it can be nutritionally risky if not done carefully, especially for people whose diet is self-limited in the first place. There's definitely a "why not try it, what can it hurt?" vibe out there.

Besides all that, dietary changes are a familiar kind of intervention. Who hasn't gone on a diet at some point or another? And it's something that's possible to attempt without a prescription. There's plenty of do-it-yourself GFCF advice available, on the web and in books and in support groups.

There is value in hope. There is value in parents feeling empowered and feeling that they are helping their child. And the GFCF diet obviously works for some people with autism, as it works for some people without. Some people with ASDs do have dietary sensitivities, just like their typically developing counterparts. When you address those sensitivities, people feel better. When people feel better, they behave better, learn better, and interact better.

I'm open to the thought that there may be more food sensitivities than we currently understand. But as both the *Pediatrics* consensus paper and a systematic review in the July 2010 issue of *Research in Autism Spectrum Disorders*[9] demonstrate, right now there is not enough evidence to recommend the GFCF diet as a primary treatment for autism, and there is no current proof of the existence of autistic enterocolitis. My personal prediction is that the evidence against the leaky-gut/autistic enterocolitis hypothesis is going to start to pile up. Autistic enterocolitis as a concept is under a shadow already, in that its originator Andrew Wakefield has been de-licensed by the U.K. General Medical Council, and his 1998 paper[10] that fueled much of the speculation has been retracted by the medical journal in which it was published, *The Lancet*.

The outsized role of parental enthusiasm in promoting the GFCF diet, as with other non–evidence-based interventions for autism, makes for unfortunate peer pressure situations. Parents are made to feel guilty if they agree with the current scientific consensus and choose not to try the diet for their children with autism. Or, if they try the diet and don't see any benefits and quit, they may well be told that they didn't try long enough or that they must not have been doing it right. It can make for a lot of unnecessary self-doubt and hard feelings.

A parent's recommendation may be enough to cause one to "automatically try" a new toothpaste or a twenty-dollar Baby Einstein DVD. When it comes to autism treatments, though, there are many more questions to ask. The list from the LEND assignment is one fine place to start. As a parent, I found it empowering to have access to the questions being used to educate the up-and-coming professionals! If conflicting claims online feel too overwhelming, consider taking your questions to the professionals in your child's life.

When a mom says something works for her child with autism, congratulate her—but don't let your search stop there, as you work to sort out the snake oil from the truly useful, and make your well-informed decisions on what is really worth trying.

—

A version of this essay appeared on elvis-sightings.blogspot.com.

[1] Greenfield, Karl Taro, "The Autism Debate: Who's Afraid of Jenny McCarthy?" *Time* 8 March 2010; 175(9):40.

[2] www.aucd.org/template/page.cfm?id=473

[3] Assignment questions courtesy of MCH-LEND, University of Wisconsin-Madison, Waisman Center. Used with permission.

[4] M. Valicenti-McDermott, M et al., "Frequency of gastrointestinal symptoms in children with autistic spectrum disorders and association with family history of autoimmune disease," *Journal of Developmental and Behavioral Pediatrics* 2006; 27(2 suppl) (2006) :S128 –S136, www.ncbi.nlm.nih.gov/pubmed/19027584

[5] S. Ibrahim, et al., "Incidence of Gastrointestinal Symptoms in Children with Autism: A Population-Based Study," *Pediatrics* 124 (2009): 680-686, www.ncbi.nlm.nih.gov/pubmed/19651585

[6] T. Buie, et al., "Evaluation, Diagnosis, and Treatment of Gastrointestinal Disorders in Individuals With ASDs: A Consensus Report," *Pediatrics* 125 (2010): S1-S18, www.ncbi.nlm.nih.gov/pubmed/200480837

[7] S. Hyman, et al., "The Gluten Free and Casein Free (GFCF) Diet: A Double Blind, Placebo Controlled Challenge Study," International Meeting for Autism Research, Philadelphia, PA, May 22, 2010. imfar.confex.com/imfar/2010/webprogram/Paper6183.html

[8] JH Elder, et al., "The Gluten-Free, Casein-Free Diet in Autism: Results of a Preliminary Double Blind Clinical Trial," *Journal of Autism and Developmental Disorders* 36 no. 3): (April 2006): 413-20, www.ncbi.nlm.nih.gov/pubmed/16555138

[9] A. Mulloy, et al., "Gluten-Free and Casein-Free Diets in the Treatment of Autism Spectrum Disorders: A systematic Review." *Research in Autism Spectrum Disorders* 4(no. 3): (July 2010): 328-39, www.edb.utexas.edu/education/assets/files/ltc/gfcf_review.pdf

[10] A.J. Wakefield, et al., "Ileal- Lymphoid-Nodular Hyperplasia, Non-specific Colitis, and Pervasive Developmental Disorder in Children," *Lancet* 351 no. 9103): (February 28, 1998): 637-41. Retraction in *Lancet*, 375 no. 9713): (February 6, 2010): 445, www.ncbi.nlm.nih.gov/pubmed/9500320

Coming to Terms

Kev Leitch

It's now been nearly seven years since Megan, my eldest daughter, was diagnosed with both autism and a comorbid "severe learning difficulty" (known in the U.S. as intellectual disability—it means her measurable IQ is less than 70). Those six years have been a personal journey for me as I first came to terms with Megan's autism, got lightly involved in the "cure autism at all costs" movement, and then as I saw the results (or non-results) of this movement, genuinely came to terms with the fact Megan was autistic and got involved in the neurodiversity movement.

In those days, 2003, there was very little online regarding autism. No blogs existed that I could find, very few forums, and little to no email lists. To get your "Google Ph.D." in those days, one had to dig very hard indeed. And boy did I dig. Every word I didn't understand was written down for a further search session, every name carefully Googled with every permutation of keywords I could think of. Early names I came across in those days may tell you something of the type of information. Lenny Schafer, Mary Megson, Andy Cutler, Amy Holmes. These names and their associated online sites colored my thinking about autism and my perception of what it was. I can remember talking excitedly with a friend about this new autism treatment that I'd read about called "chelation" and how I was going to do my damnedest to get Meg involved. However, that search proved fruitless in the United Kingdom. In 2003, I'm not sure any U.K. chelationists existed. Lucky Meg.

But what really caught my eye was the Gluten Free Casein Free diet. The way the information was written about on the web, all I had to do was get Meg on this diet and she would be cured of her autism. I bought a book from Amazon and joined a web forum recommended by the book. With great expectations, we began the diet.

While Meg was on the diet, we learned a few things about our daughter. We learned that she liked bread and really objected to not having it. We learned that in biomed circles, this was known as a form of addiction and our daughter was essentially going "cold turkey." We learned that Meg was far cleverer than her official IQ of 70 allowed, as many times she managed to sneak foods she wasn't supposed to be having. We learned the power of positive thought over the power of truth as we re-began the diet every time she did this. We learned how to reorganize our kitchen, and we learned that even re-organization wasn't enough and so bought locks for our fridge and cupboards.

In short, what we were learning was one of the first basic truths about any biomed-based approach: it takes over your life.

And even now, in these early days, I was beginning to question. Here's a quote from a blog post of mine from June 2003:

> "I wonder what scientific basis there is for these claims and anyway the trends in what is acceptable in relation to food alter so quickly it's impossible for u to be sure. So what we intend to do is take it step by step. We'll start by removing Dairy foods from Megan's diet and see how we go!—probably making Gluten the next on our 'hit list.'"[1]

And so on we went. We carried on excluding certain foods from Meg's diet—more successfully now we had locks on the fridge and cupboards!—and she carried on making her displeasure known. We waited and we waited and we waited for some unknown, unspecified point when we would see that her autism was receding.

Nothing happened.

Dr. James Laidler, also a former GFCF advocate, sums up how we were beginning to feel:

> My younger son was still on a gluten- and casein-free diet, which we both swore had been a significant factor in his improvement. We had lugged at least 40 pounds of special food on the plane with us. In an unwatched moment, he snatched a waffle and ate it. We watched with horror and awaited the dramatic deterioration of his condition that the "experts" told us would inevitably occur. The results were astounding—absolutely nothing happened. I began to suspect that I had been very foolish.[2]

We had done exactly as we were told. We had given the GFCF diet the time it was recommended we should do for it to begin to work, and nothing had happened. Nothing at all.

Like Jim Laidler before me, after I felt foolish, I began to get angry. Angry at myself (as well as guilty as to what I had insisted we put Meg through), angry at some of the parents on the biomed forum I attended, and above all, angry at those who were not just "researching" this treatment but making a hell of a lot of money from it.

It was now I began to notice that there were other things that could accompany the GFCF diet—nutritional supplements, megadoses of vitamins, various detox methods, and as 2003 became 2004 and we moved into the summer of that year, my own anger became a determination. A determination that I—and through me Megan—would not get caught out again—"won't get fooled again," as Roger Daltrey famously sings.

I started reading scientific abstracts on autism and the vaccine connection, and a connection that had once seemed not just possible but likely melted away in the same way a mirage does—as you get closer to the truth, the lie fades away.

If the abstract was highly technical, then I would write to the authors and ask for an explanation. Nine times out of ten, the authors would be more than happy to talk about their work and would walk me through what they had done, how they had done it—and of course above all: what it showed.

I also became familiar, online, with a group of autistic adults and began to have my assumptions about the overriding necessity for "cure at all costs" challenged. I was highly impressed with people like Jim Sinclair, Frank Klein, Clay Adams, Amanda Baggs, and of course the now sadly silent Autism Diva.[3]

This set of circumstances led to what I (rather pompously) think of as my autism awakening. I was being exposed to proper science in terms of causation and treatment, and at the same time, was being exposed to a new way (to me) of thinking about autism.

This new way of thinking about autism included the really rather radical idea that just maybe autistic people might not choose to be "cured" of their autism (assuming one day a cure ever existed). This put them into direct conflict with those who chose a pure biomed way of treating autism, designed as it was—however badly—to cure autism.

One of the aspects of the biomed movement that I had once shown was a burning desire to rid my daughter of any aspect of her autism. To the biomed movement, any approach that is

a) Not grounded in biomed principles and

b) Not set up with the end result of removing all traces of autism from a person

was simply invalid and should not only be mistrusted but actively attacked with what Jim Laidler describes as: "Utter nonsense treated like scientific data…theories made out of thin air and unrelated facts."[4]

And lo and behold, when I tried to post on a biomed group citing science regarding the autism/vaccine non-connection, I was attacked in what was—to me at the time—a surprising and intense amount of vitriol. I was accused of being insane and of "trolling" the group (trolling is an activity that sees an individual trying to annoy the regular participants for no reason other than the chance to see them annoyed).[5] Needless to say, I wasn't trolling. I was (I thought) providing the group with much needed realistic information.

I soon discovered that there was a defining set of properties that characterize a biomed follower. I discovered this by taking my evolving ideas about autism and my discussions with scientists onto my blog:

- An overriding desire to "cure" their autistic child at all costs
- An overriding belief that vaccines cause autism in some (any) way
- A willingness to listen and act on the advice of other parents only
- An unwillingness to want to hear the thoughts of autistic adults
- A deep-seated mistrust—almost a hatred—of mainstream science
- The need to see everything that doesn't agree that vaccines cause autism in terms of an Illuminati-type conspiracy organization
- The need to see those that directly disagree with them in terms of persecution
- Member veneration of the leaders of the movement and attacks on anyone who questions them
- Frowning upon dissent and questioning-type behaviors

In a lot of ways, biomed groups display cult-like behaviors,[6] and it was somewhat surprising to myself to think that I had been—for however short a period of time—a member of something that could be described as cult-like.

But now I was coming up full force against these people. Wherever one went, in the comments section of a news story, on a web forum—even in the comments section of my own blog—you were coming up against someone—usually several someones!—who were committed to the biomed movement and all that that entails. These discussions usually generated a lot more heat than light, and I'm sure I did my share of biting back (in fact I know I did), but I had become a firm proponent of science and the idea that autistic people had rights and that that one of those rights was their right to be autistic,[7] and I saw it as a duty to my friends and my family to tackle misinformation wherever I found it.

My blog has evolved over the years to fit this view of the world and now tackles science and pseudoscience on a regular basis. I believe that a purely biomed—and particularly the more extreme biomed such as chelation—treatment regime is not only grounded in bad science, but it is dangerous. People have died and been injured. It is past time we got back to the idea that well-designed science can help expand our knowledge of autism.

[1] www.leftbrainrightbrain.co.uk/2003/06/nutitional-asd, retrieved on June 11, 2010.

[2] www.autism-watch.org/about/bio2.shtml, retrieved on June 11, 2010.

[3] www.autismdiva.blogspot.com, retrieved on June 11, 2010.

[4] www.autism-watch.org/about/bio2.shtml, retrieved on June 11, 2010.

[5] See en.wikipedia.org/wiki/Troll_(Internet) for more details.

[6] See www.csj.org/infoserv_cult101/checklit.htm for more information

[7] See www.nytimes.com/2004/12/20/health/20autism.html for one of the original articles (published in 2004) responsible for the change in my own beliefs. Retrieved June 11, 2010.

Autism and Environmental Chemicals: A Call for Caution

Emily Willingham

Pardon me for a moment while I get a bit sciencey on you. In a former life, I was a scientist who conducted research in the field of endocrine-disrupting compounds. We focused on compounds that accumulate in body fat. The list of these compounds is long, almost endless, and many of these chemicals occur in what we consume, wear, sit on, wash with, and eat from.

The term "endocrine disruptor" doesn't even encompass the physiological systems that some of these compounds affect, and one system that interacts and overlaps with the endocrine system—the two cannot be separated, frankly, and I dare anyone teaching physiology to try—is the neurological system. Our neurology and our endocrinology are integrated, and compounds that influence or disrupt one often will do the same to the other.

It all started with what we used to call environmental estrogens. Then it expanded as we realized that the effects of these compounds weren't always estrogenic—some were anti-estrogenic, anti-androgenic, androgenic, thyroid-inhibiting, thyroid boosting, adrenal affecting, and, yes, neuroeffective. While my focus was the influence of these compounds during embryonic development on sex development—gonadal development and penile development, specifically—there are hundreds of other endpoints that these chemicals can affect.

The key factor that these compounds—and pretty much any chemical that has an influence on a developing organism—share is that they may seem to have little in the way of negative effects on an adult, but they can have permanent disruptive effects if the exposure is embryonic. That makes sense if you think about alcohol—ethanol. You can go out and get knee-walking drunk and suffer the acute effects the next day, but that single episode of exposure likely won't do you lasting harm. But do that to a fetus, and the processes in motion at the time of exposure may be disrupted in ways that do not allow recovery.

Another feature of the chemicals is that the doses required to cause an effect in an adult organism can be many, many orders of magnitude greater than the doses that disrupt normal development. In my research models, it would take as little as a drop in a trillion drops of some compounds simply to shift the sex development of the embryo from male to female. One. Drop. In. A. Trillion.

For several years now, I've had these compounds on my mind as I consider human neuroendocrine development and my own scientific work. It's hard to formulate any firm hypotheses while the jury remains out on whether or not autism rates are genuinely on the increase because of a real increase in autism or whether or not the increase is the result of better diagnostic criteria and recognition. Until that question is decided, it will be difficult to identify any real correlation that would lead to a hypothesis of causation of any specific compound.

And as anyone in endocrine-disruption research will tell you, a single compound can be difficult to tease out of the thousands to which we're exposed every day. However, there are some prime candidates for human exposure and developmental disruption. These include phthalates (used to soften plastic toys), bisphenol A (BPA), PBDEs (polybrominated diphenyl ethers, otherwise known as flame-retardants), and PCBs (polychlorinated biphenyls). These have all been identified as having endocrine-disruption capabilities. But results vary about which tissues they effect, what the effects are, what doses have these effects, what the timing of the dose is to have an effect, and more. The PCBs alone constitute a class of hundreds of separate chemicals. In other words, endocrine-disruption research is extraordinarily complex.

The few solid human-based studies have identified some of these at high levels in women—in breast milk, in particular—and also have identified them in umbilical cord blood of infants, meaning that they passed from mother to infant. So, yes, we're exposed. And for most of these, there is a great attraction to fat, which is mobilized at some of the worst times for exposure for children, as when we breastfeed.

Thus, it comes as no surprise to me that mainstream science is paying attention to this potential link[1] between these exposures and autism. A handful of chemicals—not of the kind we're passively exposed to but of the kind we take therapeutically—have already been linked to autism. These include valproic acid (an anti-convulsant sold under the name Depakote), which also is an endocrine disruptor.

What we need to be careful about is talking about any links as established before the work has even been done. Nicholas Kristof in the *New York Times* tries to make this argument, but I'd call it a fail from the get-go, as the headline itself is a screaming warning: "Do Toxins Cause Autism?"

Kristof states, and he's right, that "these are difficult issues for journalists to write about. Evidence is technical, fragmentary, and conflicting, and there's a danger of sensationalizing risks." It's quite true. The studies of the effects of these compounds in humans are mind-bogglingly complicated, with endpoints that may be under the influence of a host of confounding factors. And once again, we can't hypothesize an influence of any environmental factor as being an actor in the rise in autism rates unless we've established that the rise is genuinely an autism increase, rather than an increase in diagnostic accuracy. And the jury is still very much out on that, although most evidence points to the latter explanation as valid.

Where does that leave us? I advocate for simply doing the best we can to remove these compounds from the environment or at least to stop contributing them. Whether they are a factor in autism or not, they're patently not safe for developing vertebrates, and we should be addressing that. Period.

And as someone who has seen the power of these chemicals to alter vertebrate development, I can only tell you what I do now. I do not use cosmetics, and I do not use shampoos or soaps on my children that contain phthalates, tea tree oil, or lavender oil. We do not use plastics with bisphenol A. I am careful about my purchases of fish oils and other fat-related items, checking to see if the persistent organic pollutants have been removed. I almost never microwave in plastic.

That said, I have to note that after all of my work with endocrine-disrupting compounds, including the study of congenital urological malformations in boys, I have two children who have urological malformations and at least one child who has autism. The thing is, I can't determine whether these outcomes are a result of genetics—the urological problems run in the family, and I can see clearly where my children get some of their spectrum-associated manifestations—or whether they're the result of what I, the mother, have been exposed to simply through living in modern times and through my laboratory work. We already know genetics contributes strongly to autism. The question is, what else, if anything, does?

And that's not an easy question to answer—if it can be answered at all. Certainly, there won't be an answer that a single, sensational headline can encapsulate.

This essay was originally published at daisymayfattypants.blogspot.com.

---

[1] journals.lww.com/co-pediatrics/Abstract/publishahead/What_causes_autism__Exploring_the_en vironmental.99878.aspx

Questionable Autism Approaches: Facilitated Communication and Rapid Prompting Method

Kim Wombles

Sorting out communication and education pathways for nonverbal or limited-verbal children with autism can be daunting. Augmentative and Alternative Communication (AAC) strategies are often a viable means to help nonverbal and preverbal individuals communicate. But two methods, Facilitated Communication (FC) and Rapid Prompting Method (RPM), are not supported by evidence and are instead a potential drain on autism families' limited resources.

The idea of Facilitated Communication is a noble one and as defined by Biklen (1991) sounds entirely reasonable:

> Facilitated communication involves hand-over-hand or hand-on-forearm support of students as they point to pictures, letters or objects to augment communication. The facilitator does not guide the students to selections but rather stabilizes the student's movements and in some cases actually slows the person's hand as he or she points to a "Choice."

But most reviews of Facilitated Communication find that it is not a reliable, effective, or legitimate communication tool. Kerrin et al. (1998) found:

> This study supports the findings of Eberlin et al. (1993), Myles and Simpson (1994), Smith et al. (1994), Vazquez (1994), and others who have tried to discover objective evidence in support of FC. The participants responded more accurately when the SLP/facilitator could see, in spite of the fact that the SLP/facilitator did not think she was influencing the students' responses and did not intentionally do so.

Miles and Simpson (1996) noted that the evidence indicated that FC was not a valid method, tested whether it had any value as an educational tool, and concluded that it had absolutely no use. Mostert (2001) notes that Biklen:

"...believed that people without communicative ability, generally regarded as lower functioning than those having some use of language for communication, could not be assumed to be lower functioning because of their obvious expressive deficits" (p. 288).

This is an important concept and one well worth exploring, although it appears that Biklen may have been overzealous in his assumptions that individuals with no exposure or formal education could somehow be hyperlexic and that FC was the way to expose this. Mostert writes: "The assumptions of FC proponents, while not well formed and severely challenged (e.g., Hudson, 1995; Jacobson et al., 1995; Shane, 1994), have precipitated several empirical reviews of the effectiveness of FC" (p. 288).

If parents are still interested in FC despite its being debunked as both a communication tool and an educational tool, how else to convince them to be skeptical about this approach? Perhaps by considering that Finn et al. (2005) analyzed various forms of treatment for communication disorders based on ten criteria for pseudoscience and found that facilitated communication met eight of the ten criteria for pseudoscience: untestable, unchanged, only confirming evidence, anecdotal evidence, inadequate evidence, disconnected from well-established models, grandiose outcomes, and holistic.

Additional evidence demonstrates FC facilitators unconsciously co-opt communication while attributing it to their clients. Moreover, the potential for harm does exist, particularly if unsubstantiated allegations of abuse occur using FC. The *American Academy of Pediatrics* (AAP) (1998) provided the following statements regarding FC in the journal *Pediatrics*:

> Many families incur substantial expense pursuing these treatments, and spend time and resources that could be used more productively on behavioral and educational interventions. When controversial or unproven treatments are being considered by a family, the pediatrician should provide guidance and assistance in obtaining and reviewing information. The pediatrician should ensure that the child's health and safety, and the family's financial and emotional resources are not compromised. (pp. 11-14)

The American Psychological Association (2003) updated its 1994 statement regarding the lack of scientific support for Facilitated Communication and noted that:

> ...most schools and treatment centers stopped using the technique in the mid 1990s. Perhaps the saddest part of this story is that the most vocal advocates of this technique continue to use it and insist that it is effective—despite the disconfirming evidence. As one parent said, even if the technique is merely an illusion, it is an illusion that they wish to continue.

Given that there are many valid Augmentative and Alternative Communication (AAC) methods for nonverbal children that do not risk the facilitator co-opting the communication and that have demonstrated their effectiveness for fostering genuine communication, Facilitated Communication should be avoided.

Another method, one that claims to be an educational tool for nonverbal individuals with autism, is Rapid Prompting Method (RPM), or Soma® RPM. Soma® RPM was created by a parent, Soma Mukhopadhyay, in an attempt to help Tito, her son with autism, communicate. According to Halo, the organization Ms. Mukhopadhyay set up, her method, "is academic instruction leading towards communication for persons with autism."

"RPM is an empirical and rational teaching method, based upon how the brain works. Academic lessons are intended to stimulate left-brain learning, leading towards communication. 'Behaviors' or stims are used to help determine the student's open learning channels."

Despite the claim of empiricism and rationalism, there are only two mentions of RPM in the scientific literature or academic databases: Van Acker (2006) and a brief mention in a case study by Gernsbacher (2004).

Van Acker (2006), in a monthly newsletter covering the latest educational research, writes this about Rapid Prompting Method:

> RPM is an instructional technique designed to develop academic and communication skills in individuals with severe autism (*CBS Broadcasting, 2003*). It is "a 'Teach-Ask' paradigm for eliciting responses through intensive verbal, auditory, visual and/or tactile prompts." This intervention program was designed by Soma Mukhopadhyay, a teacher and a mother of a child with autism. As in FC, the RPM employs the facilitation of the person's hand or arm as he or she types, points, or writes the responses. To date, RPM has yet to be empirically validated.

In discussing an autistic person with the pseudonym RH, Gernsbacher (2004) briefly mentions RPM and Soma Mukhopadhyay:

> RH's mother then had the opportunity to visit with the mother and son in the United States (Mukhopadhyay, 2000). Although RH's mother was unwilling to go to the extreme measures that the Indian mother had used with her son, RH's mother was very motivated to explore the possibilities of RH using even a gross style of handwriting for augmentative communication.

The website for Halo/RPM, www.halo-soma.org, provides no solid evidence for how this instructional method works. Instead, vague phrasings assert that "Of course RPM is real." And FAQ assertions that science is providing information regarding how autistic individuals think are contradicted:

> Teaching and learning is an age-old process. It does not take scientific research to realize that children must be taught if they are ever to learn and improve. ASD [autism spectrum disorder] students need not be deprived of teaching and learning opportunities because of diagnosis, differences, or doubt about a student's potential.

Though the Rapid Prompting Method has been in use for approximately a decade, there are no studies on this method's effectiveness at helping individuals with autism communicate or master academic material; there are only testimonials. Therefore, it is not possible to assess whether individuals with autism legitimately benefit or gain skills from RPM.

It is also not possible to assess whether RPM responses come from the person with autism, or are a result of the facilitator/prompter's co-opting. Many YouTube and Google videos show facilitator effect with RPM. And the Rapid Prompting Method has never been subjected to the rigor of a scientific study.

Both Facilitated Communication and Rapid Prompting Method are unsubstantiated and—due to the need for facilitators—expensive attempts to help nonverbal children with autism learn academic materials and communicate independently. Both methods should be avoided by parents, especially in light of available AAC strategies that do not introduce the opportunity for facilitator co-option. Ensuring that our children's gains are honestly their own and that the communication they engage in is genuine should be the priority.

References

Finn, P., A. Bothe, and R. Bramlett. "Science and Pseudoscience in Communication Disorders: Criteria and Applications." *American Journal Of Speech-Language Pathology / American Speech-Language-Hearing Association* 14(3,) (2005): 172-186. Retrieved from MEDLINE database.

Gernsbacher, M. "Language is more than speech: A case study." *Journal of Developmental and Learning Disorder* 8 (2004): 81-98.

Green, V. "Parental Experience with Treatments for Autism." *Journal of Developmental and Physical Disabilities* 19(2,) (2007): 91-101. doi:10.1007/s10882-007-9035-y.

Kerrin, R., J. Murdock, W. Sharpton, and N. Jones. "Who's doing the pointing? Investigation facilitated communication in a classroom setting with...Focus on Autism and Other Developmental Disabilities" 13(2,) (1998): 73. Retrieved from *Health Source* - Consumer Edition database.

Mostert, M. "Facilitated Communication Since 1995: A Review of Published Studies." *Journal of Autism and Developmental Disorders* 31(3,) (2001): 287-313. Retrieved from Psychology and Behavioral Sciences Collection database.

Myles, B., and R. Simpson. "Impact of Facilitated Communication Combined With Direct Instruction on Academic Performance of... Focus on Autism and Other Developmental Disabilities." 11(1) (1996): 37. Retrieved from *Health Source* - Consumer Edition database.

Van Acker, R. "Outlook on Special Education Practice. Focus on Exceptional Children" 38(8), (2006): 8-18. Retrieved from *Academic Search Complete* database.

—

A version of this essay was originally published on www.kwomblescountering.blogspot.com

How I Know Vaccines Didn't Cause My Child's Autism

Devon Koren Alley

Eleven years ago, as I lounged in my mother's apartment at the tender age of twenty, overwhelmed by the heat of the summer combined with my final trimester of pregnancy, I finally settled on a name for the creature who kept poking her tiny feet into my ribcage, the creature who was poised at any moment to completely and irrevocably change my life. I decided on a name derived from the Irish language—"Aisling," which meant "Dream," and "Stoirm," which meant "Storm." A Dream Storm. At that moment, I had no idea how completely that name would end up describing my beautiful, blonde-haired daughter, who would spend much of her time lost in the dreams inside her head, and who would also grow to rage against the confusing world around her. I did not realize that the child in my womb would be diagnosed with high-functioning autism.

For some reason (I'm assuming due to the controversial and heated nature of the discussion), many people, upon learning that Aisling is autistic, ask me if I believe her early childhood vaccinations caused the condition. My answer to this is always, emphatically, "no."

Aisling did receive all of her vaccinations on time and would occasionally become slightly feverish and irritable after those first few sets, but I personally never saw any evidence that Aisling regressed in development, nothing that seemed out of the ordinary compared to the little checklist of probable side-effects that the health department sent home with us.

The reason I decided to write this essay is because a friend of mine suggested that I share my experience and perspective when it came to possible "causes" of Aisling's autism. The current debate seems to often pit extremely concerned parents against the scientific community. It would be nice, he suggested, to present a different perspective. So, on request, I'm offering up my own experience.

First, a little disclaimer—I am not well versed in the scientific research or the debate surrounding this particular issue, so I'm not about to try to "prove" or "disprove" that childhood vaccinations cause autism in children. What I am absolutely certain of, however, is that childhood vaccinations did not cause autism in my own child. As Aisling would say, "I need some strong supporting details, Mom!" so I will flesh out this essay with the reasons I never suspected vaccinations as the cause of Aisling's autism.

Aisling was diagnosed at a very early age—she was only two years old when she started receiving speech therapy, and only two and a half when she was officially diagnosed with autism. I was relatively certain that she had autism before we ever got a diagnosis, from my own personal research on the topic.

Once I knew what the symptoms were, I was able to backtrack through Aisling's life and see evidence of the disorder everywhere. I could remember how difficult it was to get her to breastfeed when she was a small baby because she seemed to dislike being snuggled up to me. I remembered how I'd heard all these stories about how breastfeeding brought you closer to your child, because they'd make eye contact with you, interact with you, "bond" with you during those early moments. I remembered feeling like I must have been doing something wrong, or that she simply wasn't interested in me, because she would actively avoid eye contact with me when I was breastfeeding her and would only eat when she was very, very hungry or when she wanted to go to sleep. I remember feeling as if I was just a "food machine" a lot of the time—Aisling really only seemed interested in interacting with me when she wanted something and couldn't get it. As a young single mother, I'd actually tried to initiate co-sleeping because I'd figured it would make night-feedings much easier. However, Aisling would have none of it. She was extremely uncomfortable. In fact, she would cry and scream unless she was on a bare mattress with no blankets, stuffed animals, or anything else touching her.

Aisling also only wanted to wear onesies or pajamas all of the time. She detested shoes with the heated passion of a thousand fiery suns. What she loved most? Spinning in circles or bouncing up and down, or swinging back and forth on her swing. Some things never change.

I wasn't the only one who noticed these "oddities" about Aisling. My entire family commented on how "serious" she always seemed, and how interested she was in just "doing her own thing." In some ways, she was an incredibly easy and low-maintenance baby—she never really demanded attention or interaction from anyone. She would respond to her name or smile at a game of peek-a-boo occasionally, but quite honestly I ended up being so overly animated in my "games" to try to get Aisling's attention or to get her to laugh that it sometimes bordered on the creepy and grotesque. She also walked very early (at seven-and-a-half months), and I'm convinced that this was because she couldn't figure out how to ask for things and needed to move around and get what she wanted for herself.

And all of these things started from the first day I held her in my arms at the hospital, long before any vaccinations, long before she was exposed to anything. I am completely convinced that my child was simply born with autism. Whether or not her autism was caused by genetic factors, or stressors during my difficult labor with her, or some combination of the two, I may never know. But I do not believe that any of this had anything to do with the vital vaccinations she received and that have protected her against several deadly childhood diseases.

Furthermore, I maintain that children should continue to be vaccinated against these diseases. I definitely respect opinions that differ from my own, and I also support continuing research into the cause of autism. However, I think we need to be careful not to get so caught up in trying to determine the cause and hoping that it leads to a "cure" that we pull much-needed services, therapies, and research that help assist autistic individuals interact with this loud, confusing world—and also that help this loud, confusing world learn to be more gentle and accepting with them!

Which brings me to another, important point of this story. When Aisling was a small baby, there were many indicators I "missed" due to ignorance about autism. However, I did notice that my child was "different" and had her unique personality at a very early age. All of that still holds true—my daughter still is a different person with her own unique personality, which is often delightful and sometimes quite challenging. Autism didn't "happen" to her; autism is very much a part of who she is, who she's always been. I feel she's imperfectly perfect just as she is, and I wouldn't change that for the world. And while I wish it was easier for her to exist in this world, to interact with people, to deal with changes, and to understand the nuances of everything around her, I am perfectly content to continue to work to make that possible for her, to make it just a little easier for her every day. I am so very proud every day that I am her mother, that I was blessed with the amazing gift of having her as a daughter.

—

A version of this essay was previously published at
www.community.advanceweb.com/blogs/ot_9/default.aspx

Autism and Biomed Protocols:
A Primer on Pseudoscience

Emily Willingham and Kim Wombles

Emily's family has kept their biomed treatment—or any treatment excepting occupational and behavioral therapies—to a minimum, primarily because of some inherent skepticism. Their current biomedical interventions are limited to fish oil, probiotics, and some vitamins.

The Wombles brood has generally taken a similar approach, although they spent four years gluten and dairy free before admitting that it made no difference for them whatsoever, except that there were five much happier people once they went off the diet.

Many autism parents investigate biomedical or "biomed" approaches as a way to ameliorate negative manifestations of their child's autism. These parents can also find themselves overwhelmed by biomedical protocol possibilities. Sorting through these protocols can be a daunting task, which is, of course, one reason for having a *Thinking Person's Guide to Autism*.

What follows are analyses of three of the most overpromising biomedical approaches: the Cutler Protocol, the Yasko Protocol, and the Bioset Protocol. We urge readers not to rely solely on what they read here: please review these protocols on your own. We also strongly recommend that you do so in the context of pseudoscience awareness, as detailed at UK-Skeptics.com and Quackwatch.org. Pseudoscience signs include:

- A clear monetary reward
- Requirements for paying more as you go along
- A central personality rather than a core science supporting the therapy
- Use of sciencey-sounding but often nonsensical terms
- A promise to cure a number of unrelated disorders

Understanding what constitutes pseudoscience versus true science or scientific practice will help you avoid a number of biomed pitfalls.

The Cutler Protocol

The Cutler Protocol, created by research chemist Andy Cutler, is based on the premise that autism is mercury poisoning—which Cutler implies can be cured by his specially timed chelation system. If an individual has any dental amalgams containing mercury, these amalgams will have to be removed before the protocol can be begun. In fact, Cutler has made available a book and a special term (pseudoscience alert!) about "Amalgam

Illness." Cutler claims that he himself "got mercury poisoning" from his fillings, as detailed at www.noamalgam.com.

Cutler asserts that: "Many conditions, from Parkinson's disease and autism—widely recognized as terrible afflictions—to those like chronic fatigue and fibromyalgia which, though equally serious, are disparaged as 'Yuppie flu,' can be undiagnosed mercury poisoning."

This laundry list of disorders is a typically a key sign of a practitioner of pseudoscience. Naturally, his protocol for removing mercury from your body is available in his book, which he describes as a "practical guide to getting well." Plus, if you add up what he recommends as a timeline for "treatment," Cutler's protocol may take years.

We won't get into Cutler's list of things that "mercury does to you" or the distinction between the chronic and acute effects of mercury poisoning that he describes on his site, because mercury poisoning is not a viable causative agent in the development of autism. For a recent study finding no elevations of mercury in autistic children compared to nonautistic children (a first requirement for it to be causative), please check out a freely available, full-text 2009 paper in *Environmental Health Perspectives*, a well-respected, peer-reviewed journal.[1]

The Cutler Protocol involves the chelators DMSA and DMPS and alpha lipoic acid (a fatty acid), which will supposedly reach the mercury deposited in the brain. The Protocol requires some testing of hair and/or urine to demonstrate that you have high levels of mercury. Unfortunately, these tests are basically useless[2] as they don't produce worthwhile information. Hair testing is entirely unreliable and misleading, while urine testing for mercury will give you one of two outcomes, depending on the circumstances:

1. You will have mercury in your urine because everyone does; we carry it in relatively steady states, and your urine tells the story of your past mercury burden.

2. You'll do the test after a chelation protocol, which releases an abundance of heavy metals, including mercury, into circulation for dumping in the urine, so you'll get elevated levels that aren't a valid indicator of what you're experiencing on a daily basis without chelation.

This kind of provoked testing is common in the biomedical world, and it's a poor guide for anyone to use in determining a treatment for mercury poisoning. And as long as we're on the topic, chelation can kill,[3] and the FDA recently warned consumers[4] about another form of chelation involving the chelator OSR#1.

Let's put it this way: if you've got mercury poisoning, you'll know it. It's not subtle. You won't be looking online for a book to order; you'll be at the doctor or hospital. Symptoms include "impairment of the peripheral vision; disturbances in sensations ('pins and needles' feelings, usually in the hands, feet, and around the mouth); lack of coordination of movements; impairment of speech, hearing, walking; and muscle weakness" (from *www.epa.gov/hg/effects.htm*).

If you're looking for more information on mercury toxicity, see Medscape's *eMedicine* website.[5] Note that the Public Health Service has concluded that dental amalgams are not a threat to public health.

The Yasko Protocol

The Yasko Protocol (*www.dramyyasko.com*) is a protocol sold by Amy Yasko, who has determined that something called the "methylation cycle" can have defects that contribute to a whole host of diseases and disorders (an expansive and unrelated list of applications is a typical sign of pseudoscience), and autism is one of these disorders. If you want to know more, you'll have to buy her books and DVDs. To select the appropriate individualized treatment plan, customers can order health tests (some for hundreds of dollars) and then base their ordering of various supplements and RNA products (also hundreds of dollars) on the test results.

We note here that usually, biotech companies specializing in "RNA products" produce their offerings at great expense and with a great deal of accumulated laboratory expertise to ensure that the products retain their RNA integrity. We infer that Yasko would know this because she once was involved in such a company, called Oligo. RNA is a molecule notorious for its ability to degrade, and the things you have to put it in to keep it from degrading are often not things you want to ingest. Yet the information at the time of this writing uses terms and assertions that don't make scientific sense. The text contains a lot of sciencey-sounding terms that most readers likely won't recognize as nonsense. The use of empty but scientific-sounding verbiage is a pseudoscience red flag.

It's easy to see how Yasko attracts people, though. Her site included, at the time of this writing, a few complex-looking graphs that purport to show the "methylation cycle," which appears to involve in some mysterious way the amino acid methionine, and the Krebs cycle, which is one of the steps of harvesting energy from glucose. In a very roundabout manner, she appears to be talking about folic acid deficiency. The solution to that is usually to take more folic acid.

Yasko (or "Dr. Amy," as she warmly calls herself) does offer a nice example of the way practitioners of pseudoscience reel you in and keep you. According to *Discover* magazine,[6] "She monitors biomarkers of detoxification in the urine as often as every week or two and tweaks supplements accordingly." So in case the things she's sending you aren't producing any noticeable effect, send in some urine and money—as often as every week or two—and she'll respond by tweaking the supplements you need to purchase. Parent bloggers have noted that they've paid thousands of dollars each month to comply with this protocol.

The Bioset Protocol

The Bioset Protocol is sometimes recommended by DAN! (Defeat Autism Now!) doctors as a supplementary treatment for food intolerance or allergies. It was originated by Dr. Ellen Cutler—or "Dr. Ellen" as she calls herself on her website, unless she's calling herself "The Empress of Enzymes." Dr. Ellen promises that her "system" will help the buyer with a laundry list of ills, ranging from herpes to migraines to "childhood illnesses or recurring infections." This is a pseudoscience alert. These disorders, vague as the list is, have nothing in common—neither causes nor treatments. "Bioset" also turned up no hits in the scientific literature databases listed above. Cutler offers a list of articles on her website,[7] but not one is a peer-reviewed research publication.

According to AllergyEscape.com, Bioset, or "Bioenergetic Sensitivity and Enzyme Therapy," is an energy-based allergy elimination method:

> Originated by Dr. Ellen Cutler, this allergy elimination method views the body holistically, similar to the Chinese approach. This view accepts the fact that there is an energy system in the human body that is separate from the cardiovascular system and nervous system. This system, which is comprised of "meridians," has everything to do with the way the body maintains its overall health.

AllergyEscape.com goes on to further explain Bioset:

> Bioset practitioners utilize Meridian Stress Assessment (MSA), for allergy testing, or they may use muscle testing (applied kinesiology), two non-invasive techniques that are both safe and reliable. MSA is a computerized device that detects energy variations in the body.

The concept of meridians has been debunked,[8] and based on Dr. Ellen's own website and our searches in scientific literature databases, there is no evidence to demonstrate a physiological basis for the Bioset protocol, much less any effectiveness with respect to Dr. Ellen's laundry list of Bioset-treatable disorders.

———

As a parent or a spiritual person, you may be thinking that there are more things in Heaven and Earth, Emily and Kim, than are dreamt of in the philosophy espoused here. Indeed, there are. But there are also many clearly established scientific standards, ones that have been demonstrated repeatedly. Examples include the disease-development pathways of many of the disorders that the above practitioners claim to cure.

What has not been demonstrated in any way—and could not be, even if we moved Heaven and Earth to do so—is that these peddled protocols, along with affiliated books and pills, have any effect whatsoever. All they ultimately do is take money from the pockets of parents desperate to do something for the children they love.

Please, if you're considering any of these protocols, or any therapy or intervention—take a critical look at it, as we have done here, before you reach into your pocket—or inject or dose your child.

---

[1] Hertz Picciotto, et al., "Blood Mercury Concentrations in CHARGE Study Children with and without Autism," *Environmental Health Perspectives,* 118 no.1 (January 21010): 161–166. Available online at *www.ncbi.nlm.nih.gov/pmc/articles/PMC2831962/?tool=pubmed.* Accessed September 19, 2011.

[2] R. Baratz, "Dubious mercury testing," *Quackwatch.* (2005). Available online at *www.quackwatch.org/01QuackeryRelatedTopics/Tests/mercurytests.html.* Accessed September 19, 2011.

[3] "Boy with autism dies after chelation therapy," MSNBC.com. (2005). Available online at www.msnbc.msn.com/id/9074208. Accessed September 19, 2011.

[4] Trine Tsouderos. "FDA: Autism Therapy 'Illegal.'" (2010). Available online at *www.latimes.com/news/health/sns-health-illegal-autism-therapy,0,747838.story.* Accessed September 19, 2011.

[5] B.M. Diner,, "Mercury Toxicity in Emergency Medicine, *Medscape.* (2009). Available online at *emedicine.medscape.com/article/819872-overview.* Accessed September 19, 2011.

[6] Neimark, Jill. 2007. "Autism: It's not just in the head." *Discover Magazine.* Available online at *discovermagazine.com/2007/apr/autism-it2019s-not-just-in-the-head.* Accessed September 19, 2011.

[7] www.drellencutler.com

[8] C. Kressler, "Chinese Medicine Demystified (Part III): The 'Energy Meridian' Model Debunked." (2010). Available online at *chriskresser.com/chinese-medicine-demystified-part-iii-the-energy-meridian-model-debunked.* Accessed September 19, 2011.

Why My Child With Autism Is Fully Vaccinated

Shannon Des Roches Rosa

Do you still wonder about a link between vaccines and autism? Then ask yourself: have you or would you ever let your child travel by airplane? If your answer is "yes," then you should re-examine any concerns about vaccinating your children. Flying and vaccination both carry risks, but those risks are statistically unlikely to affect your family.

You should also know that Andrew Wakefield, the researcher who launched the autism–vaccine panic via a 1998 press conference, had his related research formally retracted and his medical license taken away. You should know that the mainstream media, after years of "considering both sides," now yawns when yet another study fails to find a link between vaccines and autism—and that gossip sites like *HollywoodLife.com* want to know why anti-vaccination activist Jenny McCarthy won't publicly end her campaign against children's health. You should consider that decreased vaccination rates put everyone's health at risk; people can and do die from vaccine-preventable diseases, and those diseases are resurfacing with increasing vigor.

Still, no amount of evidence seems to satisfy parents who continue to believe in vaccine–autism causation. I understand fears like theirs, as I've been there myself. I remember the stone age of 2003: my two-year-old son Leo had just been diagnosed with autism, and I was desperate to help him.

My first action was to enroll Leo in an Applied Behavioral Analysis (ABA) program—the only method proven to help children with autism gain skills. But ABA is hard work and doesn't promise miracles, and I wanted changes, fast, so I started exploring alternative autism therapies.

And indeed, I found many self-appointed autism professionals who wanted me to look past the loving son I already had, the boy who needed my support so badly, and focus on a theoretical Recovered Boy of the future. I also found myself looking past their promotion of scientifically questionable approaches and focusing on one of their popular theories: they thought mercury in vaccines caused autism.

Those anti-vaccination people were passionate about "curing" autistic children. I was passionate, I believed them when they told me I should try to "cure" my autistic child. I did what they told me.

I stopped vaccinating my kids.

My youngest child was born in 2004, 18 months after her brother's diagnosis and during the thick of my alternative-treatment frenzy. Almost every autism activism resource I found implied or proclaimed that Leo's autism was likely caused by an injected environmental factor. I freaked out and decided there was no way in hell my new baby girl was getting a shot of anything. Not even vitamin K.

As that fortunately healthy baby grew and thrived, so did the evidence refuting a thimerosal/vaccine/autism link. Unfortunately, so did the rates of preventable and potentially lethal diseases. Turns out I wasn't the only parent who'd been scared into tossing aside my kids' vaccine schedules.

I wanted proof that vaccinations had in fact affected my son, so I formally investigated a possible relationship between Leo's autism and the vaccinations he'd received as an infant and toddler. I enrolled him in a University of California, Davis MIND Institute study on autism and regression that tracked the emergence of his autism symptoms via home videos, medical records, and my own journals.

The result: there was no evidence that Leo had regressed into autism after being vaccinated.

I thought long and hard. And decided that the risks of vaccinating my children were acceptable.

I started slowly, under the supervision of a pediatrician willing to listen to my concerns. My youngest child initially got only one shot at a time, only when she was healthy, and with one month between doses, because I wanted to see how she reacted to individual vaccines. She had no adverse reactions, so I began to allow vaccinations in small batches. I also resumed vaccinating my son—you know, the one with autism. Both kids remain fine, or at least no quirkier than they were before their shots.

Mine is not the only vaccination perspective you should be familiar with, however. As you likely know, there is no talking about vaccines and autism without mentioning "safe" vaccine advocate Jenny McCarthy. Ms. McCarthy once declared:

"If you ask a parent of an autistic child if they want the measles or the autism, we will stand in line for the f***ing measles."

Really? If we're going to celebrities rather than experts for medical advice, I have to counter with the *Law and Order: SVU* episode "Selfish," in which a child too young to be vaccinated died from encephalitis as a complication of measles; measles acquired at a neighborhood park from an asymptomatic carrier kid whose mother refused to vaccinate him.

I'm sorry, Jenny, but Mariska Hargitay, Christopher Meloni, Ice-T, and Stephanie March say that measles kills and that we need to vaccinate our kids not just to keep them healthy but also to protect other people's kids.

And because the SVU team members are celebrities too but outnumber you, I'm going to side with them.

I kid, but only slightly, as I really do prefer my son alive. And I seriously doubt Jenny would volunteer to give her son measles—or pertussis (whooping cough), diphtheria, tetanus, or polio, if she'd actually seen these diseases affect a child, or considered that acquiring the diseases is much riskier than getting vaccinated for them.

Jenny is not alone in underestimating the critical role of vaccines or the diseases they prevent. In 2010, I participated in a conference call with Every Child By Two, a non-profit dedicated to educating the public about vaccine-preventable disease. I listened as Danielle Romaguera described her infant daughter Brie's 2003 death from pertussis—a disease herd immunity was supposed to protect the baby from, as she was too young to be vaccinated; a disease vaccine campaigns had squelched so successfully that her doctors didn't recognize it, not until it was too late. A disease that caused baby Brie so much pain and suffering that a Romaguera family friend chose to fully vaccinate her child who has autism.

A disease that, seven years later, was declared an epidemic in California. Katharine Mieszkowski of *BayCitizen.org*, using her organization's excellent interactive California immunizations statistics database, observed: "Marin and Sonoma Counties have reported the highest rates of whooping cough in the Bay Area this year. They also have the highest local rates of personal-belief [vaccine] exemption."

When I talked with Katharine, she said that budget-challenged California schools don't always have the resources or a school nurse to properly monitor immunization compliance. She also said parents who took out personal-belief exemptions were worried about possibilities like their kids' immune system being overwhelmed—which, to me, means they probably weren't consulting a pediatrician on the matter. And a personal-belief exemption doesn't differentiate between skipping a few vaccines, and skipping all of them—so while we have data on vaccination non-compliance, we don't have complete information on specific vaccination rates. All we know is that California parents are choosing to put their children at risk.

We live in a culture where some people make critical health decisions for their children based on the opinions of celebrities rather than pediatricians. I'm asking you to help right the balance, to ensure that science-based viewpoints counter earnest but misinformed sensationalism in the autism—and parenting—communities' information flows.

I know that some people will never vaccinate their kids, no matter the argument or evidence (and we are now in a banner era for both scientific evidence and court decisions debunking autism–vaccine links). I also know some kids can't be vaccinated due to health issues or because they are too young. Herd immunity will compensate, will keep the unvaccinated kids safe from disease *if* enough other children get vaccinated. That is why we must reach out and talk to parents who are still formulating their immunization opinions, educate with facts rather than furor, have the confidence to spread the word about what we know, and keep blasting away at the fast-crumbling wall of harm the anti-vaccine movement keeps trying to prop up.

6 Acceptance & Inclusion from the Parent/Neurotypical Point of View

Behavior is communication. That's it. That's all. That's everything.

—Shannon Des Roches Rosa

The Autism Path

Jean Winegardner

I feel that when I got my son Jack's autism diagnosis, it was as if I had been given directions to a trailhead that started us down a path. The path was different than the one I'd planned on, and this path was rockier than the one I left behind, but still, it was a path. Walking along this autism path was better than milling around aimlessly in a meadow, unable to find a trailhead of any sort.

When I think of Jack's autism and where it takes us, I can actually see this path in my mind. It is made up of dirt and rocks and it winds through and up a mountain pass. I'm walking it with Jack, and my other children walk on either side of me. Sometimes the rocks in our path cause only Jack to stumble, but sometimes they are spread out so all of us trip and struggle.

Here's the thing about this difficult autism path though: it's beautiful. There are trees and ponds to the side, and every once in a while we see a deer or a squirrel. Yes, the terrain is bumpy, but the setting is gorgeous. This is how I see my life with Jack. Parenting a special needs child brings so much love, joy, learning, and amazement. Some days, when we trip and fall, we see a beautiful flower under a rock that we wouldn't have seen had we not stumbled.

Often times our children with autism forge straight ahead through the hardest section of the trail, but sometimes they notice that there is an easier way around. Every time they take that easier way, every time they learn that they should look for the possibility of an easier way, the sky seems to get a little brighter.

We're not alone on our path either. There are special needs families strewn all over this trail, walking with us. Sometimes we hold hands as we struggle up a steep incline, and sometimes we catch each other as we slide down a scree-littered down-slope.

No matter where our paths are taking us—and they stretch all over the mountain—we all started from the same trailhead, more or less. We all saw that signpost with the words, "Diagnosis: Autism" on it.

Some of us set off with purpose in our hearts and our heads held high. Some of us feared the heavy trees and that initial almost-vertical climb. Some of us tried to turn around to find a different trail. Many of us had hope. And we needed it too, because that first couple of miles? They are a bitch. The terrain is unpleasant and the overhanging trees block the view. There is so much to learn about how to climb, and we often forget to look for the bright spots hidden among the boulders.

But we keep going because someone a little bit ahead holds out a hand, or we see a beautiful rock that a previous passerby dropped for us on the ground. We keep going, because our child keeps going, and he needs us to keep up. He needs us to remember that even when struggling up that path on unsteady legs, he is still the same child who days ago was frolicking in the meadow before someone said "autism" and pointed toward this trail.

There are people who are much farther ahead of us on this path. Through the special needs parenting grapevine, word comes back that there is a really steep hike coming up. The word warns us to work hard and keep trying but don't despair, because there is a lovely flat section after you reach the top, and oh my God, you won't believe the view from up there.

These paths wind all over the mountain of autism, intersecting, diverging, and running parallel to each other. There are times when I am on my path, picking my way around trees, when I can see my special needs friends on their paths below and above me. Some of them are struggling, some of them are running, and, look, that guy there is sitting down nursing a bruised knee.

But we all get up and we keep walking.

Sometimes the path is dark and scary. And sometimes its beauty takes our breath away. Sometimes we gaze at the path of neurotypicality on the valley floor and wish for those easy slopes and the way all of those paths run close together, providing easy company. There are some beautiful plants and geographic formations down there, that's for sure. We forget that there are hazards down there as well, that they are merely different from our own.

There are days that we don't envy those valley-floor paths, however. Those days we realize that those trails don't wind around high-altitude lakes, stunning in their beauty. Those paths don't force their walkers to fight through a bramble of thorns, which means their travelers don't get to feel the surge of pride and victory when they emerge back into the sunlight. We don't get to experience the same beauty as those walking on the valley floor, but our scenery is gorgeous in its own right.

Everyone's path is hard. Everyone has to struggle up and down the trail on which we have embarked. We struggle over the uneven ground and hope that around the bend there is a nice flat section or a tree stump, upon which we can take a rest and enjoy being with our fellow travelers.

But after we sit, after we rest, we stand up and we keep walking. We continue to find ways to help our kids avoid the most difficult pitfalls and we keep on in our search for that small, beautiful flower or the overwhelming gorgeous view.

We're tired, but we keep going because we get to be with our children and they make the walk oh so worthwhile.

—

This essay was originally published at Washington Times Communities' Autism Unexpected.

I Want to Tell You a Secret About Autism Awareness

Shannon Des Roches Rosa

I want to tell you a secret about Autism Awareness. I'm telling you because you have a stake in the autism community; whether you touch one or many lives, you can change them, and you are powerful. And, like me, you care. You want to make a difference—for yourself, for your child, for someone you love, for someone who depends on you. And you can make a difference, you will, if you keep this cornerstone of Autism Awareness in mind at all times. Ready? Here it is:

Behavior is communication. That's it. That's all. That's everything.

If you put your mental backbone into behavioral awareness, into trying to understand why a person with autism, or a person associated with autism, behaves the way he or she does—if you can make yourself truly aware of that person's needs—then that is when the connections will happen, that is when you will make a difference, that is when awareness can leapfrog goodwill, and translate into real-world benefits and positive actions.

If you're a parent of a young child with a new autism diagnosis, a behavioral awareness mindshift can be hard. It's not how most of us are taught to think about parenting. And you're already struggling with so much right now: you love your child, want the best outcome for your child—yet you've been handed an autism label with all its associated baggage and media fear mongering.

You need to remember that an autism label is just that—a label. It can help describe your child, but it doesn't define your child. You need to set the label aside, enlist it as needed, and instead hyperfocus on what your child does, and why they do it. You'll probably have to jettison some lingering hopes and dreams about your child's future to focus on your child's reality—but since parenting always involves a large amount of eventual ego-disentangling, assure yourself that you're actually ahead of the curve.

You can learn a lot from parents who actively practice behavioral awareness, parents like Todd Drezner, who directed the must-see autism understanding and acceptance movie *Loving Lampposts*; Kristina Chew, mother of the legendary and now teenage Charlie; Jennifer Byde Myers, whose son Jack has a constellation of diagnoses besides autism; and author Laura Shumaker, whose son Matthew is legally of drinking age.

But the behaviors! They don't always make sense, not on the surface, not if you've never encountered anything like them before. Does your child scream if she can't wear her favorite shoes? Can he talk happily (and indefinitely) about sprinkler systems or precious gems or superheroes?

Does she enjoy fondling material of certain textures without regard for where or on whom that fabric may be located? Does he fear the toilet, the market, the dentist? Make understanding those behaviors the focus of your approach. Decide which quirks are quirky, and which are legitimate impediments to learning, self-care, health, and socialization—then put your energies into helping your child get past the roadblocks.

Get professional help if possible, from a behaviorist who can explain that yelling at a child to stop unspooling toilet paper or "punishing" a child by ousting them from circle time may actually be exactly what that kid wants—you may be unwittingly helping perpetuate undesired behaviors. But know that not all professionals are going to be in tune with your child's behaviors, no matter how much training and experience they've had. Be careful about ceding authority to a professional whose own behavior is more about showcasing knowledge, and less about applying observation skills to help you or your child.

Most autism community members who practice behavioral awareness will eventually encounter autism parents who disagree about best autism practices. And that's okay, too—if you understand those parents' behavior. Are they truly interested in giving their child the best life possible? Do they fight hard for educational placements and evidence-based supports? Are any of their chosen therapies actively harming their child? If the answers are "yes," "yes," and "no," then you likely have more in common with those parents than not, and the relationships are worth pursuing. You don't have to agree with autism parents about every last thing—I doubt that any useful, forward-thinking community is a Shangri-La of consensus. But you do need to be wary of parents who place their egos, their fear of autism, and their desire for a "typical" child above the needs of the actual children in their care. Still, you should support those parents by listening, if they'll let you—with enough positive role modeling, they may swing 'round and start investing in behavioral awareness, their kids might receive respect in addition to love, and our community will strengthen and become more whole.

When I feel the need to better understand my son Leo's behaviors, or when I'm feeling low because despite his and our best efforts, we cannot solve his behavioral crises, I seek solace in the experiences of autistics. Sometimes I use Twitter—a great resource for queries both specific and general (many of my Twitter conversations have deepened into cherished friendships). Sometimes I search those same autistics' blogs or message boards as a grateful lurker. I don't always find agreement—people's backgrounds and experience vary, as they do in most populations. And not all autistics are interested in being role models or sounding boards for parents like me, which is fair. But I almost always come away with greater understanding, useful information, and a renewed awe for the generosity of the autistic community.

Behavioral awareness is not a magical mitigation tool. We still have tough times: Leo finds summers and their schedule disruptions disorienting and distressing, and sometimes he is inconsolable. My husband and I do our best to understand why Leo gets so upset, and sometimes Leo tries to tell us. But our boy doesn't always have the language he needs; at times, he cries himself to sleep out of frustration and exhaustion. It breaks all three of our hearts.

I know these episodes will get easier as Leo's communication skills improve. I also know that they used to be commonplace, especially when Leo was little, before we understood so many of the behaviors that make our wonderful boy tick, and before we had the awareness to appreciate our son for exactly who he is.

———

A version of this essay was previously published at BlogHer.com.

Buying Hope

Jennifer Byde Myers

Lotions, potions. A special chair for eating, a special chair for learning at home. Shoe inserts, leg braces, seat cushions with no grip, a lot of grip, seat cushions with little bumps, seat cushions with little bumps and gel inside, and a backrest. Fancy forks with bendable handles, child-sized forks, spoons with holes in the bowl, bowls with grips on the bottom, bowls with the side cut out, and special chopsticks, and sippy cup after sippy cup with any number of parts and combinations to mess up.

Small piano keyboards, and larger piano keyboards, and a keyboard you can walk on, just like in the movie *Big*. A touch screen monitor, an adapted computer, an adapted tricycle, an expensive German tricycle. Jackets that zip with a nice big tab, pants with an elastic waist that are easy to take off, overalls that are difficult to take off, and hook and loop shoes, always another try for the best hook and loop shoes.

An art easel, another art easel, another art easel, another art easel. A tambourine.

Crayons for the tub, foam letters, magnets in the shape of the alphabet. Vitamin E, vitamin B, fish oil, grape seed oil, gluten-free, flavor-free foods, straps and Velcro bands. A single-button talker, a four-button push talker, a talker that lights up, a button that makes the toy move, cars that go when you barely shake them. Books that talk, books with special flaps for little fingers to turn pages with ease.

Honey oil, lavender shampoo, and a wet suit. A car seat, a booster seat, a bigger car seat, a car seat that can only be purchased through MediCal. Fat crayons, triangle crayons, multicolor crayons, finger paints, paint that sticks to your fingers, brushes that attach to a child's hand. Weighted vests, extra weights, leg weights, and bands that go around his torso to keep him sitting up straight. A laminator and special software. A pool float to keep him above water, and special swim pants to keep everything sanitary, and shoes to wear in the water so he can keep his balance. Small plastic brushes and a folder to document each time we brush, and another folder that is a special color to track everything, and while we're at it a new computer to better document his life and his doctor appointments.

A toothbrush that goes on my finger to brush his teeth, an electric toothbrush, a toothbrush that lights up, a toothbrush with Dora, with Spiderman. Ski hats, headphones, an iPod, an iPad, tape recorders, a booster seat with headphones already built in. Cup holders that attach to strollers, and wheelchairs, and windows. Cup holders that go into other cup holders for an easier reach, and strappy water bottle carriers that sling over seats and on to wheelchairs. Flashcards, and puzzles, and every brightly colored spinning, honking whirly toy we could ever find.

My house is filled with piles of hope.

Some things we bought all on our own, most were purchased because someone else thought we should, or we saw it work for another family. They were birthday presents from grandparents, and things we bought off Craigslist.

When things are going well, the toys and books and projects around my home are like little pieces of inspiration, a future where Jack's communication will be unlocked, and he will be able to ask for the four other toys in the bin. On hard days, this jumble of disaster we call home is a minefield of disappointment, the closet barely holding in all of the unsuitable gifts my son has been given over the years, and the house, a tripping hazard of wasted money.

Jack comes with cerebral palsy on top of his autism, which makes us a target for all of those neurologically stimulating things for autism, plus all of those special devices that might serve a purpose for improving his balance, coordination, and bilateral movement. When he was younger, when some people thought Jack was just going to "snap out of it," we often felt desperate, and there was always a steady flow of suggestions about what to buy.

This over-buying is not limited to parenting a special needs child; we all want more for our children. Families with typical children go through ballet lessons and move on to soccer before settling comfortably at softball. Blocks lay abandoned when more intricate building materials and model planes arrive. The difference is that those families can be finished with the blocks because their child has grown out of them, whereas my child just never did master stacking blocks more than three high, and I bought the next set of toys because I thought perhaps they would be the object of desire for my son.

How many years, how many dollars did we spend before we realized we shouldn't try, and we couldn't "fix" Jack. Jack is not sick. Jack is not broken. Jack is whole and beautiful and amazing exactly as he his. And if that sounds like we've given up hope, we haven't. Instead we have given up paying for someone else's notion of hope. We're doing our best to stop trying to buy our way out of the constant guilt we feel that we aren't doing enough for our children.

We've given up purchasing every single thing that worked for some other kid with autism. We focus now on what our family needs. Can Jack really use it? Will it improve his quality of life? Can we afford it? Does it align with our family's value system? Can we buy it locally? Can we borrow it first from someone else, to see if it really works? Because most of the time we are left to struggle through purchase after purchase, never knowing whether something will work until it's paid for and assembled, and not returnable.

It took a few years, but we have crystallized several thoughts, ideas I go over when I am confronted with an opportunity that feels like: if I get it right this time, it will forgive, somehow, the thousands of other dollars we've wasted.

- Always borrow the item first if you can. If you can test drive the item, or a very similar item, you can avoid making costly mistakes, and purchase the right size or style the first time.

- If an occupational therapist, a physical therapist, or some other professional suggests you purchase something, make sure that medical insurance, or a state program doesn't already cover that item before you pay out of pocket. Budget cuts and unfriendly coverage mean that it might not be covered, but you might as well ask.

- Think about whether the device will work for your specific child, and do not purchase it solely because of another family's success. This has been my number-one purchase instigator, and it is always the most depressing thing when the item doesn't work for my kid.

- Steer clear of snake oil and false prophets. If the therapy, device, or supplement says it treats autism *and* several other things ranging from dyslexia to ADHD to sleep apnea, look more carefully, and make sure it's really what your child needs.

- Use your crafty, MacGyver-like skills to adapt regular items for extraordinary uses rather than pay for the special item from the special catalog. The hardware and fabric stores have many ways to make things useful, less expensively. We have Velcro, duct tape, and a variety of bands and clips available at all times in our workshop.

- Do not let the sorrow or the guilt of other family members influence your purchasing decisions. Grandparents, for example, have the weary task of being our parents, and our child with autism's grandparents, and they want all of us to be happy. Their need to "fix" things can make everything seem necessary.

- Use the Internet. Research the item carefully before you buy. Get the best price, the best one of its kind, and the exact thing you need. I often type in whatever I'm looking for, and the words "awful" "terrible," or "never again" so I can find the specific complaints others may have had. (This trick also works for hotels and restaurants.)

- Build on your successes. Look to see what you already have that didn't work or gave you great success, and build from there. Several items we purchased as a cure-all for our three-year-old boy were disappointments then, but have become hits now as he has gained more skills.

What I realize, as my son turned ten last week, is that the most important item I can garner for him, the most valuable thing I can do, is to be the best parent I can to him. Encouraging his strengths and helping adapt his world to accommodate his deficits are mostly done with words, and patience, and affection, and those don't cost me a thing.

——

A version of this essay was originally posted at www.jennyalice.com

The Keeper: A Tale of Late-Childhood Asperger's Diagnosis

Mir Kamin

For the first time in a very long time, it felt like things were okay. Good, even. Things were going to be great, in fact, and once I got the kids settled in to our new town, new house, new life...things would only get better.

So there I was in the office of the one and only psychiatrist in town that our new health insurance would pay for, who would also see children younger than twelve. My son was only seven, but for the past year he'd done well on an anti-depressant to help control his anxiety. I'd had reservations about medicating him—of course I did—but it helped. It helped a lot, actually. All I needed from this doctor was a new prescription for the medication that we already knew was working fine.

I'd brought his medical records and his neuropsychiatry evaluation results. In answer to the doctor's curt questions, I explained that he'd been a colicky baby but then a charming, social, active toddler. By the time he entered preschool he never cried; he loved school, adored his friends, and other than being a little clumsy, and maybe just a little more sensitive than the other kids, he appeared to be perfectly normal. It wasn't until kindergarten that the tantrums began. And it wasn't until first grade that a kind teacher asked us if we'd ever heard of Sensory Processing Disorder (SPD), and recommended we have him tested. Testing bore out her suspicions: he had a pretty classic case of SPD, combining both hypersensitivity to touch (the slightest brush against him could result in wounded howling of "You hit me!") and large proprioceptive deficits (he struggled with balance and just generally knowing where his body was in space).

I explained all of this to the new psychiatrist. I detailed how we'd tackled the issue on all fronts; in addition to medication for the anxiety, my son had been receiving regularly occupational therapy and attending talk therapy, as well. He was doing better. Combining all of those things together, I told him, he was practically back to the old version of himself, the one who was all smiles. To punctuate my point, my son—who'd been sitting next to me, fiddling with a couch cushion this entire time—turned to the doctor and flashed him a wide grin.

The doctor took notes and nodded and asked a few more questions, and then asked to spend fifteen minutes talking to my son. I agreed, but when I didn't move, he added, "Alone." Embarrassed, I headed back to the waiting room, hearing my son launch into a detailed explanation of his favorite Pokémon character as the door closed behind me.

When fifteen minutes had passed, the doctor walked my son back out to the waiting room and asked him to wait for me, and then invited me to come back in without him. Back inside his office, the door clicked shut as I settled back down on the couch. "Did you learn a lot about Pokémon?" I asked, trying not to laugh. It was my son's current obsession and I knew he'd given the doc an earful.

"Oh yes," he laughed. "More than I ever knew before! He's quite the charmer."

"Thanks," I said, smiling. "I think we'll keep him!" That had always drawn a chuckle whenever I'd said it before, but the doctor merely made a note on his pad, expressionless. Then he set his pen down, looking up to lock eyes with me.

"So," he said, then. "Your son has Asperger syndrome." He said it as though he wondered why I hadn't told him.

"What?" I said, sure I'd misheard. He was still looking at me, taking in my flustered response. "He...no he doesn't," I continued, briefly wondering when it had gotten so warm in his office. "He has Sensory Integration Disorder. He was just tested last year. That's all. Sensory stuff. He's not autistic."

"Why do you say that?" he asked me, cocking his head to the side. I stared back at him, baffled into silence. "I mean," he continued. "You seem...almost offended."

"I...uh..." I groped for words. "I guess I am a little offended?" It came out as a question. I tried again. "You just spent less than an hour with him. His testing last year didn't say anything about that. He's extremely verbal. He's extremely social. He's never had an issue with eye contact. He has tons of friends and plays well with others. He's incredibly compassionate, always the first one to run over and ask if you're hurt or get upset if someone else is upset." The doctor was still just looking at me, waiting for me to run out of steam. "He's very social," I repeated. "Aren't people with autism...you know...not?"

"I haven't fully evaluated him, obviously," he said, "but I've seen kids like him a lot. We call them Little Professors. It's a kind of high-functioning Asperger's where yes, they don't have problems with eye contact and they love people, but they talk like brainy old college professors in spite of being fairly immature in other ways. Kids like him care when you're upset, but they have no idea why you're upset. They're rigid and specific about how they want things to be, though, which is the most common source of the kinds of meltdowns you describe him as having." I tried not to gape at him. Fifteen minutes. Fifteen minutes this man had spent talking to my son, and he claimed that trumped the extensive testing he'd had the previous year? Oh, I was starting to hate this man and his smug little theory.

"He's okay right now," he continued, as if he hadn't noticed the horrified look on my face, or just didn't care. "But it's going to get worse before it gets better. I'm telling you this not to scare you, but to prepare you. It's already starting to happen—his peers are maturing in ways in which he is not, and it's causing some social tension. In first, second, maybe even third grades? It's not a big deal. But in fourth and fifth grade you'll see the gap become a chasm, and relationships will become increasingly difficult for him. Middle school is usually the worst for kids like this. It will be bad, and you'll have to really be vigilant in making sure he's okay. For kids with Asperger's who are socially inclined it's actually worse than for the kids who are happy on their own, because they want to be part of the gang and they just...can't. You need to be prepared for that."

We looked at each other, across the few feet separating his chair from the couch where I sat, and anger burned brightly on the edges of my vision, blurring and narrowing my gaze, which after a few seconds of silence I purposefully shifted to a point on the wall behind him.

"Okay," I finally said, in a tone that no doubt suggested it was not even a little bit okay, "can you write us a new prescription or not?"

"It's not my intention to upset you," he said, confused. "I'm sorry if I did. I thought you knew." My reaction was unexpected, and he was clearly not a person given to comforting others.

"I know what's on the paperwork I handed you," I snapped. "There's nothing about Asperger's there. This is the first time I've heard it even suggested. It's been kind of a long day and I just want to get his prescription and go home if there's nothing else." I realized I was trying very hard not to cry.

The doctor nodded slightly, wrote the prescription, and told me he'd see us again in a month, and then we could go to every three months after that. I nodded and thanked him and all but stormed out of his office.

At home, my husband patiently endured my resultant diatribe. Because how dare he and who does he think he is and what kind of mind game is he playing here? I was furious. I never wanted to see him again, him and his smug, split-second diagnostic powers. What a jerk. As if my son didn't have enough on his plate.

But he was the only doctor our insurance would approve who could monitor and prescribe my son's meds. So we kept going to see him.

That first year, I kind of set my jaw and endured each appointment. Everything was fine, yes. Same as before. New prescription, please.

The second year, my son struggled. We changed meds. We added another med. We went back to the original. Every appointment seemed to find me detailing some new problem or other. Compulsive behaviors cropped up. His temper flared. His "filterlessness," as we'd always called it, had him blurting out more and more inappropriate and even offensive things. The anxiety was back. My memory of our initial meeting with "that stupid doctor" poked at my increased worrying with more and more insistence.

As we headed into the third year—which was now my son's fourth grade year—everything seemed to come to a head. My son was getting in trouble at school, friends were telling him they didn't want to play with him anymore, and he was so anxious I couldn't decide who was more miserable—him or me. At our next regular med check I sent my son back to the waiting room for a minute, and then I turned to the doctor. "Do you remember our first appointment?" I asked him, before he'd even closed the door. "Do you remember when you told me you thought he has Asperger's, and I thought you were nuts?"

"Yes, I do," he said, calmly, settling into his chair.

"I think it's time for you to say 'I told you so,'" I said, trying not to choke up. "He just…it's like all his friends are growing up and he's still five. He can read on a high school level but he can't cope with the most basic of social interactions without ending up convinced that everyone hates him."

To his credit, he never said, "I told you so." And it probably won't surprise you to hear that these days I find myself rather fond of the no-nonsense doctor, in an odd way.

We had the evaluation, and the Official Diagnosis, and the countless Individual Education Plan (IEP) meetings that followed. As I write this, my son is about to start fifth grade, and I pray daily that it will be an improvement over fourth, which was truly the hardest year of his life thus far. I also know that it might not—probably won't—be. I know that we will likely opt to homeschool him through middle school. I know we have miles to go before he will feel truly comfortable with who he is.

But I also know that that the more we embrace exactly who he is, the closer he gets. Since becoming "official," we've talked about it a lot, and read books together, and made an effort to meet fellow Aspies. This past year brought the unexpected gift of a best friend who is "like me, Mom!" which had the incredible side benefit of bringing me a fellow local mom who Gets It. We can watch our boys together and neither of us needs to apologize or explain away their quirkiness; they're just our boys, and we love them.

I'm not going to lie; I still often think that if I had the option to take this particular cup from my son, I would. I'd rather he be dumb but happy, I've confided to just a few trusted loved ones in the past, than have this amazing, brilliant mind that so badly wants to connect with other people but often can't seem to decipher them. I know, I know that he will find his way and be an amazing adult, but to watch him now, while it's so hard for him…it's heartbreaking. Someday all that is hard to remember when today so often takes all your patience, you know?

Talking to Aspie adults has been a lifeline in keeping my hope afloat. While the psychiatrist was quick to tell me "it gets worse before it gets better," it's those folks who've walked out the other side who can actually tell me about the "better," and assure me that it's real. Every "I wouldn't want to be neurotypical" comment is a gem I hold onto and savor.

I can tell you the exact moment when I knew he'd be okay. We'd gotten together with some folks the kids had never met before, and they brought their kids, too. I happened to overhear my son, just a little while into the visit, saying, "I have something called Asperger syndrome. So, you might think I'm a little weird. That's okay. Sometimes I don't realize I'm talking a lot, or I'll say something rude by accident. Just let me know if I do. I really want us to have fun today." The other child took this little speech in stride, and they ran off to play together. No one else had heard the exchange, and I smiled to myself, even as I blinked back tears.

I think we'll keep him.

All His Base Are Belong to Him

Susan Senator

When Benj was a very little guy, he used to sit on my lap at the beach, holding on tight to some little palm-sized truck or being. He did not like to move from there. I was his base. He took a long time to get himself into the sand, and even longer to play in the waves the way he does now.

It worried me, of course. All the other little kids were sitting on their fat, puffed-up diapers and digging, crying, yelling, laughing, pointing. Benj could do all of it; he just had to do it from my lap. I tried pushing him off, prying him loose, setting him down, showing him how to play, but generally, he preferred my cushiony self. Sweet Baby. But oh, God, was I worried. He wasn't like his brother Nat, who has autism, but he wasn't like his other brother Max, who doesn't. So what was he?

He was always content to play on my lap. He was always content to sit in the big armchair with kitten Beanies or drawing tiny palm-sized pirate ships over and over and over again. Sometimes he'd ask me to play with the kitten Beanies with him, but he always had such a firm idea of what the game was that it was tough to get it right. He had such plans, so much going on in that adorable head, such an intense stare, thumb plugged into his mouth as if to help keep it all to himself. Why did he have to keep so much to himself? Why did he enjoy solitary play so much? Why was I the main playmate, for so long? Why was it always his idea that had to win?

Of course I had him evaluated. Wouldn't you, seeing that Nat was autistic, hearing all of the Early Intervention warnings/statistics? I learned that he was not on the autism spectrum. He was "normal, but stubborn." I was instructed to break into his solitude with other little kids and other games: to gently insert my own ideas and steer him off his internal path. But the psychologist also pointed out that she knew our family, so she knew the chances of my actively changing my behavior, into this play therapist mommy, would probably not be stellar. (We are all islands in this family. We all have our laptops open at all times, and Ben's desktop is always on with a project of his.) Dr. W. knew us very well and she smiled, saying it would all probably be okay.

That was a great thing for her to say. He is indeed what she said, and then some. He is not Nat, and he is not Max, and he is not easy. No diagnosis, but life comes to him kind of hard anyway. He's "got" Life-Comes-At-Him-Hard-Ism (LCAHH).

I started thinking about a friend whose second child was also found to be on the spectrum: and also another friend who fears it. I know of so many who did a sib study program somewhere because of one child on the spectrum. And so much of the time, the sibling turns out to have a diagnosis of some sort, but much more minor. I was thinking about Little Benj as well.

I had a thought that was kind of radical for me, and please don't let it offend you: what good does the diagnosis do in some of our children? We all reply, "Well, of course you want to know. You need the services. You need to know what you're dealing with." But do we? Do we need to know? Does hearing, "He has Asperger's" give you relief, does it change how you parent him? Really? How? Weren't you already creating structured routines, rewarding good behavior, using five-minute warnings for transitions? Or did it only make you sad and unsure of what this means? Weren't you already worried about some stuff, like where was he going to be in five years or ten years? Or how would I take him to the supermarket? Or can he have sleepovers, if he's on the autism spectrum? Relationships? Did the technical certainty from a doctor bring you relief, make a positive change? Probably not.

Okay, you need the label for the services. I'm not going there. Nat has come so far with the services he's gotten. And then there's the argument for Early Intervention (EI), the nip-it-in-the-bud argument. Yes, a good one. But—

What bothers me is that the worship of EI has gotten to be so fervent that people believe it to be fundamental in Making a Difference Later On. Pay now or really pay later. But sometimes EI didn't make a difference later on. And no one knows why. Did the kid get misdiagnosed? Did the schools fail him? Did the parent screw up? Does it matter? What matters is that there be supports and structures in Later Life so that he can live okay as an adult. No matter what the diagnosis, if someone is struggling, they're struggling, and they could use a little help. You might have an Aspie who simply cannot be left alone. You may have an adult with Down syndrome who can live independently. Life is full of surprises.

What bothers me is when the label confirmed what you already suspected, and made you feel worse. Made you now think your kid had a limitation that he doesn't necessarily have. Changed his childhood into one with services and therapies, with assessment and appointments. If that's what's needed, okay. But I am here to say, don't let the label change how you see your child. It's just words. You already knew who he was, his difficulties. Your child is different, you know that already. Okay, the therapies may help some of that. But what you need to do the most is give your kid a childhood to the best of your ability—and his. You have already been adjusting to the way that he plays (or doesn't), the odd language (or lack thereof), the eccentric behavior, all the difficulties. Okay, that's the disability part. You'll do what you can, and he'll do what he can.

But you don't know what will be. Benj wasn't like Nat, and he wasn't like Max. He is Ben!

So do you have a future, an entire life with your kid. And a few letters cannot change that, one way or the other. He's got you, his base on the beach.

The Crucial String

Liane Kupferberg Carter

My husband and I had grown increasingly uneasy about our second child, Mickey. Though a warm, engaging baby, he showed no interest in playing Peekaboo, How Big is the Baby, or waving bye-bye. At monthly visits the pediatrician assured us all was well. But by eighteen months, Mickey had only three words, which is why fourteen years ago we finally found ourselves sitting in a cubicle at a major teaching hospital. A team of unsmiling experts spent two hours poking, prodding, and measuring our son, asking him to draw a straight line, stack cubes, put pegs in boards. I perched forward to catch the doctor's words more fully, hoping to hear how adorable, how promising my child was. Instead, she said:

"Don't expect higher education for your son."

It felt as if we were looking down an endless, dark tunnel. Our radiant little boy had just been diagnosed with an autistic spectrum disorder. How could she make such a prediction about a child not yet two? we asked. There was no doubt, she said, that he was "special." A puzzling word. For if he was special, did that make our other, older son, Jonathan, ordinary?

Just as you go through predictable stages of grief and recovery when someone you love dies, so too, learning to scale back your expectations and dreams for your child is an equally painful process. We began the endless rounds of therapy: speech, occupational therapy, sensory integration, physical therapy, auditory integration therapy, behavioral therapy, play therapy, dietary and biomedical interventions. At first my mood was only as good as the last therapy session had gone. It was a lonely time, as I stumbled around in an unlit room of my dark imagination. I felt isolated by my anguish, as friends and relatives rushed to dismiss my fears. "Einstein didn't talk till he was four. Give him time and he'll snap out of it. Boys talk later. Don't compare your children."

In the next year and a half, Mickey learned to recognize letters and numbers, and showed a keen interest in reading signs and license plates. I was waiting for a "Miracle Worker" moment, a breakthrough where he would suddenly begin speaking in paragraphs. Naively, I still assumed that with enough intervention he'd be fine by the time he reached kindergarten. One night at bedtime, he offered a first full sentence: "Mommy, snuggle me," and my eyes filled.

Disability seeps into all the cracks, the corners, of one's life. It becomes the emotional center of the family. Sometimes I felt as if other, "normal" families were feasting in a great restaurant, while the four of us were standing outside, noses pressed to the glass. Birthday parties for other children were sometimes unbearable, as my child, so clearly different, was unable to bowl, do gymnastics, or participate in any other activity. People often stared at him. Equally painful were Mickey's birthday celebrations; I couldn't help remembering just how much his older brother, Jonathan, had been able to do at a comparable age.

I was adrift in a foreign country, without a guidebook, and I didn't know anyone else who lived there. Those first few years with Mickey were like living with someone from another culture, and it was our job to teach him the ways of our world. Slowly, we learned the language, as I dogged my son's therapists with questions and requests for more information and articles, reading voraciously, going to workshops and conferences, acquiring a new vocabulary.

You adapt. Mickey was impulsive, and would often dart away in public or dash out of the house; we put a special lock on the front door. He frequently dumped every book and toy from his shelves; we stripped his room to a minimum of play materials. Loud noises—even the whir of elevators—disturbed him so much he would cover his ears and hum; we avoided crowds and learned to take the stairs.

And yet, for all that he could not yet do, there was so much about him that was intact. He was unfailingly sweet, carrying his collection of Puzzle Place dolls everywhere, hugging and kissing them, feeding them pretend food. He would line them up under the bed covers, whispering "Shhhh, take a nap." Given the depth of his issues, his affect, his warmth, and his sheer vibrancy seemed extraordinary.

The summer before kindergarten, Mickey lost his first tooth. We hadn't even known it was loose, because he still lacked the words to tell us. It was a bittersweet milestone. I remembered vividly the flush of excitement when his brother Jonathan lost his first tooth. Though Mickey seemed pleased to show off the gap in his teeth, and we cheered for him, there was no elaborate celebration this time. The tooth fairy was too abstract for him.

The age of five was also the magic cut-off point I'd always imagined when all would be well. On the first day of kindergarten, I stood in a huddle with the other mothers and watched through the window of the special education classroom as Mickey lay on the floor and said repeatedly, "I go home." But in the next year, he learned to follow classroom rules, and began to read. Later that year, when he told us his first knock-knock joke, we celebrated.

As the years have passed, I have learned to wear emotional blinders. I stay tightly focused on Mickey, celebrating every change I see. I try to tune out what other, neurotypical kids his age are doing, because the gap is still too painful. Mostly, I try not to compare him with his brother Jonathan, an excellent student who is athletic, funny, and well-liked. Their trajectories are so different. It was hardest when Mickey was a toddler; if I did not remember every one of Jonathan's developmental milestones, there they all were, lovingly chronicled—by me—in his baby book. Comparing the boys is sometimes tempting, but dangerous. I must hold separate, realistic expectations for each.

Most support comes, not surprisingly, from other parents of children with special needs. When I finally connected with them after those first hard years, it felt as if I could take a deep breath after holding it too long. Today we talk with bottled eagerness, like war veterans sharing their foxhole experiences. And though each of our tours of duty is different, we all long for our discharge orders.

How do you do it? I am often asked. I give the same answer each time. I wasn't given a choice. I just do it, one foot after the other. I have to be his advocate, because as wonderful as the therapists and teachers are, they go home every night. We are his ultimate teachers, the ones who are in it for the long haul. There's nothing particularly noble about it. We do it because it has to be done.

Acceptance doesn't mean giving up, and it isn't a constant state. Grief and anger still rear up unexpectedly. I still get tired of the relentless effort, the struggle for normalcy, the endless round of therapies and school meetings and fights with the insurance companies. This process of healing is a destination without an arrival. There is no cure, no magic bullet. Joy and grief are joined in lock step.

Ultimately, what buoys our family is hope. When I look at this child, I do not see "autism." I see my child: an animated, endearing, and handsome fifteen-year-old with a mischievous sense of humor, who, despite the early dire predictions, has learned to speak and read and do math. Parenting this trusting, gentle boy has deepened me immeasurably. But would I trade in my hard-earned equanimity and expertise if someone could magically make his autism go away tomorrow?

In a heartbeat.

A few years ago, I heard a story that changed the way I framed my feelings about having a child with a disability. Itzak Perlman was giving a concert. He made his way on crutches to the stage, seated himself, and took up his violin. He began to play, when suddenly a string snapped. Perlman looked around, seeming to measure the length of the stage, how far he would have to go on crutches to fetch a new string, and then seemed to decide that he would do without it. He lifted his violin and began to play, and even without that string, this man with a physical disability not only played; he played beautifully.

This is what it is like to have a disabled child. It feels as if you've lost a crucial string. And then, painstakingly, you must learn to play the instrument you've been given. Softly, differently, not playing the music you'd intended, but making music nonetheless.

Meeting Maddy

Jennifer Byde Myers

It was almost dark when we pulled in to the campground in Ohio. I went to the door of the manager's office, and the sign said, "Will return 9:00." I am an eternal optimist (Ha!) and hoped that it meant in eleven minutes at nine p.m. instead of twelve hours later. We had a reservation, called in hours before, but there were no instructions left for us taped to the door. Most RV parks and campgrounds will do this so you can still find your way in the dark.

As I stood there on the porch, looking back at the RV, knowing that my children were probably yelling at my tired husband because they so desperately want to *get out* of the RV when we stop, I thought I might die of exhaustion. I wilted a little in the heat and began to survey the campground, hoping I could figure out a solution on my own.

Out of the brightly lit laundry room next door, Maddy and her sister Lila appeared. Chattering like little monkeys, they peppered me with questions: Where was I from? How long were we staying? How many kids did I have, and can they go to the playground?

Without waiting for my answers, they told me just about everything they could: parents divorced, mom's boyfriend has a camper, staying for two weeks, actually thirteen days, trying to do laundry, but missing a few quarters. Lila is older. Maddy is younger. They live nearby with their dad. Lila just completed a babysitting course. They have bikes.

And they knocked on the door of the manager's office spouting that it was "worth a try."

The manager came to the door, gave the girls some quarters, then looked at me. I admit I was a little embarrassed, wondering if she thought that these not quite rude, but not well-mannered children were mine.

I told her my name and she welcomed me in to the office/general store, and shooed the girls away. As I checked in, we chatted and she let me know that the girls, while sweet, were not monitored very well, so I should expect to see them at all hours of the night (she wasn't kidding).

After we landed safely in our space, I let my husband Shawn put out the slides, put up the jacks, and make ready our camp for the night while I took the kids to the park, just an earshot away from our numbered space.

Sure enough Maddy and her sister were there at the little park. Katie made friends immediately, identifying easily with other motor mouths. I let go of Jack's hand when I found a pile of gravel. He settled down, and went about sifting the land through his fingers, getting back in touch with earth after so many hours on the road.

He tilted his head to the side, as he often does when he is very interested in something before him. He watched the girls play. He stood up a few times, dribbling pebbles to the ground slowly, and then went down on one knee to grab a few more.

By this time it was mostly dark. I could see the outline of the three girls, but I could no longer distinguish faces.

Katie lost a shoe. I had been very specific about her not taking off her shoes while playing on the playground. I heard Katie whimper a bit. Lilly pulled a flashlight out of her babysitter emergency kit and searched the grass with Katie. They found her shoe, and Lilly sat with her while she put it on.

Maddy came over to where Jack was playing.

"Hi. Um, how old is your boy?" Nine and a half.

"I'm the same age. When's his birthday?" October.

"Will he play with me?' Yes. Sort of. Let me explain…

"I've never heard of autism."

Never. Heard. Of. Autism.

There are still people who've never heard of it. I don't remember ever not knowing about autism, but whatever the statistics are, whatever the numbers that people throw out there, the numbers that make autism seem as ubiquitous as heartburn, there are people who have never heard of it, and my family, in this case, will shape forever what autism means, what autism looks like, for this little girl. And this is where I am most comfortable; teaching, advocating, changing the hearts of people one family at a time. If I do this right, Maddy will know that Jack is different, but the same, that he is as important as she is. She will know that he plays and laughs and has a mom and a dad and a little sister, and feelings, and deserves to be acknowledged, and treated with respect in our society.

I answered every question she asked, her stream of words, more river than creek. Some of her queries were hard: How do you know what Jack wants to play? What is his favorite color?

And some were easier to answer, even if I don't know the answer exactly: So does he understand me? Can he see okay? What is his favorite food? (For the record, we believe it's ice cream.)

The most remarkable part about the conversation was that she was playing with Jack the entire time she was asking the questions. When he got up to wander, she followed him, backwards, even lightly touching his hand every now and then, and when he bent to slip his hand in a pile of sand, she copied him, right down to the same crouched position he favors. When he stood to run, making those sounds that Jack makes, she asked if he was happy, because it "sure sounded like happy."

It was dark now, dark enough that I wasn't more than two feet from Jack anymore. Shawn walked over from the campsite with a flashlight.

I started to get distracted, the dark, Jack loose from my grasp, Katie chirping to her dad about her new friends, and losing her shoe, and finding her shoe.

Maddy quietly said to me, "I hope no one makes fun of him, ever. When I was younger I couldn't see out of one of my eyes and people made fun of me."

I told her I was sorry that that had happened to her, and asked her about her vision now. "Is that why you asked if Jack could see okay?"

"Yeah, I was wondering if we were the same, 'cause I know how it is when you can't see—when you're different."

It was time for us to call it a night. We said our goodbyes.

Maddy walked up to Jack and put her hands on his shoulders, facing him.

"I'm glad I met you Jack. Have fun on your trip."

7 Autism—Adult Voices

I do not want a single child to slip through the cracks and suffer being unsupported, through school and throughout life. I do not want them to suffer even a fraction of the damaged self-esteem, heart-broken pain, overwhelming confusion, exhaustion, and self-loathing that I clawed through.

—Corina Lynn Becker

What I Want People to Know

Corina Lynn Becker

In my time browsing the online community, I often get asked about my story, what it's like to be a late-diagnosed Autistic, and what I want people to know. This is rather odd, because I'm not in the habit of showing off my scars, but there are some things that I think that I can talk about.

I want to be very honest with you. I am an adult living on social assistance, in a shared accommodation run by a non-profit housing organization. Despite being highly educated, I find it difficult to find and maintain a job on my own, and I'm not even sure that I ever will. I struggle to survive with few to no supports, mostly my family and the little that some organizations have been able to provide. It is, at times, very and extremely hard. There is a lot to remember, and each minute, each second, costs me. It costs me strength and energy to maintain social skills, to remember how to do things, to process information and formulate answers. It takes a lot of work, as I'm sure most parents of autistic people can understand.

I am an autistic adult who was diagnosed with Asperger syndrome when I was 17, in 2002. I wish I had known sooner, and that I knew as a child what I know now.

Maybe I wouldn't have felt like a defective monster, or that I was too lazy and just needed to work harder for most of my life. Maybe it would have shielded me from the taunts of bullies, and helped to soothe the tears I cried into my pillow for nights on end. Maybe it would have helped me and the other children to better understand so that maybe I wouldn't be bearing the scars of social blunders. Maybe it would have mended my mother's broken heart as she watched me desperately calling up every girl in my class, trying to get someone to play with me for a weekend a month away. Maybe my teachers wouldn't have been so confused, and helped me more than the little ways they snuck into the classroom. Maybe I would have gotten better supports sooner, and would be more comfortable with accommodations, and more willing to ask for help when I'm in trouble. Maybe my parents would have understood me better, and would have been better prepared to help when I started coming home with meltdowns and severe panic attacks every day.

I could go on with all the "maybes" and "what ifs." But maybe just knowing, just having a diagnosis, would have made all the difference in my life. Or maybe it wouldn't have. I can't say for certain, the same way I cannot predict the future or outcome for any child, autistic or not.

What I do know is this: I do not want a single child to slip through the cracks and suffer being unsupported, through school and throughout life. I do not want them to suffer even a fraction of the damaged self-esteem, heart-broken pain, overwhelming confusion, exhaustion, and self-loathing that I clawed through.

Once, I went to South Africa for a course and met with anti-apartheid activists. To make a change, they told us, take up a cause that is personal. This is about as personal as I can get, that I share my experiences and advice from those experiences so that others may learn. And so, I go out and try to find parents and caregivers who would welcome what I have to say, in order to make a change. Change, for a better future, not just for the next generation, and the present generation of autistic children, but for the entire autistic population including autistic adults.

I do not tell my story too often. It is very painful to relive it, and I am thankful that I can focus on using my experiences to think of positive applications to my knowledge.

I want you to understand, that from my point of view, I did not suffer from autism. That is, autism does not cause me pain. It creates struggles and challenges, yes, that can be disabling, but the pain and suffering that I went through happened because of two things: being undiagnosed and not having the knowledge for supports and accommodations.

In other words, I struggled because nobody knew exactly what I was struggling with, and because I did not have the words to describe my difficulties. For me, the rising autism rate represents a rising rate in awareness and knowledge and a hope that fewer and fewer children will be mis-, under- and un-diagnosed, until not one child slips through the cracks. With that hope, there is a chance to make a difference, to ensure that each child gets exactly what he or she needs and requires in order to succeed.

To me, each child is a unique person with unique strengths, weaknesses, and needs. This is all children, and all people. We all grow up with different cultural backgrounds, with different parents and experiences, and become unique people. At the same time, one autistic individual will require unique supports, just as she or he has unique abilities.

I may not be able to speak on behalf of the entire autistic population in terms of my beliefs and experiences, but I do my best to apply what I know to each situation I come across on the Internet, to see whether I can be of any assistance, even if it is just to provide encouragement. By doing so, I hope that my feedback can provide support to parents and caregivers, who in turn support my fellow Autistics.

As I do this, I hope that people remember the following:

Have understanding. Sometimes just knowing that we are having a hard time is enough. Be aware of what affects each of us and understand that we try very hard with what we have, even when we have nothing left. Even if it does not lead to supports and accommodations, just knowing and giving us a little more room to work can make a big difference.

Have patience. A lot of us can take longer than others to develop and learn things. But autism is a developmental disorder, not a delay. So we do develop and grow, but we need your help, and you need to keep your cool. It may take a saint's level of patience, but we need someone stable that we can depend on, a steady hand to help guide us when life gets more confusing.

Be caring. More than anything, we are still your children and students. We are still people capable of feeling, of loving, and of being hurt. Make sure to not just be a service provider or educator. Be our friends, our family. Learn what we love, and use that to speak to us that you care. Learn how we can show you that we also care for you, and to look for how we communicate to you.

Be positive. This is really hard to do sometimes, with all the challenges that arise, but it's very important. We tend to pick up our attitudes from those we're around, either being oversensitive or undersensitive, and so your attitude becomes ours. With all the difficulties we face together, it's very easy to be discouraged. Do what you can to keep a positive perspective on things.

And finally, be good to yourself. You and I are only human. We aren't perfect. It's okay if you make mistakes. Forgive yourself, and take the time to take care of yourself. If you need to, seek respite and take a day off. We all need personal time to rest and recharge. So when you feel yourself worn thin, don't be afraid to reach out for help and take a break.

I don't believe I am alone when I say I don't expect you to be superhuman. Raising children and taking care of others can be very hard, and sometimes it's hard to find help. But there are people who can help, and we want to be there for you.

I hope that my words reach people and provide help in some way. While I strive to make big changes, I believe that all that I've gone through and all that I work for is worth it if I can make even just one small change. Maybe that small change can make all the difference.

Grieving the Dream and Living What Is

Rachel Cohen-Rottenberg

When I first began delving into the words written by parents of autistic children, I found myself troubled by phrases like "the heartbreak of an autism diagnosis." At the time, I was just beginning to develop a positive identity as an autistic person, and I felt offended that people would feel heartbroken at having a child like me. At the same time, I recognized that the grief was sincere, and that I couldn't possibly tell someone that his or her feelings were wrong. I've been known to argue with an outlook or an idea, but not with a feeling. Feelings, in my view, are not open to disagreement.

I've come to understand the grieving, I think. I've come to understand it because, having received a diagnosis at fifty, I've gone through my own grieving process. And what I've come to learn is that my grief is not about being autistic. I don't feel that it's unfair to have been born autistic. I don't feel as though some terrible tragedy has descended upon me in mid-life. I don't curse my fate and wish I were just like everyone else. I've never asked who I might have been were it not for my parents' abuse, and I have no inclination to ask who I might have been without being autistic. Being autistic is intrinsic to my life experience, to my insight, and to the gifts I bring. The One Above made me just as I am, and I respect that.

And yet, I grieve. I grieve the loss of the person I thought I was—the person who could navigate the world like everyone else, the person who could do anything she wanted if she worked hard enough. I grieve the things that I've always wanted to do but am physically unable to do. I grieve the loss of my apparently privileged status as an apparently neurotypical person. In short: I'm grieving what was never there to begin with. I'm grieving an idea of myself and of my place in the world. I am not grieving what is or what was. I am grieving what doesn't exist and what has never existed, except in my own thoughts.

This understanding came into focus in the days after I met with a woman at a local civil rights organization. She works in the area of disability rights, and I approached her in my role as the leader of the Vermont chapter of the Autistic Self Advocacy Network (ASAN). When we set up the meeting, I told her about my auditory processing condition and about the kinds of accommodations I need—namely, a quiet space and a slow conversational pace. She was quite welcoming and offered to meet anywhere I wanted so that the environment would work. We ended up meeting in her office, which is just five minutes from my house.

In some ways, the two-hour meeting went very well. She was very friendly and very dynamic. I learned that she works as an advocate for parents, attending IEP meetings and helping to protect the rights of children. I learned that she does a great deal of anti-bullying and anti-harassment work, running compliance trainings for schools throughout Vermont. I learned that, as a person of color, she had been through severe racial harassment as a student, and that much of her work is powered by the conviction that no child should ever go through bullying at school.

The downside? She spoke very, very fast and provided a great deal of verbal information. I was able to see, right away, that asking her to slow down would not have worked. I don't think she would have been able to do it. Her work is very stressful, and she was clearly up to the task, but what made her so good at her work also overwhelmed my auditory processing system. As the meeting progressed, I felt more and more overstimulated, and less and less able to find the words I so badly wanted to say. And because I've never seen a nonverbal signal in my life, words were all I had. Without nonverbal shortcuts, the process of listening and speaking became exhausting. I probably should have cut the meeting short, but I wanted so much to make connections with other people working on disability rights that I stayed glued to my chair. Needless to say, I needed a few days after the meeting to get my nervous system back into a state of calm and balance.

Helping to advocate for the rights of parents and children, especially bullied, harassed, or otherwise vulnerable parents and children, is something I've wanted to do all my life. I have a fire inside me when it comes to injustice, and much of the recovery work I've done for twenty-five years has been aimed at being able to go out there into the world and fight the good fight. I want to go to IEP meetings and be a supportive advocate; I want to be able to walk into any situation and do workshops and trainings. When it comes to making right the wrongs of the world, I've got the spirit of a warrior. And yet, no matter how patient, how brave, and how intelligent I am, I can't make my auditory processing system do what it isn't made to do. I can't change, by an act of will, the way I process speech and sound. I can't see a nonverbal cue, and no amount of explaining is ever going to get me to.

As I've looked at what happened at the meeting, the truth has become clear: I am an experienced and conscientious researcher, writer, and editor. I am highly intelligent. I am very sensitive. I am absolutely tenacious. But there is something I cannot do: I cannot implement my work in a chaotic or dysfunctional environment. In the quiet of my own home, I can put together a fact sheet about children's rights. I can interview people and develop materials on bullying and its impact. I can help to create an anti-harassment workshop. I can gather large amounts of information and organize it in myriad ways. I can do the behind-the-scenes work, but I cannot go into the thick of things and be effective.

It's not that I'm incapable. It's that I cannot find an environment in which it would work. An IEP meeting is not such an environment. A compliance training session is not such an environment. Any situation in which people are under stress, not at their best, and talking at cross-purposes is not such an environment. In those environments, almost by definition, accommodation for my disabilities becomes impossible. After all, if the situation were friendly, functional, and fair, there would be no need for me to be there in the first place.

This realization represents the end of a decades-long dream, and there's sadness there. I imagine that it's an emotion similar to what a parent feels upon receiving an autism diagnosis for his or her child; it's the end of a dream, and there's sadness there, too. I remember how many years I planned for the birth of my daughter, how many years I dreamed of all the fun we would have, how many times I told myself that I couldn't determine the future and yet found myself looking forward to a multitude of things. Being autistic, I might have had an easier time with an atypical child than most, because I've always been the one who is different. But a typical parent has typical dreams, and there is grief in letting go.

In large part, those dreams have to do with life being safe and welcoming to a child, and, as we all know, the world is often not a safe and welcoming place for autistics. I have been bullied, and ignored, and left behind, in many different ways, all my life. And yet, I don't wish I were different. I wish the world were different. I wish that more people defended the bullied rather than the bullies; I wish that more people took the time to get to know me and find out what a great good friend I am; I wish that more people were sensitive to all the things that autistic people need in order to live our lives with more joy and less fear, more inclusion and less loneliness.

The grief I feel is for what never was and for what has yet to be. It's not for who I am. And I imagine that, for parents, the grief is for the dreamt-for child and the dreamt-for plans; it's for the opportunities and the safety and the welcoming that the world does not yet make possible. And it's absolutely right to grieve that child and those plans and the state of the world as we know it. But grieving all those things is different from grieving that we are autistic. I want to say to parents, "The child who is here does not need to be grieved, any more than I need to be grieved. There will be new dreams, different dreams, dreams that are based on what is real—not on the doomsday prophecies of doctors with God complexes, not on research that barely scratches the surface, but on the child you see in front of you, whose life you are committed to nurturing. That's the only basis for a dream—your flesh-and-blood child, longing for a way to manifest his or her reason for being in the world."

Each of us is here for a unique purpose that no other person can ever serve. There is so much to be done. So let us grieve our dreams. Let us carry our grief with dignity. And let us get to work.

Being Employed With Asperger Syndrome

Michael V. Drejer

When I was diagnosed with Asperger syndrome in 2003 at the age of twenty-five, I had already pretty much given up hope of ever finding and getting a job that was right for me. All I had to show for my job skills was a high school diploma with a lousy grade average, plus a few exams that I barely passed when I tried studying to become a school teacher and when I tried getting a bachelor degree in English at the university. (I did not finish either course.)

Apparently it is difficult for people with Asperger syndrome to get a job or keep a job, which was exactly what I had experienced as well. Fortunately, it does not have to be like that. In fact, hiring "Aspies" (as some people with Asperger's refer to themselves) for certain niche jobs can be of a great mutual advantage both for the Aspie and for the company hiring.

I found such a job, through complete and unbelievable luck, by reading an article in a local newspaper about a company that specializes in hiring people with an autism spectrum diagnosis. All my co-workers are diagnosed as being on the spectrum, mainly as having Asperger syndrome.

I started out in a five-month trial period, where I was given assignments that were designed to expose my strengths and weaknesses regarding my work skills. Doing follow-ups on assignments was important, as was discovering what sort of work environment was optimal for me. Personally I prefer to work in a room without any direct, bright light, and I don't like to sit with my back towards a door or where people can look over my shoulder. These things make me really uncomfortable and distract me from my work.

After the trial period was over, the company offered me a job as an IT consultant on "flexi" time, which means I work 20 hours per week, four days per week, five hours per day, and get Wednesdays off. I get paid as if I had a normal full-time job: the company pays me for the twenty hours per week I actually work, and the local municipality pays the rest.

Our company's main niche area of expertise is software testing. We test programs and applications for use on the Internet as well as software to be used in other industries, for example, software for windmills and software for hospitals. Doing a methodical and structured test of a piece of software is something that fits right in with a lot of the strengths of most Aspies . We are good at spotting even the most minor irregularity that could potentially be a fatal flaw in the software—this is something I have experienced personally in my work, and that is when I know I have done a good job.

The downsides of hiring Aspies: it requires a lot of patience on the employer's behalf. But having been employed for over two years now, my experience tells me that it is worth the patience.

The first thing is that Aspies have a lower stress threshold, or we are worse at recognizing the warning signs of stress. This causes us to have a significantly higher number of sick days than most people, and usually this means the Aspie gets fired. This is a big mistake for the employer. Let the Aspie have a few days off to cool down again, then talk to him or her and find out what caused the meltdown. Chances are it has something to do with the work conditions not being optimal. In my experience, under optimal working conditions, an Aspie will work harder, faster, and better than just about any "neurotypicals" or NTs out there, out of sheer loyalty and personal perfectionism.

The second thing is that potential clients tend to be rather skeptical when they hear that the employees are disabled. It does not matter to them that the product they will be getting in return will generally be of a higher quality and usually will be finished quicker than if they got it somewhere else. (However, our prices are on competitive market terms. This is not a charity company; our services are not cheap just because the employees are diagnosed with autism.)

But work can be scarce, and "quiet" periods can be extremely stressful for us, which leads back to the first thing.

At the company where I work, we have two main solutions for this situation. The first solution is a game room where the employees can go and play a game on a video game console (in our case a Nintendo Wii). The second solution is that the employer lets people go home early, no strings attached, no reduction in pay that day, just go home early, get some rest, and come back tomorrow. When this happens to me, I usually stay at the office until after lunch and then go home (because the lunch is pretty good at work compared to my miserably empty fridge at home).

I share an office with three other guys. I think it is important to be aware of who gets put together in the same office. Obviously, if there is somebody in your office you have a bad problem with, that is not going to get very productive. On the other hand, if it is an Aspie you get along with too well, you probably won't get a lot of work done either. It is a delicate balance, but it can be done. The guy I get along with "too well" sits in the office next to mine. We talk during breaks, or if neither of us has anything better to do. The guys I share the office with and I talk more casually and maybe more often, but because we don't have as much in common, it is easier to focus on getting back to work.

The feeling I get when I go home from work, knowing that I have done a good job, made a difference, and contributed to business life as a professional, and getting paid and recognized for my work, is incredible. I went from having no hope back in 2006, to recently starting to think about how to improve my career.

Having Asperger syndrome does not prevent us from getting jobs; in fact it can be an advantage and huge strength both to ourselves and to the employers. The future of Aspie employment has never looked brighter than now, and I believe that this is still just the beginning.

—

A version of this essay was originally published at www.aspieteacher.com.

Reflections on Mature Autism

Rory Patton

I love it when someone asks me to write a guest piece about my experience of autism because it compels me to think about it in a way I don't in my blog. On this occasion, the invitation has been more or less coincidental with a recent blackout and even more recent meltdown. I don't pretend to be an expert on autism; sometimes I am not certain I am even an expert on me!

There has been some debate over whether Asperger syndrome should disappear as a discrete diagnostic category and instead be subsumed into the more general description of Autism Spectrum Disorder. I personally prefer the label Asperger's—much more socially acceptable than autism—but recent events have reminded me of just how firmly we are part of the autism spectrum. I am very much inclined to believe that the key difference between Asperger's and high-functioning autism is only the early acquisition of speech. I am also not entirely sure how we measure the level of function. I am high-functioning Asperger's, but give me the right level of sensory overload and you might be hard put to distinguish me from someone with intense autism. My recent meltdown reminded me very forcibly of just how autistic I am.

As someone with high-functioning Asperger's I have found myself—like others of my kind—on the receiving end of hatred from some parents of more severely affected autistic children. I find this upsetting largely because it seems so unjust. I accept that on occasion I may express opinions too forthrightly and I don't realize how other people will react, but I do actually try to understand them.

I have just bought a book called *Mindreading* by Sanjida O'Connell, which explains Theory of Mind, so I may soon understand why some people hold the ridiculous belief that they can know how someone else thinks and feels. I do not like that they discount my experience and opinions; I am as entitled to express an opinion as they are. It is funny how many neurotypical people around the autism field get fixated on one point of view. This piece will probably upset people; if so I apologize in advance as it is not my intention. If you do get offended please don't just have a go at me, but explain what I have done to upset you.

One of the areas in which I have been abused is my support for vaccination. I accept that some children's onset of autism symptoms is coincidental with vaccination; whether the vaccine is the cause is unproven. Personally I am certain they are not the primary cause. I incline rather to believe that autism is part of the process of evolution. I do not believe that we should not vaccinate, but I totally support those calling for more independent research into the triggers that precipitate the onset of autism symptoms. I have a theory—based on nothing but vegetarian prejudice—that the trigger is chemicals used in meat products, but until the research is done, who knows? Perhaps it's pesticides, and exhaust fumes probably don't help either. All that having been said, I sincerely believe that vaccination in the majority of cases provides protection from disease for both the individual and society.

I do believe that the autism community should work together to seek the causes rather than fight for one exclusive point of view—at the end of the day it won't matter whose position is right as long as we find the truth. Perhaps instead of starting with a theory and looking for evidence to support it, we should start with autism and try to understand it.

Many parents hope for a cure for their children. I suppose that's understandable. I don't want a cure and I certainly don't want antenatal screening, and this causes a degree of argument. I believe what we can agree on is that we all want the best for people with autism. I think we should be designing a world that is a good place for people with autism to live in. We should be finding the best ways to lessen the undesirable symptoms and we should not allow orthodox science and logic to close our minds to the possibility that alternative therapies may help some people. There is a tendency by some scientists to discount the experience of parents—anecdotal evidence is still evidence and should be taken into account but not to the exclusion of experimental data. I personally am skeptical of homeopathy and consider it illogical, but illogically my chronic heartburn has responded so well to Bio-chemic Tissue salts that I am off my four-to-eight-a-day Gaviscon habit. We would be rash to discount anything out of hand.

If—as I believe—autism is an integral part of humanity's evolutionary process then we cannot comprehend it with our old beliefs but need to develop new ways of thinking. We are moving into a new technological era where a level of autism may well be a positive advantage, certainly an age where traditional social skills are becoming less relevant and the ability to be on one's own is an asset. There is a blog with the wonderful name *Adventures in Autism*—the name is inspiring, the content you must evaluate for yourself as I am not prepared to comment on it. As someone with high function, my autism is an adventure and a journey of discovery; every day is a challenge and I am—to some extent—glad of that. Is autism an adventure for those less able? I don't know, but neither does anybody else except themselves.

Before anyone decides how life occurs to someone with autism, may I make a personal point? I love my spinning tops and yoyos and my cameras, my routines and repetitive behaviors give me a lot of comfort, my collection of cables is reassuring, I enjoy touching things—and if I choose not to display emotions or indulge in pointless chit-chat, it would not occur to me that it is a problem, just as I am perfectly happy not to have to suffer other people's displays of emotion. Being on the spectrum does present difficulties but it is by no means all bad. The people about whom you worry may not be as unhappy as you suppose—obviously they could be but in many cases they probably aren't.

So What's the Fascination With Autism and Sex?

Lindsey Nebeker

A slight uncomfortable laughter was shared among the crowd of mothers sitting in a circle as one mother said quietly, "I'm really trying to avoid bringing up the topic of sex with my son. I hope that day doesn't come up soon."

This was during a recent speaking engagement I gave to a parent support group. I arranged for all of us to sit around in a circle since the group was small enough to pull that off. I often find that with circle-style seating, the conversation becomes more open-ended, and I hear more from my audience. And the conversation can get very interesting—such as when it turns into a conversation about autism and sex.

I was tempted to chuckle at the level of discomfort these mothers had in linking the words "autism" and "sex," but kept to myself and gave a quiet smile. I understand why they would feel that way. Parents often find it awkward to have the "sex talk" with their kids. For a child with a developmental disability, it can be even more awkward for parents to initiate the "sex talk." Whenever I ask parents about this, the number-one reason they give is that they are unable to tell the level of ability their child or teen will have in grasping such topics. And with such a spectrum of cognitive levels, who can blame these parents for wondering? There is no single formula to educate an individual with autism on sexual topics, and the teaching approaches will vary from person to person.

What we can't deny, however, is that individuals with autism and developmental disabilities go through puberty, experience hormonal changes, become curious about their own bodies, and are sexual creatures by nature—just like anyone else. Some people are asexual, and some people never desire to seek a romantic companion. However, just because an individual has autism does not mean they lack hormones and the natural development of a sex drive.

In the autism community, all this is well known. The parents and professionals who work with adolescents can tell you about it, and the adolescents and adults with autism can share that as well. Even though my brother, James, is nonverbal and has not established the skills of romantic companionship, my parents and I know he is aware of his hormonal shifts and the natural development of his sex drive. Then there are other autistic individuals (and plenty of them) who do have a desire to seek a partnership, get into relationships, and even marry and raise children of their own. When you attend an autism conference, you will find several books, DVDs, and other media materials on the subject of autism and sexuality, distributed by specialty publishing companies such as Future Horizons, Autism Asperger Publishing Company, and Jessica Kingsley Publishers.

To the general population and mainstream media, autism plus sexuality is an unfamiliar phenomenon. But as the topic is gradually introduced to the limelight, people are becoming more aware. One really good example was when the movie *Mozart and the Whale* (starring Josh Hartnett), loosely based on the love story of Jerry and Mary Newport, came out in 2005. Shortly after, their book *Mozart and the Whale: An Asperger's Love Story* was published. This was the first major story on autism and relationships I can recall that really stood out in the mainstream media. The movie and the book had come out right around the time Dave and I started dating, so they definitely served as inspirations to me. I wished for more stories like that to reach out to the general audience.

That is why Dave and I were ecstatic to share our story when we were approached a few years later by *Glamour* magazine. I hadn't really paid much attention to the content in women's interest magazines in the past, but we both knew it was a major publication and were aware of how big an opportunity this was. It was an opportunity to tell the world that there are individuals with autism who do find love, who do have sex lives, and experience the ups and downs of a relationship—just like any other couple. But as much as I was eager to share this with the world, I was also nervous. I knew not all the feedback would be positive, and I understood why. I try hard to tell people that although not everyone will find love, the possibility and the concept of autism and sexuality exists, and is very real.

Since then, other stories have broken into the mainstream, such as the movie *Adam* (a fictional portrayal of a young man with Asperger's and a woman who is neurotypical), and *The Seattle Times* article on the real-life love story of Emilia Murry Ramey and Jody John Ramey (who have also co-written a book called *Autistics' Guide to Dating*). There have also been stories about the complications a person can face in seeking love and establishing a sex life, such as the story Paul DeSavino and his family shared with ABC News' *Nightline*.

In addition, countless individuals and other members of the autism community have posted blogs, uploaded YouTube videos, and written articles about the concept of autism and sexuality, in efforts to continue promoting awareness to the general public.

The fascination and curiosity have no limits when it comes to autism and sexuality, leading to questions regarding what goes on behind closed doors. Sometimes, it leads to taunting. A woman from Queens, New York, posted an entry on her blog about flipping through her copy of the March 2009 issue of *Glamour* on her bus ride back home and coming across the article about me and my boyfriend. In reaction, she wrote: "Autistics having sex?!?!? I can't believe it!! I'd pay to see that—a couple of mental retards f***ing!!"

Sad to see? Yes, it's always sad to see ignorance. But I've learned that is part of the price one pays for exposure, and the best thing you can do in negative criticism is to ignore it and move on.

Besides—I think this woman from Queens would be quite disappointed if she ever did have the chance to witness two autistic people having sex. It's pretty much like two nonautistic people having sex.

—

A version of this essay was published on Naked Brain Ink,
www.nakedbrainink.com

Why Closed Captioning Isn't Just For Deaf People

Sandy Yim

Thanks to the excellent advice of a friend, closed captioning is one of the most helpful discoveries I've made. I didn't even know until recently that you could get closed captioning on any TV show just by turning it on in your cable settings!

For a long time, my husband and I have been really frustrated by the ratio of how much we paid for cable to how little TV we watched. And then, oh my God, I discovered closed captioning. I could finally read TV instead of just watching or listening to it—what a revelation!

See, following a conversation is pretty complicated:

You have to be able to hear what's going on.

There's also the assumption that the language being spoken is one you understand.

There's the question of whether you can parse the words correctly, or tell where they begin and end. And that has to happen in real time unless you want to be mentally playing back your "recordings" and missing new ones.

Do the utterances have meaning to you?

And can you remember everything you've just heard?

Yes? That's great. But—can you do all that and fit it into a social and emotional context too?

When there's a glitch at any point in this process, a person can have a really hard time following speech or conversations. In the end it has social ramifications and I've gotten used to looking kind of dumb in social situations because it's not realistic for everyone to pause for as long as it takes me to replay their utterances and then process them. Some days I'll go with sweet but dumb, some days I'll go with aloof. I can't watch TV shows with a lot of speech and intense social situations, especially when they're heavily dialogue-based. Too often the plot will hinge on an important line or joke that I'll never fail to miss.

(This is not because I'm Asian! Too many people assume English is my second language so they'll start gesturing wildly or not even talk to me, until I open my mouth and put them to shame.)

But now that I have closed captioning, a whole new world has been opened up to me. I'm able to read very quickly and process several words at once, so I can keep up pretty well with dialogue. I wish I had closed captioning for everything everyone said in real life; maybe I wouldn't feel so stupid every time I had conversations with people.

The captioning system isn't perfect yet; often there's a delay between the speech and the text, and sometimes the spelling is downright atrocious. I hope this will be changed soon, along with people's negative stereotypes about closed captioning. Someone once came over to my home and asked mockingly if a deaf person lived there because of the captioning. I was so mortified that I could find no words to explain.

I'd highly recommend giving closed captioning a try—it's much easier to set up on cable than you'd think. And if you're making a YouTube video, maybe you'll consider adding captions, because there are so many people with invisible disabilities out there who need that text badly.

—

This essay was originally published on Aspie Teacher,
www.aspieteacher.com.

For the 85 Percent of Us Who Can't Work

Clay

I can't say I'm surprised to learn that most autistics have a great deal of difficulty getting and maintaining a job for more than six months. I believe it, because I know just how hard it has been for me. I saddled myself with a wife and two kids before I even got out of the Navy, and for quite a while, the subject of my wife getting a job wasn't even discussed, because our generation wasn't much into that. Instead, I took whatever job I could get, starting as a low-paid parts clerk, until I accepted my stepfather's offer of helping me get a job at an iron ore mine (which paid much more). After I recovered from a huge accident, I returned and worked there for another three years. They gave me some hard and nasty jobs for awhile, such as wrestling with fifty-five-gallon drums and getting other heavy supplies for drill and shovel crews, until I had some seniority to claim an easier job just driving a labor crew around. All of my time there was rough, as it involved interacting with mostly ignorant rednecks. They had all heard rumors that I had won a big settlement from the company for the accident, which wasn't true, but they all believed it and gave me a hard time.

They also gave me a hard time because I lost thirty pounds after the accident, and it took me a couple of years to tip 140 again. The Mexican co-workers called me flaco (skinny), and the Oklahoman rednecks called me "little perfessor." I was smarter than all those bastards, my vocabulary and maybe some of my comments gave me away, and they weren't much appreciative of that. No single "big thing" ever really happened, because it was a large company operation, and also a union place, and no one wanted to lose their job. Still, there was that time when I was sent to the warehouse to pick up a "skyhook." (Hey, I was only twenty-two, and fresh out of the Navy.)

Okay, that parenthetical remark up there was just an excuse—to hide the embarrassment. The reason they did it and got away with it and all those other fool's errands was because they saw and knew that I was just that naïve. This was back in 1969, thirty years before I was diagnosed with Asperger syndrome.

I can skip over some of my worst moments: working at a car wash, flipping burgers at Jack-in-the-Box, spending nine months whacking, stacking, and burning weeds in 110 degree heat; slaving away in a factory where we would often be locked in, in order to finish up another couple coaches; working on painting crews; making salads and sandwiches; and sanding and oiling pianos, where I heard my foreman tell another foreman, while both of them were watching me, "It's true what they say—hire the handicapped. They're cheap, and fun to watch." I still have no idea what I was doing "wrong;" that was about sixteen years before I got a diagnosis. I also finished donuts, and—God, I'm getting dizzy remembering all that stuff.

It wasn't only the hard work, but all the crap I took from the co-workers, with the refrain of "little professor" repeating itself. Yeah, I did know a lot of things, the academic sort of things that 99 percent of my co-workers would never understand. A Mensa test I took in 1980 said my IQ was 150. But the tests I took for diagnosis in 1999 showed that my "performance IQ" was two standard deviations lower. There were other results that showed similar discrepancies in abilities.

I gained a new determination after my father died in 1988. I was 41, had only enough money for the next month's rent, and had been fired the Friday before Christmas of 1987, but I realized I had to take a stand, had to stand up to bullies who just wanted to see me leave my job. I earned my spot, through talent, skill, and working very hard and long hours. The owner (employer) was the only one who was glad I was there. After making several of my coworkers back down, embarrassing one in front of the others, and playing a sneaky trick of just disposing of another worker's timecard, I was impervious to their shenanigans. I began to think of myself as a "winner," because of skill and determination, and by refusing to back down. I was finally in a pretty good position. The redneck foreman was not my boss and couldn't tell me what to do, or how to do it. (It always really bothered me when people would try to tell me how to do something.)

I have a female cousin, maybe a year older than me, and when we were young, we were told she was the "R-word." Nobody knew much about autism back then, but at the time, it was the only explanation for her behavior, the way she spoke and thought. I'm sure that if Lynne were diagnosed now, it would come up as "autistic," of the Kanner variety. I've often wondered if I was little bit "R-word"-ed. Certainly, my naïveté and inability to communicate or socialize was pretty pronounced. And yet, I was smarter than most of the people I met, and I'm not bragging. I also know that that would not have been so if I were in any actual academic circles.

I have another invisible handicap: scoliosis. "They" knew about it as soon as I took my first physical, before I even joined the Navy. I should have been classified 4-F, but they didn't do it. After spending some long days of typing, I went to see about my back problem, and they finally told me about it. Even though I had just re-enlisted, I spent the next year fighting the Navy to get out. That scoliosis gave me a big problem with just about every job I ever had, because most of them were manual labor jobs.

I've been retired for nearly two years now, and because I retired four years early, I get a very small Social Security check. It does cover my bills, and for anything more than that, I just don't give a rat's ass! I'm perfectly happy doing nothing, because, well, doing nothing is what I'm best at! I'm just so happy to be free, not to have to go to work every day, not to have to eat somebody's shit just to keep my job, not to have to worry about pleasing anyone other than myself (okay, and my cat), and I've always been free of greed, desire, or jealousy of what others have.

I can look back on a lifetime of some small accomplishments, most of them in the past 23 years (since I got really determined), and it does give me some comfort to know that I was able to support my family, and then just myself, despite the many problems I had because of my invisible disabilities: scoliosis and Asperger's. In being able to remain employed, through about fifty different jobs, I now realize that I beat some long odds, like the ones that state that 85 percent of us are unable to hold a job for more than six months. I've counted them up, and just twelve of those jobs lasted as long as a year, or two, or three. The longest was the last one, health aide, which lasted sixteen years. Six years before diagnosis, and ten after. So yeah, maybe my biggest accomplishment was just being able to support myself, without any safety net, against such long odds. It makes me feel a little better, even though I don't have a lot to show for it.

The trick is in not needing much.

I hope that those who want a job, who want to be able to support themselves, just for the satisfaction of doing it, will be able to do it. It's a great boost for one's self-esteem. I will support anything that comes along that helps people to become independent, because that's a good feeling to have. In the meantime, until that happens, I would say to them: Be happy for what you have. Be happy that you have your freedom, have no boss, no co-workers to hound you for being different, to hurt your feelings, to work against you trying to get you fired. If you have a government check (and are able to live on it) but are living with relatives to make ends meet, then find some way to "pay your way" by doing worthwhile things around the house. There are more ways than just earning a living to gain self-respect.

Finally, I know that not having a job when you know that you could work under the right conditions, is just downright depressing. Living in need is in itself depressing. If someone has never been able to work, for whatever reason, depression can turn into despair. That sucks, it totally does, but I would remind you that people's problems are all relative. I'd venture that whacking weeds, and stacking and burning them in 110-degree heat also sucks big time! Most of those jobs I had were pretty damned bad, and the near constant hazing from co-workers made them all the worse.

I just want to repeat something I said to the first email list I joined, almost eleven years ago: "We are, each of us, responsible for the thoughts in our heads." We have the power to choose whatever thoughts we wish to entertain, and negative thoughts can only give birth to negative situations. The same goes for the flipside. I choose to be happy with what I have, and I am. I thank God every night for all that I have (not that I think He hears me) because I know the mechanics of how prayers can actually work. I know that we are the "authors" of our own lives, we ourselves create our own worlds, and we are happy in them (or not) as we choose. Go and be happy, with all your might.

8 Autism—Parent Voices

I've turned my attention away from the past. I no longer fret about how or why things turned out this way. My son has autism. And it is what it is. I can't go back and will a different outcome. I can't conjure him a brain that makes the right connections 100 percent of the time any more than I can fly to the moon. So I've learned to more or less take it in stride, to trust my instincts and my judgment, to parent my son the only way I know how.

—Kristen Spina

Shifting Focus: Eight Facts About Autism the Media Is Not Covering

Holly Robinson Peete

Over the years many parents have reached out to me for emotional support after their child was diagnosed with autism. I particularly remember getting Jenny McCarthy's phone call shortly after her son's diagnosis. Like most moms and dads, she needed to connect with somebody who knew firsthand the swift gut-kick of this difficult diagnosis, somebody who had been in the trenches for seven years already.

We cried. We cussed. We even managed to laugh. We spoke for eight hours. She was naturally frustrated with the lack of answers about autism. I was there for her as I'd be for any parent, and I told her she was blessed to get such an early diagnosis. Her passion was palpable and I could tell she was going to grab autism by the horns, making it her mission and focus. I knew she'd help spread autism awareness like nobody else could and the media would pay attention. Since that phone call, she has created a very successful platform with her powerful opinions, blogs, and books on vaccine safety, diet, and recovering her son, among other things. It has been a courageous, controversial, and fearless ride. Miss Jenny is not scared to get in the ring with the big boys!

Though I share many of same concerns, I feel compelled to shed light on the fact that families affected by autism are struggling on multiple levels. We need a shift of focus to share the spotlight with other, often overshadowed issues that profoundly impact families daily.

To that end, below I highlight eight things about autism the media is not covering enough. They are not hot-button, provocative, or headline-grabbing, but with 1 in 110 children affected by autism (and rising), these issues desperately need more attention:

1. Autism Is Unaffordable

I'd love to see more media focus on how ridiculously expensive it is to treat a child with autism. You can counsel folks all day long to get early intervention, but who in the world can pay for it? Therapies can average over $100-$150 an hour—many require up to fourteen or more hours a week. With insurance companies still not covering the vast amount of therapies needed, too many families are forced to pay out of pocket for much of these expenses. A 2006 Harvard study puts the average cost of services for an individual with autism at $3.2 million over his or her lifetime! A total of $35 billion a year is spent on services for individuals with autism in the United States. The numbers have climbed since then. Bottom line is treatment is completely and ridiculously unaffordable and can financially bring a family to its knees—even in good times. Families live on pins and needles with hopes that they're doing the right thing. But the fact is for too many, the things we want to do are simply out of reach financially. I can think of no worse scenario than not being able to afford to help your child.

2. Parental Guilt

So if you are blessed enough to afford it, in my experience it seems that some kids can improve tremendously with a mix of intensive behavioral, biomedical, and other treatments. But the fact is so many likely will never be "recovered" and nothing, I mean nothing, makes a parent feel more guilty than thinking you could've "fixed" your kid but—well you didn't or couldn't afford to. If you have a child who is nonverbal and severely impacted by autism, for example, and all you want to hear is him or her speak or just use the word "no" appropriately, it can be maddening to hear that someone else did x, y, or z and now their kid is no longer on the spectrum at all. So many parents have shared with me how badly they feel about this. And although I personally have broken my butt for my son and though he has overcome many challenges we were told he would not, he still has autism. What could I have done better? Oh the guilt! Don't get me wrong, I am always elated for any child's success in this journey, but it can be very hard to swallow at times—making you feel like a failure. Just one mom's opinion, keeping it real. Alas, accepting my son's progress or lack thereof is the key to moving forward with my head up.

3. Puberty Plus Autism Can Be a Volatile Mix

Our son is almost thirteen and has entered puberty. Oftentimes kids on the spectrum can start puberty prematurely, and it can be an extremely jarring experience.

A dear friend of mine and autism "Superdaddy" explains puberty's effect on autism like this: "[Puberty is] an 'oy vey' for a normal child but it can send hormones racing in a child with autism that they don't know how to deal with."

The hormonal surge can cause violent and unpredictable behavior. Stress and depression can develop accompanied by social ostracism. Our son has suddenly regressed recently after making so much progress, bringing us a new set of challenges we hadn't anticipated. We always, always remain extremely hopeful and have been blessed beyond our wildest dreams with what he has been able to overcome to this point. But puberty has been a challenge more parents need to be prepared for. It can be a completely different dynamic at this age. Let's get that out there, please.

4. Minority Children are Diagnosed with Autism Years Later Than Other Children.

There are a lot of mysteries about autism. But one thing we know, according to a study covered by CNN: "If a child is diagnosed with autism as early as eighteen months of age, offering the toddler age-appropriate, effective therapy can lead to raised IQ levels and improved language skills and behavior." That's why the fact that African American, Asian, and Hispanic children tend to be diagnosed much later than other children (sometimes two to five years later) is an extreme concern that needs more attention. One reason these children are diagnosed later is that there are more barriers for socio-economically challenged families to access information. Certain developmental milestones are ignored, unknown, or overlooked. Another part of the reason is that there are some cultural and social stigmas about mental health and a fear of talking openly or seeking help for them. So the hope often is that the child will just grow out of it. We just need way more infiltration of autism information and support in minority communities, which will hopefully result in earlier diagnosis. I've visited black churches with this message, letting them know they can be extremely helpful in this effort. We can't allow the window for "age-appropriate, effective therapy" to close on these kids.

5. Autism Can Be Tough on a Marriage

Autism is not a divorce mandate. Often it can bond a family tighter. But too often the financial and/or emotional toll autism can take leaves some couples feeling distanced from each other. This was the case with our marriage. My husband and I narrowly survived statistic status. But over the last ten years I have marveled at his ability to evolve as a father and husband during this bumpy ride that he chronicled in his book *Not My Boy! A Father, A Son, and One Family's Journey with Autism.*

I want to shamelessly plug my former NFL quarterback's evolved, honest account of his pain of dealing with this diagnosis. His personal revelation was that he had to adjust his expectations of his son. Our hope is that *Not My Boy!* will help so many dads (and moms) confront these challenges without feeling so alone. Rodney has taught me that men process things so differently. I could have been more patient and empathetic with respect to that. A book like this might have offered me that insight earlier on.

Couples digging deep to find the strength and resources to take on this fight together may be rewarded by actually connecting more deeply through this journey instead of being fractured by it.

6. Autism's Effect on Siblings

We don't see too much coverage about what the siblings of autism endure.

Ruined play dates, family outings cut short due to a brother's or sister's public meltdown, feelings of neglect, life planned exclusively around the affected child, social stigma...the list goes on.

It can be devastating for a typical child to have to grow up in such an environment. Sibs are often overlooked and really need a bit of attention; parents need tips to help the siblings cope.

I'm so hopeful this will change a bit with *My Brother Charlie*, a children's book co-written by my daughter and me. (We've been a busy family!) Told from a sister's perspective, in *My Brother Charlie*, Callie acknowledges that while it hasn't always been easy for her to be Charlie's twin, she advocates lovingly for her brother, letting people know about all the cool things he can do well. I pray this book will go a long way towards fostering autism acceptance among children and mainstream schools. We found it hard to believe that there wasn't already such a book in children's libraries, considering the rising number of children on the spectrum. We are thrilled that Scholastic stepped up enthusiastically to embrace this important effort.

7. Adults Living with Autism

The face of autism is changing. Our children grow up. Understandably, every parent stresses about what will become of their child with autism in adulthood. It's my own personal recurring nightmare. We ask ourselves: How will he make it in this cruel world without me? Will he live on his own? Will he ever get married or have meaningful relationships? Who will protect his heart? Our fears in this area can consume us.

Here are a few sobering facts:

- More than 80% of adults with autism between 18 and 30 still live at home (Easter Seals).
- There is an 81% unemployment rate among adults with autism (CARD).
- 78 % of families are unfamiliar with agencies that could help them (CARD).
- At least 500,000 children with autism will become adults during the next decade, and they will need homes, jobs, friends, and a future.

The good news is many adults living with this disorder live very fulfilling lives, but too many face a variety of difficulties including anxiety, depression, anger, and social isolation.

We must create meaningful, respectful futures for adults with autism that include homes, jobs, recreation, friends, and supportive communities. They are valuable citizens!

How glorious would it be to get more media attention on this particular issue.

And bravo to Fox Searchlight Pictures for their beautiful and enlightening film *Adam*, which gave great insight into what it is like for a young man with Asperger syndrome to live and thrive on his own.

8. Autism Advocates Who Actually Have Autism

What a concept! Rarely do you hear any stories in the media about people actually affected by autism ever weighing in on the issues surrounding it. Because people on the spectrum may seem disengaged, they hear you talking about them and can develop frustration at not being able to respond to issues that affect them. We all need to remember that.

I have had some enlightening and profound conversations with folks on the spectrum who have made it very clear that they feel completely excluded from any national autism conversation. I've had some ask me to be very mindful about my language when speaking about autism. For example, several have said to me they cringe at the word "cure." Many have expressed that they feel this was their destiny, that they were born this way, so stop trying to "cure me." Whatever our views or personal agendas, we have to respect that.

Others have been frustrated by the polarizing issues disproportionately covered in the media and would prefer for us neurotypicals to focus that energy towards trying to understand their world, how they see things. "Come into my world!" one 25-year-old young man with Asperger's told me passionately.

My friend, fourteen-year-old Carly Fleischmann, has autism, and has taught me more about it through her expressive writings than I've learned in any book! You go, Carly!

I am also so grateful to HBO for the sensational film *Temple Grandin*, finally giving us an image in the media of an adult with autism advocating beautifully and articulately for others like herself.

Bottom line: Their opinions should be heard, valued, and included.

So here's to breaking off eight rays of the media spotlight towards some other important autism issues. Autism families deserve more than just fiery headlines; we deserve a 360-degree, multifaceted conversation. Spread the word!

This essay was previously published at The Huffington Post.

(Extra) Ordinary Days

Kristen Spina

I hang back, following but not too closely, watching my son and his two best friends through the viewfinder, my face hidden behind the awkwardness of a zoom lens. As I watch the boys cross the red wood bridge, I snap half a dozen photos. And then again, as they settle in on the dock, taking turns casting, tossing pieces of bread to a giant turtle bobbing on the lake's surface.

There is little to show here for my son's differences. He is simply one of the guys, enjoying a bit of freedom and fun on a weekend in the Catskills. I scan the lake and the mountains beyond, the grey clouds sitting low in the sky, and think about how remarkable the scene really is—how its very ordinariness is something to celebrate.

I take a few more pictures, then leave the boys to their adventures. Later, they will head for the pool, to toss themselves again and again down the twisty waterslide. They will walk to the barn and feed the rabbits and pigs, play baseball, climb the playground equipment and sit side by side in the dining room, buttering their own bread, pouring their own milk, weaving themselves in and out of the tangled knot of parents and grandparents, friends and family surrounding them on this late spring weekend.

When I look at the shots taken that rainy morning by the lake, three boys and a fishing pole, I am struck by their body language, the ease and comfort of a hand on an arm, two heads dipped to the side to share a quiet word, three young boys standing shoulder to shoulder, their bodies overlapping in a way that is at once familiar and relaxed.

There was a time when I could not imagine the beauty of it. Could not picture my son walking away from me to follow his friends across a green meadow, chasing the wind and the rain and a giant turtle by the side of the lake. For the boy who missed nearly all his developmental milestones, didn't walk until he was 16 months old, and could not tolerate noise or chaos of any kind, his fortitude is nothing short of a wonder to me. When I think about where we started, I am overwhelmed by how far we've come.

There was a point when I thought it would never be okay. When the tantrums and tears and the sleepless nights took away our smiles and our joy. At three years old, my son could not walk down a flight of stairs or attend preschool without a one-on-one aide. He wasn't speaking in a coherent or understandable way and he spent his days frustrated and angry, lashing out at the world around him. The sound of a hair dryer or car alarm crippled him, a light hand on his shoulder led to screams of pain. He was off-the-charts sensory sensitive, unable to complete the simplest art project or play with other children. He lined up his toys and cried if anyone else moved them. We were lost and scared, and yes, I was completely in denial.

But he's eight now. And I've turned my attention away from the past. I no longer fret about how or why things turned out this way. My son has autism. And it is what it is. I can't go back and will a different outcome. I can't conjure him a brain that makes the right connections 100 percent of the time any more than I can fly to the moon. So I've learned to more or less take it in stride, to trust my instincts and my judgment, to parent my son the only way I know how.

I've come to think of his actual diagnosis as nothing more than a formality. Like shaking hands on a deal that was decided long ago. I didn't want to see it at first, but I know now it was always there. I wanted to believe well-meaning family and friends; the pediatrician who said my son was "a bit behind the curve, but still making progress." I pushed my concerns aside, couched my worries. And told myself that all kids have mega-meltdowns.

By the time we had a workable diagnosis, my son was nearly four years old. We started then down the tried and true path of speech therapy, occupational therapy, physical therapy, and social skills training. My son balanced Cheerios on his tongue and practiced waiting his turn. He did exercises to build muscle tone and learned how to hold a crayon. It was non-invasive, behaviorally driven, and somehow, in ways I don't even fully understand, exactly what he needed.

There was pressure early on to pursue other therapies. Things both proven and unproven. Family members would pull me aside to ask about his diet; whether or not he seemed "allergic" to wheat or milk. Many swore that adding this or that supplement could curb his behavior. Others talked about discipline, no doubt whispering to each other that my husband and I were too soft on our son. But none of these suggested remedies seemed wholly directed at what ailed him. Applied Behavior Analysis (ABA) therapy felt too rigid for our family, the Gluten-Free, Casein-Free (GFCF) diet too unnecessary, and the skeptic in me steered clear of anything too risky or too expensive.

I started to do my own research. I read Dr. Stanley Greenspan's book *The Child with Special Needs* and *The Sensory Sensitive Child* by Karen Smith and Karen Gouze. I understood things in a new way. I sought the counsel of my son's occupational therapist, and worked with her to cobble together a little bit of this and a little bit of that, a behavioral approach that could help us remediate in a positive way. I began to see things through his eyes, to change my response to his behaviors and to follow his lead. I learned to trust my son and to listen to what his behavior was telling me. We slowed our family way down. And then when it felt like he could handle more, we ramped things up—looking for ways to raise the bar, to help him grow, stretch and narrow the developmental gaps. We inched our way forward through his toddler and kindergarten years, working in tandem with our school district and trusting in the experience of his therapists and teachers.

But it is never easy. For every two steps of progress, there are three steps of regression. The bulk of my son's challenges fall under the larger umbrella of processing issues, self-regulation, and motor planning. His standardized evaluation scores are just beginning to climb out of the single digits. When you look at who he is on paper, you very nearly can't believe the boy before your eyes.

Today my son is a quirky, exasperating, delightful, funny, interesting, charming, friendly, emotional, sensitive, awkward, and sometimes extremely frustrated third grader with a diagnosis of Pervasive Developmental Delay-Not Otherwise Specified (PDD-NOS) and sensory processing disorder. He still struggles with his ability to handle the unexpected, to cope with disappointment, and I continue to remind myself that delays are not permanent stops. We apply band-aids and tourniquets as needed—continuing to tweak our behavioral strategies to meet the challenges of grade school and beyond.

When he wasn't reading, we found him a tutor and consulted a developmental optometrist. Because he couldn't tolerate the pace or competitiveness of our community-based sport programs, we enrolled him in a league for kids with special needs. And as he struggled to overcome emotional growing pains, we added a social worker to the mix.

What all this has taught me is that—for us—there is no *one* thing. No one strategy or approach or end-all plan to fix things. It's a sliding scale. More of this, less of that and back again. It is an evolution in progress. One my son is even beginning to have a say in as he learns to accept and deal with the hand he's been dealt.

There are days when I wonder—worry—about the future. Will he graduate from high school? Go to college? Be able to live on his own? But I've set aside previous notions of success and found I'm happiest when I live in the moment, appreciating the forward motion, the hills and valleys, of my son's life.

There is no substitute for the lessons he learns when he is out there, taking part in his world. And I am grateful for the small group of friends who stand by him through thick and thin.

On our last day in the Catskills, I ask the boys to pose for a final picture. My son's two friends—brothers—stand to his sides, their arms draped over his shoulders, his slung low behind their backs. The boys tilt their heads to the middle and the three of them look up and grin—silly, toothy grins. I see them then, through the years—young boys and the men they will become—standing on the threshold of something.

I search my son's eyes as he looks into the camera. He is relaxed, completely at ease. Happy. There was a time when I could not imagine him in this moment.

And yet, there he is.

Just Passing Through

Christa Dahlstrom

If you spotted my six-year-old son on the playground or at recess, he wouldn't stand out from the other kids. Like most boys this age, he loves playing any made-up game that involves running, shouting, fighting bad guys, fighting robots, or fighting bad guy-robots.

If you were to watch him, you might even be impressed at the way he's able to invent elaborate imaginative play scenarios and enlist other kids—kids he's never even met—to join in the story. "A born leader," you might think. "What an imagination." You might also be impressed by his sophisticated vocabulary, peppered with "suddenly" and "meanwhile" and "actually" and maybe an occasional "shall" substituted for "will" for extra flair. "Smart kid. Polite, too," you think, as you watch him introduce himself to kids and adults and request their names with an Emily Post-ian correctness.

But if you hung around the playground for a while longer and watched carefully, you might see his confidence and exuberance shift to frustration. As the other children take the made-up story in another direction, or no particular direction at all, he will run after them shouting, "Wait! Stop! Come back!" Red faced and neck veins popping, on the verge of tears: "You're not *listening* to me!" he accuses.

The other kids are simply tired of trying to remember which part of the blacktop is the lava and which part is the alligator swamp and just want to swing on the monkey bars. He might yank their arm, or even shove them aggressively when they ignore his directives.

Now you (okay, maybe not you, but someone) might have a different view: "Geez," you might think. "Bossy as all get out, that kid. He's out of control. Probably spoiled rotten at home."

And if you hung around even a little longer, you'd see something else entirely. You might see my son all by himself, walking back and forth over a railroad tie, happily talking to no one in particular.

—

It's not immediately obvious that my son is on the autism spectrum. Like so many people who sit, toes dangling, on a certain end of the spectrum he often "passes" for neurotypical or "NT."

Great, right?

Yeah, great. Except it's not that simple.

When a child doesn't show the obvious outward signs that have come to signify autism, and when that child is precociously verbal, obviously bright, and has a strong social urge, we often assume that the child doesn't require specialized support. Behaviors that result from challenges with social interaction, language differences, or sensory processing difficulties appear as plain old garden-variety bad behavior.

After all, he doesn't look disabled. A kindergartner who reads at a third grade level, after all, should know better.

When we go to birthday parties or social events with families, I'll find myself striking up a conversation with another parent I've never met or barely know. I go through a set of mental gymnastics to try and determine if I should "disclose" or not. The longer the conversation goes, the harder it is to engage honestly without saying something about my son being on the spectrum.

When I do, often the conversation continues easily without a blip.

But occasionally, when I say something about Asperger's or autism, I've gotten an eye-rolling response that goes something like this:

"Oh, I just hate all those labels they give kids these days. Why do they have to turn every little problem into a psychological condition?"

The optimist in me wants to hear this as supportive (let's not pathologize differences!), but the paranoid, parent-on-the-defensive in me hears it as dismissive:

"There's nothing really different about those kids that a swat on the behind wouldn't cure."

"They're old enough to know how behave."

"You're just excusing bad behavior by giving it a fancy name."

With these imagined judgments ringing in my ears, watching my son mix it up with a crowd of NT kids feels like watching him perform a high wire act. I scrutinize his steps watching for the tiny bobble or misstep. I run around underneath him with the net rather than gazing up and marveling at the amazing feat.

Will he fall? He almost fell. Oh, God, please don't fall.

—

Let's go back to that imaginary playground I was telling you about. What would you see if you—or that generic someone—were to watch me?

I might not be among the parents who are chatting with each other or enjoying their novel on the bench. You'd see me lurking somewhat close to the action. Occasionally, you might see me prompting my son to answer another child's question or helping to interpret the what's going on: "It looks like they're changing the game. They want you to join." And sometimes, I might interpret my son's behavior for other children: "I don't think he heard you. Can you ask him again?" or "I think he wants you to follow him."

My son is at an age where having a lurking mom isn't yet the ultimate uncool stigma. But soon, my well-intentioned attempts to help him fit in—to pass—will only make it more difficult for him to do so.

So here I stand, on the playground, at the birthday party, taking the somewhat complicated position that, "My kid is just like yours. Except when he's not.

Wanting him to be "just one of the guys," but hoping he'll feel proud someday to claim his differences.

Wanting him to be independent, but hoping he'll be able to get support when he needs it.

Wanting him to develop the skills he'll need to do things that don't come naturally, but hoping that he surrounds himself with people who let him know it's okay when he can't.

Wanting him to fit in, but hoping he'll always let his quirky light shine.

I guess I'm the one trying to pass; the one who is conflicted about dual identities, the one who worries that I stand out as the lurker mom and not the cool sidelines mom.

But it's not about me. It's about him and the ways in which he will shape his own identity, however he chooses to do that, when I'm not there holding the net.

———

Author's note: I've barely scratched the surface on this idea. Please check out these amazing posts for more thoughts and insights about the blessings and challenges of almost fitting in:

MOM-NOS on "A Matter of Perspective":
www.momnos.blogspot.com/2010/06/matter-of-perspective.html

MOM-NOS on "The High Cost of High Function":
www.momnos.blogspot.com/2006/10/high-cost-of-high-function.html

Squidalicious on "But What if Your Kid Can Pass?":
www.squidalicious.com/2008/07/but-what-if-your-kid-can-pass.html

Just about anything by Drama Mama at Like a Shark:
www.likeashark.blogspot.com

The Eyes of Autism

Brenda Rothman

It was a coolish summer day, no humidity, a perfect day on the porch. We have an old-fashioned front porch, meant for eating, for socializing, for calling out over the railings to neighbors and friends. A large, narrow-planked porch with columns, rockers, sofas, ceiling fans, and lemonade. We dragged the sand box, literally a box filled with sand, to the middle of the porch. I lugged buckets of water from the kitchen and kaplooshed the water into the water table. I fetched a spoon and a tin of baking powder and Jack was set.

Jack: Then a little salt and a little more sand and stir, stir, stir.

I could watch him do this all day. When he was three and the other three-year-olds at preschool were doing this, Jack wasn't. He wasn't talking, he wasn't interacting, he wasn't playing. And he was worried. More worried than any three-year-old should be. So, yeah, I could watch him do this all day long.

After Jack had cooked and watered and sploshed mud puddles, he was ready to wash up and relax. We retreated to a darkened living room to watch Baby Jack videos. I've watched very few of Jack's baby videos, just for sheer lack of time. He doesn't enjoy the infant videos so much—not enough action—but he does like the toddler videos. Reluctantly, he agreed to watch a few minutes of an infant one. Daddy and I begin to notice a theme to this video. Scene after scene of Daddy filming baby Jack lying on his back in his crib with the mobile on. We laugh about it. The only way you can tell it's a different day is by Jack's change of onesie. Daddy is a very, very proud father.

And we also notice another theme. Jack looks at the mobile with his head turned to the right. He's looking at it with his left eye.

Before Jack was born, while I was having wispy, cloud-filled dreams of chubby babies, we visited friends at their house. They had two adorable blond boys toddling around. The youngest wore glasses and I remarked to the mom that I always thought that having to put glasses on little kids was the saddest thing. She looked at me, puzzled. "Why?" she asked.

Why?

Call it arrogance. The arrogance of ignorance. That moment still shames me. At the time, I thought the worst thing was having to put glasses on an adorable baby face. This is coming from me; me, who has had glasses since third grade and needed them well before that. That was just my thing, my hole, my wound. It wasn't a real problem, a child needing glasses. It was my view because I hadn't lived through any real health problems with kids.

Then came Jack. Jack spent six weeks in the NICU when he was born. He had pulmonary hypertension, among other issues, which meant he couldn't breathe on his own. He was on oxygen and that can lead to eye problems. So Jack's had to have eye examinations since birth. At one year old, he got his first glasses. Did I flinch? No way. He needs to see. He needs glasses? Then he needs glasses. Nothing like a slap upside the head from God to get you over the little things.

But—you want to know how hard it is to get a one-year-old to wear glasses? Oh, let me tell you. We're not talking any one-year-old here. We're talking a one-year-old who hates things to be on his face or his head. Who, though he could barely manage to work his arms, pulled the oxygen tubes off his face every chance he got. And those tubes were secured on his face with Band-Aids. That would become unsecured and unsticky on one side, requiring me to pull them off his face and reapply new ones. Oh, dear mama.

After several attempts at putting brand new glasses on our brand new one-year-old, who screamed and pulled them off each time, I went back to the pediatric ophthalmologist.

Me: Are there any head straps or any suggestions for keeping glasses on a baby?

Oh, you gotta hear this.

Doctor: "You'll have to put splints on his arms so that he can't use his arms at all."

Oh, yeah. He said that. Even for a typical kid, I can't believe he would suggest splints. But Jack had been diagnosed with cerebral palsy when he was eight months old. We'd been working like crazy in physical and occupational therapy for him to learn to *use* his body, not *stop* using it!

Our occupational therapist at the time, a graceful, Zen presence, thank God, said, "Splints on his arms? What kind of message is that sending your child? Why not find a gentle introduction?" Exactly.

Do I seem a tad peeved? Even after five years? Oh, yeah.

So, I found my own way. Every day, twice a day, starting out at two minutes, Jack and I went out to the porch. We'd sit on the sofa to watch cars. Even then, he liked watching the cars speed by. Holding him on my lap, I'd whip his glasses on and put my arms around him to keep him immobile. Then, with my utmost enthusiasm, I'd say, Oooh, there's a red car! Oh, look, there's a black car! Here comes a tan car!

It worked. Two minutes under our belts the first time, five minutes the next. Next thing you know, we were up to twenty minutes and from there it was a piece of cake. After about two weeks of watching cars, he'd gotten used to his glasses.

Splints. Huh.

And then we found out that corrected vision is not everything.

So, we're watching the baby Jack video and all the signs of vision processing problems are there, though subtle. He turns his head slightly to look out of one eye. He's fascinated by the bold lines of the picture railing against a light wall, the corner where the white ceiling met the dark wall, the tops of doorways.

As he got older, we realized that he couldn't recognize faces. He looked at the negative space in a picture, instead of the filled spaces, to identify an image. He couldn't identify animals that were cartoons or drawing.

He spent most of his time looking down.

Used to be because he wasn't looking, I thought he wasn't paying attention. Once, I set up the finger paints and swept his hand around in it. He kept looking away. I'd say, "Jack, look, look!" repeatedly, thinking he's not listening. Meaning really, he's not looking, therefore, he's not paying attention. It was a very subtle train of thought. But there it was.

It took me a long time to realize that he was paying attention. He was noticing. He was looking in his own way, not straight on, not continuously. He was taking peeks and managing his visual load; because Jack can only process one thing at a time. He's either going to feel what's on his hands, which is a lot to deal with if you don't like weird sensations, or he's going to look at the swirling colors. He can't do both.

The same with when I was explaining something to him. I'm explaining what we're about to do and he's not looking at me. Look out, here comes that train again. If he's not looking, then he's not listening; therefore, he's not paying attention.

The thing was: he was paying very careful attention to hearing me. If he had been looking at me, he couldn't have heard me. He can't do both.

Let me tell you about Michael Burry. Michael has a lot of accomplishments behind him. Though he lost an eye to a cancerous tumor before the age of two, he graduated from medical school. At 32 years old, he opened his own investment firm and made himself and his clients billions of dollars by correctly predicting and playing the subprime mortgage bond market. He was diagnosed with Asperger's as an adult—only after his son was also diagnosed.

In a *Vanity Fair* article, Michael Lewis writes this about Michael Burry:

"Grown-ups were forever insisting that he should look other people in the eye, especially when he was talking to them. 'It took all my energy to look someone in the eye,' he said. 'If I am looking at you, that's the one time I know I won't be listening to you.'"

And you already know about John Elder Robison. John was diagnosed with Asperger's when he was forty. As a child, he was sure something was wrong with him. He wondered if he would turn out psychotic, dangerous, a killer. Why? Because people were always telling him to look them in the eye...and he couldn't.

It turns out that even typical children and adults look away. Yes, they look away less often than kids with autism, but they look away for the same reasons. To turn off visual processing while concentrating on difficult cognitive tasks. To manage anxiety when facing emotional demands. And the hardest place to look? The human face. Turns out that the most visually demanding thing to look at is the human face. It's ever-changing. It's emotionally charged. It's a sensory amusement park. So, while presented with a fairly difficult cognitive task or social difficulty, people tend to avert their gaze.

It's no wonder kids with autism look away. They're dealing with an extra load of visual processing, sensory input, and anxiety. They are working hard to manage the world, the daily tasks, the things we take for granted every single minute of the day. Imagine yourself working at your most difficult task. What would it be? Climbing a mountain? Doing algebra? Playing piano? Now imagine someone asking you to look at them while you're doing it.

Now you know why it pains me to hear someone say "Look at me. Look in my eyes" to a child with autism.

———

Sources

Michael Burry: Read more of the excerpt from "The Big Short: Inside the Doomsday Machine," *www.vanityfair.com/business/features/2010/04/wall-street-excerpt-201004?printable=true#ixzz0sppCsrhu*

Robison, John E. *Look Me in the Eye: My Life with Asperger's*. Three Rivers Press: NY, 2007.

Doherty-Sneddon, G., and Phelps, FG. "Gaze aversion: A response to cognitive or social difficulty?" *Memory and Cognition* 33 (2005): 727–733.

Doherty-Sneddon, G., V. Bruce, L. Bonner, S. Longbotham, and C. Doyle. "Development of Gaze Aversion as Disengagement from Visual Information." *Developmental Psychology* 38 (2002): 438-445.

———

A version of this essay was originally published on www.mamabegood.blogspot.com

The Miracle by the Lobster Tank

J. Lorraine Martin

It was a typical, suburban day at my local grocery store. Besides loading up on Mad Housewife wine, I had other highly important plans: channeling the wisdom of Pavlov on aisle twelve as I held up a bag of Skittles—think mad housewife becomes mad scientist. What can I say? An autism mom often reaches new heights (or is it lows?) to help her child step outside of his self-imposed postage stamp zone of perceived safety.

In case conducting Pavlov experiments isn't in your shopping repertoire, allow me to explain. You see, my oldest son, at the age of nine, developed some intense fears at our local grocery store. Despite uneventful years of happy grocery shopping experiences up until that time, he one day became dramatically frightened over the thunder sound in produce when the water sprayers came on; not much later the mooing cow contraption by the dairy section also became off limits to him.

While I found the cow annoying as I imagined it was dropping hints as I pounded by with my thunderous thighs, my son began to experience it and the thunder sounds as catastrophic. Mind you, my son could theoretically sing and dance in a field of real cows in the middle of a torrential rain storm interspersed with thunder and lightning (some days I imagined that would be a fun escape for me, like an invigorating and enchanted spa retreat); however, the faux thunder and cow mooing at our store? Not a chance! If you were expecting to find logic and autism charmingly linked hand in hand, carrying a prescribed rule book of its do's and don'ts, think again, oh naïve, knowledge-seeking, autism grasshopper!

So after a few episodes of my son loudly lamenting, while others gawked, wailing and occasionally jumping up and down in mad-like stomping by bushels of lettuce and two-for-one pints of strawberries (and my own rebellious fantasies of chugging Mad Housewife wine and joining him), I adapted to a new, albeit unusual routine. While he remained unattended on the cereal aisle, eventually ruling out a majority of aisles as "too close," I madly dashed through various aisles like a crazed woman on an errant bumper car. (Highly important, guilt-reducing author note: (1) He was not a flight risk by this age, (2) His ability to yell would have the Vegas odds makers betting the house and their mother's heirloom diamond wedding ring and daddy's gold tooth that he wouldn't be disturbed by menacing kidnappers, and (3) Yes, I was quick and had the bruised cart of fruit to prove it.)

Wishing to rid my son of this phobia, I pondered. How hard could it be to break? A few weeks or—gasp—months? Talk about a naïve and foolishly hopeful grasshopper! With good intentions, I tried numerous "quick fixes" that included the aforementioned Pavlov experiment. As I held up a bag of candy, I hoped to tempt my son to walk further down the aisle and around the corner where he would have to face the dreaded cow moo. I didn't understand at the time that Pavlov is no match for autism; it's like approaching Fort Knox imagining that you can pick the locks open with an unfolded paper clip.

"I can't Mom! I can't!" echoed down that aisle. There was another echo entangled with his that only I could hear—the primal scream within: "I want to save you, and I don't know how."

So why put myself and son through this ordeal? After all, I could have simply picked another grocery store to avoid such encumbrances, or left him at home. However, autism was not limited to a store; it was pitching its grenades across numerous settings leading to school dismissals and panic attacks across parks, malls, restaurants, movie theaters and even our own backyard. Siblings grew more embarrassed and frustrated; a spouse tried to support but often was away on business, leaving far too much time for me to ponder: if I couldn't get him over the faux thunder and cow sounds at our local grocery store, what hope did I have to help him navigate the fears of the "real" world? No, I could not bear to let the doors of our grocery store be closed to my son; they became my symbolic battleground.

One day, I ran into a neighbor who mentioned she saw my son elsewhere in the store. Hmm, I wonder if she saw him talking to himself, flapping his hands and/or holding his ears? What would she think? How do I explain? Letting down my humor and sarcasm guard, I timidly shared of his unusual store fears. She inexplicably burst into laughter. Had I been in the autism world so long that the typical world was no longer fathomable to me? Sometimes it felt like I might as well be speaking Swahili as imparting understanding to those outside this world was a communication gulf I found terribly hard to cross.

I wish I could say that I delivered a witty and let-me-put-you-in-your-place-and-give-you-an-education-oh-unfeeling-and-shallow-one retort (or was I just too sensitive?). No, I quietly moved away from her, retrieved my son, and promptly retreated at home to lie on my bed to cry—cry for my son I wished to save and cry for myself...I needed saving too. Unfortunately I skipped the "Noble Autism Parent Warrior" class in college, and I endlessly punished myself for missing out on the secrets to maintaining optimistic gusto in what felt like constant heartache.

After a period of emotionally healthy and vivid fantasies of sporting Army fatigues and wielding a BB gun to launch a late-night infiltration to take out a thunder and cow machine, i.e., Operation Thunder Shock and Cow

Tipping Awe, not to mention comical ways I imagined piping in thunder and mooing sounds on a continuous nighttime feed into my lovely neighbor's bedroom (how hilarious!), I remained entirely calm, rational, and composed during this jaunt down Mad Housewife shopping lane.

I was mired in helplessness intertwined with another uncomfortable feeling: embarrassment. I longed to just feel normal and dispense with such unusual and heartrending challenges. How about one of these problems? "Johnny didn't make the varsity football team!" "Susie lost student council by one vote!" Was it possible to love a child with an accepting heart yet also crave normalcy? Did that mean I was judging him? Did that make me a less than ideal mother? It's safe to say that guilt, loneliness, and conflicting emotions were also piled into my grocery cart.

Guided by a group of insightful and loving therapists, progress was made in countless ways outside the store as my son gradually gained greater self-awareness, learning to find more productive ways to cope and problem solve through a host of issues; over time we even found a school that added more happy and meaningful moments to his life. Sometimes I still wished for a guru to arrive with the wand-waving plan to save my son, but over time I got better at steadying the ebb and flow of my hopeful longings, and grounded myself in the daily pursuit of slowly, lovingly, and patiently working to ease my son's experience of the world, savoring even the smallest of gains. Through the process, I had to work on myself, as I frustratingly often felt like autism tormented me by perpetually moving me back to the starting line with a blank slate, cast into an arrested state of the naïve and yearning grasshopper, struggling to surmount my own crippling "thunder and cow" fear: You don't have what it takes. You aren't strong enough. You're failing your son.

Autism, like life in general, eventually revealed through its rigorous curriculum that I was on a pathway with my son and family, one different than what I would have chosen, but a pathway nonetheless that was a part of life's natural rhythm to mold, instruct, and enlighten, bringing us to a location more profound and meaningful than where we began. Who was I to question the form in which such a gift of emotional and spiritual growth was delivered? And if I insisted on answers as to why my son had to suffer in such a way, I came to understand that I would be a part of a disgruntled, long line for the rest of my life waiting at an earthly door that would never open; autism didn't make me any particular stand-out when it came to feeling the unfairness of life. And how misguided to expect that others or myself should have the answers to all of life's perplexing challenges?

After a long spell of simply avoiding the fearful areas of our store, my son, under the influence of what I darkly called "Cheech and Chong's End of the Road Elixirs," agreed to sit on a bench that viewed the produce area.

As the thunder sound erupted, my son, red-eyed and forlorn, looked at me with tears running down his face. Walking out he said:

"I don't ever want to walk in this store again; it's awful. Don't make me, okay Mom?"

"Okay."

Was love and acceptance winning or was autism winning? I wasn't sure, but I honored the wishes of my son, no longer displaying the cherub face of a boy when this fear began, but now a teenager with a deeper voice and emerging facial hair.

If I could reach for the perfect tool out of my life's toolbox, it would be reflection—the constant talking through fears, setbacks and triumphs in a supportive, nonjudgmental way. Through reflection, a family found grace together, and I came to understand my own power and driving force—love. Lacking the hoped-for eloquence and perfection at times, but now interwoven with greater kindness to self and more realistic expectations, love's power grew exponentially as it sang a song that had always been in play, a song in which a heart and intellect could now not only hear, but could also finally believe in the beauty of its melodic words: You have what it takes! You are strong enough! You are helping your son and all your children find their way!

Not all tales reach the conclusion of our choosing, but sometimes, gloriously they do.

Picture my oldest son and me sitting in a car at our grocery store parking lot. With an initial plan to quickly run in as he waited in the car, I felt a small ember of hope begin to stir.

"What if we walked up to the store window and simply looked inside?"

My son thought at first this wasn't possible, but when I assured him that I would not push him to do anything more than he felt comfortable, he agreed. Breathe.

As he pressed his face to the glass, I said "Why don't we simply take a step through those doors?" I reminded him of other fears conquered, yet continued to let him know that he was in control.

He gazed some more. "Okay Mom."

Breathe. Hope.

We walked across that threshold and he stopped—six years into a fear, over a third of his life by the way, and one year since he last entered this store. I wondered which way the experience was going to go.

What was different for me is that I felt better prepared for either outcome. When a mom parents a child, especially one with special challenges, her own emotional growth is requisite, not subordinate, to her child's; they go hand–in–hand, and so literally and figuratively that's how we entered through those doors.

My son, deceptively housed in a fifteen-year-old hulking, broad-shouldered young man's body, proceeded to face his fears with a tense stance and a breathy utterance: "Okay. This is okay."

We traversed a few aisles in the vicinity of the cow, which thankfully had been dismantled and put out to pasture. After picking out a few favorite food items and watching my son peer down aisles as if painful memories were fluttering across his mind in quick succession, he asked to leave. Courage and grace, how illuminated you were in my son that day!

A few days later, he said: "I would like to go back to the store." He invited his older sister and younger brother.

I imagined the keys to the store, through much trial and error, were finally placed in my son's hands, and he now possessed the strength to unlock the door.

With tentative steps, we made our way to the lobster tank, a comforting visual distraction within earshot of produce.

My youngest son understandably grew in his own anxiety as he had been witness to many of his brother's trying times. "Mom, we should go. He's going to lose it!"

"I think he'll be okay." Nuanced gut feelings told me to gently push. We were all pushing past our natural comfort zones.

Thunder erupted. A family braced itself. Will I be consoling three dispirited kids or will we be celebrating? Inhale.

Other than enlarged eyes, my oldest son's frozen facial features revealed no clues.

The assaulting sound ended. Was it really a ten-second sound or so that had held a boy and a mother's heart in its walled-off madness for six long years?

If I could put a word to this moment it would be purity. To unite around all my children, gently held suspended in vulnerability together, was a moment that made me feel the pulse of life in all its mysterious, soulful beauty.

My daughter broke up the stillness with a calm, supportive tone: "That wasn't so bad, was it?"

We waited for the reply from the six-year-abyss.

"That wasn't bad at all." Exhale...

We gingerly took our remaining steps through the fear-laden produce department, cradling the miracle in the confines of my pounding heart. With tears glassing my eyes, I wanted to roll around on the floor and sing chants of praise that could rival a church revival! Hello Joy! Hello Triumph! Oh how I've missed you! I wanted to shout in the intercom:

"Attention shoppers! A miracle occurred right in your midst today! A boy, now an emerging young man, crippled by a fear, let it go today and freed himself!"

I've come to understand that autism, just like many major life challenges, isn't an all-or-nothing battle, stuck in the belief that if you don't find the cure, you'll never find contentment; there's a whole lot of terrain to explore in between those polar extremes. The illusion that happiness can only be found in the imaginary world of Johnny and Susie and magical gurus has thankfully been extinguished for me.

"I did it Mom! I did it! I'm not afraid anymore of the store! Are you proud of me?"

"Oh, how proud I am! I love you so much! How do you feel?"

"I feel happy Mom. I feel happy!"

Me too, grasshopper, me too.

—

This essay was originally published on cheeselesspizza.blogspot.com.

Teamwork

Kim Leaird

I clutch John's hand as we enter his brother's school. We are here to pick up Sam after week two of an after-school soccer program, a program I thought would be great after hearing that a few of his classmates were enrolled. In the five minutes it takes to find the gym, no fewer than three teachers greet us, see John, and say "Hi Sam!"

Their faces look puzzled and I watch them trying to sort it out: *Sam has a twin? Why didn't we know Sam has a twin?*

We find the gym and look inside. Eight or so boys running between two nets, a coach yelling encouragement. There are just a few minutes left and more parents are filing in behind us. John takes in the open expanse, the rolling ball, and yanks me inside. Before I can get a good grip, he darts free. At first he just runs the perimeter of the gym, but then he begins to weave in between the group of boys, his eye on the moving ball.

Sam spots him, stops playing and yells, "Coach C! Look, it's John! He's my brother! Can he play?"

Coach C pauses, glances at me. I mouth *Sorry!* But he says, "Sure, John, come on!"

John laughs and runs in and out of the group, flapping excitedly. Coach C calls the group over for a huddle but Sam won't join unless John does too. He's pulling him and pulling him and I am keenly aware of all eyes on me: the coach, the kids, and the parents.

I weigh my options: go and hoist John out of there and risk an epic meltdown or go help him sit in the circle with the other kids. I opt for the latter and as I near him, John yells all on his own, "Sit down?" and takes a seat with Sam. Relieved, I kneel behind him.

The coach talks about teamwork and the great job they did. Sam interrupts, "And my brother did really great too!" He grins at John and John throws his arms around him. At first I think John is just excited, and wants to pull Sam to the ground. But then, no, I see John's grin and realize that he is genuinely happy to be here, sitting in this gym with his brother.

We link hands to leave the gym and Sam says, "Mommy, I want John to come to *my* school, not his school, okay?

I am too choked up to reply.

—

If you think of the autism spectrum as a seesaw, then I have a boy sitting at each end. Sam is quite social, talks non-stop, and never has trouble making eye contact. John prefers his own company, flaps, and didn't say a word until he was four. When they were diagnosed with autism, I found it really difficult to believe that they had the same diagnosis. How could they? They were so different. I still had yet to learn that when you've met one child with autism, you've met one child with autism—even identical twins.

Of course I didn't know it then, but they were more alike than different. Neither of them had really babbled, neither had said a word by the age of two. Neither waved, pointed or clapped. Neither responded to his name. But Sam would seek us out with his deep brown eyes, he would laugh when he saw something funny and wanted us to share it. John was always more interested in following lights and shadows down walls and across counters. He loved to be held, but would yearn and stretch to be back at his work.

The boys began attending a class with other two-year-olds on the spectrum through our county's Infants and Toddlers program. Just two weeks later Sam started to talk. At first it was the alphabet—he'd recite it over and over. He found alphabet cards with pictures on one side, the word on the other, and memorized them. We'd awake in the morning to the sound of him spelling in his crib. His language was not terribly functional but he was a sponge. By the time he was three he could read and wherever we went he'd sound out new words.

John made very little progress, and the early intervention team decided he needed more intense therapy. We began a 15-hour-per-week home ABA program to teach him the most basic skills. We upped his speech and occupational therapy. We studied the Hanen *More Than Words* system to try to get him to engage with us. We struggled to bring him into our world and at times joined him in his but to little effect. Where Sam had seemed to skyrocket out of the difficult parts of autism, John had little interest in doing so.

What worked for Sam did not work for John.

Today Sam is mainstreamed at our elementary school while John attends the autism program at another school. Sam's diagnosis is now "high-functioning autism" or "HFA"—he's a quirky kid and he still has issues, but he's academically gifted. I am told that John is "very verbal" but he chooses not to talk unless motivated, and it is hard to motivate him. We know he can read, but he is more interested in the computer and Sesame Street and lining up blocks. I still don't know what he thinks or feels about the world but I do know he is happy—his smile is a song.

He and Sam share a special bond. I once worried it would never exist, but it's more and more evident every day. The most beautiful sight is John throwing his arms around his brother because in that instant his face betrays him: he is very much aware. In that moment I see love painted across his face. The connection John has with Sam makes me believe that he will be okay, that they will look out for each other, and that one day, John will straddle both worlds—even while I recognize that he'll never completely leave one.

Moving Day:
Transitioning to a Group Home

Laura Shumaker

My twenty-two-year-old son Matthew and I were cruising our neighborhood for garage sales early one November morning, and we weren't having a lot of luck. We needed to find furniture for the apartment that he would be moving into the following weekend.

Matthew has autism, and would be part of a supported living arrangement that we had designed with the help of our regional department of developmental services and Camphill Communities in Soquel, California.

"Supported Living Services (SLS) consist of a broad range of services to adults with developmental disabilities," said Mary, who had been Matthew's social worker since middle school.

"With a supported living program," Mary said, "Matthew will be able to exercise meaningful choice and control in his life, but with enough support to help him achieve his long term goals."

"How long term is 'long term?'" I asked.

"The services are offered for as long and as often as needed, with the flexibility required to meet a persons' changing needs over time."

Matthew told Mary that he would need to be a gardener and a landscaper, and that he'd need a girlfriend, as well.

———

Our family had become connected to Camphill, a worldwide organization with nurturing communities for the developmentally disabled, when Matthew was a teenager and we were desperate to place him in their residential school in Pennsylvania.

It was the last thing we thought we would ever do.

While painfully aware of his disability, Matthew has always wanted to be a regular guy like his two younger brothers. He didn't just want to be a regular guy, actually, but *the* guy—the poisonous plant and weed expert, and the lawn care authority of our Northern California community. He was often seen at our local hardware store with his large hands wrapped around a bottle of weed killer, studying the label earnestly, and he'd approach strangers with warnings about deadly nightshade, oleander, and water hemlock.

But just a few days into his sixteenth year, Matthew decided that he should drive a car like a regular guy and drove my car through a wall in our garage. There were other close calls. One day during his freshman year at our local high school, he observed a guy pushing his girlfriend flirtatiously and then tapping her on the head. When Matthew tried the same move with too much force, I was summoned to his school where he was crying in the principal's office. "Joe did it to Sue, and she liked it!"

Just when we thought things were calming down following the incident at school, a letter arrived from an attorney asking us to contact him about the bicycle accident involving Matthew. It turned out that while riding his bike, Matthew had collided with a young boy on his bike the month before.

"Matthew? What's this about a bike accident?"

"Who told you?"

"Someone sent me a letter. Was the boy you bumped into hurt?"

"Pretty much."

Dear God.

"Was he bleeding?"

"Probably. Am I in trouble?"

It became clear that Matthew was no longer safe in the community where he had grown up, and his impulsive actions were putting others in peril. He needed more supervision, more than we or the local school could provide. We were grateful to find Camphill, and were excited about the prospect of Matthew being a part of their community near our home in Northern California when he was an adult.

Now Matthew would be the first to take part in Camphill California's supported living program and would be living in an apartment near the community with a "roommate" hired by the Camphill program, one who could assist Matthew with daily living activities, personal financial affairs, and help involve him in community life.

Matthew would also be involved in a day program that would provide vocational training, social skills workshops, recreation, and other supports.

Putting the program together had taken months, and had been stalled by waiting periods, misplaced paperwork, and red tape tangled beyond recognition. While we waited for the program to come together, Matthew felt unsettled and lost without a routine he could count on. He lived at home and was lonely, so I hired "friends" that he could hang out with. Finally, the program gelled, and move-in day was December 1, 2008.

"I'm getting tired of all this driving," Matthew whined after 45 minutes of garage sales with nothing but knick knacks. Just as we turned the corner to head home, Matthew yelled, "*Stop! Look!* I see something good."

It was a large green sofa sitting cockeyed at the end of a long driveway with a large sign on it.

"Look!" Matthew gasped, "It's free!"

Matthew jumped out of the car before I could park it and sat on the sofa with a big grin. It seemed to be in good shape, except for a small tear on the arm. Just then, a grandfatherly type walked out and shook my hand.

"Will you take this off my hands?" he asked. "I'm moving to a smaller place and it just won't fit."

I offered to pay for the sofa, but he joked that he would pay me if I took it. He even offered to lend me is truck to take it away. I introduced the kind donor to Matthew who was still sitting on the sofa with a goofy grin.

"Guess what?" Matthew said. "I'm moving, too. Into my own apartment. That's what guys my age do."

As we loaded the sofa into the truck, I thought about the day I moved into my first apartment. I was about Matthew's age and I felt so grown up—so liberated. I remember my mother's tearful send-off when I drove away in the moving truck with my roommates. I also remember stopping home the next weekend with a load of laundry, where my mother greeting me with a hug and a smile.

I knew that Matthew would continue to need a lot of ongoing support from me, especially in the beginning of his new adventure.

But as he sat grinning on his sofa on that November morning, just a regular guy getting ready to set up his first place, I decided to worry about that part later.

Autism Contradictions

Jillsmo

I'm currently sitting downstairs in the TV room with Child Two and I can hear coming from the kitchen the unmistakable sound of a chair being slowly dragged across the room. This only means one thing: there's something (probably cookies) on a high shelf that Child One wants and he is in there bringing the chair over to it so that he can climb up and grab it. The fact that he went in there by himself without saying anything means that he knows that whatever he's going for, he's not supposed to have.

Two things go through my mind in a time like this:

• It's 5:15, he can't have cookies, we'll be having dinner soon. If he had asked me, I would have said no, which he knows, which is why he didn't ask me. He's being sneaky and devious, in addition to eating crap right before dinner. That's bad! I should go in there and catch him in the act.

• There are many things involved in this kind of action:

First, he had to spot the cookies on the shelf, which is a few feet above his head. That shows that he's paying attention to his environment.

Second, he had to decide for himself that he wasn't allowed to have them and consciously choose to not ask me for them. He's thinking, he's weighing his pros and cons, he's (correctly) predicting the probability that bringing attention to his cookie plight will mean he won't get them.

Third, he figured out, for himself, that dragging the chair over to the shelf and climbing up on it will enable him to pull down the box. He figured out the steps involved in getting the cookies down from the shelf, he worked out a plan, and he's carrying it through, without any assistance.

I remember, in ABA, working on these problem-solving skills with him. Look, the cookies are on the shelf, what do you need to do in order to get them? First, get the chair, etc. We did that kind of thing again and again when he was three, four, and five; I honestly never thought he would get it. And, yet, here he is, right now, dragging a chair across the room in the kitchen, all by himself, and getting the cookies down.

I'm pretty proud of him, actually. Good work, Child One!!!

Of course, I can't tell him that so, instead, I'm going to sit here and listen to the chair and let him get his cookies, even though it's 5:15 and we're having dinner soon.

Tree

Shawn C. Graves

We'll call him Tree—trees fascinate him. He climbs them in reality and in his dreams, fearlessly. Tree is five years old. When his mother (Mom) and I started dating, we immediately spoke of our children. I have two daughters, three and seven. Mom has two sons, five and eleven, and a daughter, fourteen. We both found out quickly that we were proud parents and shared several parenting notions and ideals. She then explained to me that Tree was autistic. Of course, I have heard of autism before. But I was to soon find out I knew nothing of it. I mean it's our nature, right? If something doesn't directly affect us or interest us, we rarely find out more about it than what the media tells us or what mainstream society thinks about it.

I honestly didn't give the issue much thought—I was a great parent and kids have always loved me. I practically raised my younger siblings; did a couple of baby sitting gigs. I can handle anything kid-related—bring it on. How hard can this be? I'll Google "autism" and read a couple web pages, check out what Wikipedia has to say about it, skim through a book Mom has lying around and I'll be good. That research method got me through college and most projects at work, so—piece of cake.

As with any new experience, I was full of wonder, curiosity, and apprehension. As a parent of nonautistic children, Tree challenged everything I knew of behavior, understanding, discipline, and development in children. Here I was, high on my horse, silently boasting of my past parenting and older sibling experiences and successes, and in reality, I was totally and utterly clueless how to deal with this amazing boy.

Tree is endearing and sweet—he will melt you where you stand. He can smile, or wink, or show me his muscles. Or a hug and a "I wuv ew" in Tree-speak. He will run and play and climb and laugh and bounce. Sometimes, it's not words at all. He'll smile and look into my eyes and I'll smile back looking into his eyes—more communication than a thousand verbal words could convey. Or, out of nowhere, he'll come up and give you a little peck on the cheek—the world instantly becomes a better place. I admire his lack of fear and his sense of adventure. Make no mistake; he will capture your heart.

I see Tree and I see his frustrations with trying to explain to everyone what goes on in his little world. Sometimes his frustrations turn into my frustrations. When he gets confused, hurt, mad, or sad, I don't know what to do. My instinct is just to talk it out with him and that doesn't always work. I realized even after all my years of effective communication, education, and parenting, all methods in my arsenal are completely useless. I try to get into his world, but sometimes there's no path for that. I have to accept that at times there will be a brick wall up and I'm not getting through. Sometimes, as he mother says, he has to "sort it out."

I have to remind myself not to confuse Tree's confusion and pain for disobedience or defiance. I try to imagine myself trapped inside my own body, where I have so much to say and express and I cannot find a way to do it. He will try to tell me something and get frustrated because I can't understand. I get frustrated when I tell my daughters to do something and they don't understand—I need to relate more to that fact.

In some ways, we all face that frustration, right? When we can't get someone to understand or we can't get someone to listen or agree. It's that for Tree, except exponentially magnified. He causes me to evaluate myself—the way I communicate, the way I adapt. I become a better person—we all do when we learn to adapt and communicate in new ways. To me, autistic development isn't just about the child learning and adapting. It's about us as adults learning and adapting. It forces us back to the basics of love, communication, understanding, and patience.

Sometimes, he gets angry and lashes out—he may scream, kick, bite, hit—gestures and actions take place of the words he cannot find. I find myself upset sometimes, ashamedly. Are my frustrations rooted in the fact that I can't figure out how to calm him or understand him? Is it out of impatience or my lack of control in the situation? Or I am frustrated out of my own ignorance? I think it's a little of all of these reasons. I am constantly challenging myself on dealing with this.

My intent is not to sound like I know anything about autism—I still know nothing. I don't pretend to know the full struggle of raising an autistic child—I don't have a clue about the trials, the pain, the joy. I am an outsider and am experiencing autism through a child and his mother. I don't intentionally make rationalizations, conclusions, or generalizations that aren't true. This is simply how I observe it so far—very early in this journey.

So, what do I do now? Is this answer in trying to get Tree to understand me, or should I be trying to understand him instead? Maybe both. This is a challenge I look forward to—a rewarding challenge. I'm amazed and enthralled by Tree and I have just scratched the surface of knowing who he is. Mom often apologizes for his behavior—the fits, the lashing out, the screaming. I think that sometimes she can visibly see my confusion and frustration. I try and reassure her that she has nothing to apologize for. It should be me apologizing for not having enough patience and understanding. I am still learning that my John Wayne (tough-as-nails, my-way-or-the highway) parenting philosophy I use on my own kids doesn't work here, at all. This is where I need to change, not Tree.

9 School and Education Issues

...making the least dangerous assumption and thus presuming competence uses resources (time, money, energy). We must come to understand that refusing to presume competence is, in the long run, more costly than making that least dangerous assumption.

—Kate Ahern

Living the Least Dangerous Assumption

Kate Ahern

Some of the most difficult things we face in our field are those things that are intangible. One of the most damaging to our students and possible our sense of purpose as educators is that our students must somehow prove themselves, repeatedly, to show they are capable, competent, and are acting with intentionality when they attempt to communicate, be it through language, adaptive and augmentative communication (AAC), or behavior. We live in a land of prerequisites and accountability, which leaves little room for *"The Least Dangerous Assumption"* as pioneered by Anne Donnellan and clarified by Rossetti and Tashie (2002). The least dangerous assumption is, of course, the premise that (in the absence of evidence) we believe we have not yet found a way to make it so a child or adult with a disability "can" instead of believing he or she "can't."

The issue, sadly, sometimes becomes that making the least dangerous assumption and thus presuming competence uses resources (time, money, energy). We must come to understand that refusing to presume competence is, in the long run, more costly than making that least dangerous assumption.

Let's take, for example, a child who at age ten is presumed to be functioning at "a six-month level" in spite of the difficulty of truly measuring the capabilities of an individual who moves only his eyes and tongue, communicates only through moaning vocalization, sleeps most of the school day and does not live in an English-speaking home. While it may be true that this individual has significant developmental delays, it also may be true that this child does *not* have significant developmental delays. When we choose not to accept the premise of severe cognitive disability and instead begin to form a relationship with the child, build trust in that relationship, respond to eye, tongue, and vocalizations as if they are intentional and then introduce assistive technology, we may find that this individual in fact is at grade level.

This is a true story and it turned out that little boy was, indeed, not developmentally delayed. One has to wonder how many stories are out there where individuals are capable of so much more than is being presumed of them. Even if it were just that this little boy functioned three, six, or 24 months higher developmentally than his initial evaluation suspected, it would have been a triumph of "the least dangerous assumption." The child would have been given the gift that presuming competence creates. And what a marvelous gift it is.

How *do* we go about living the least dangerous assumption and giving the gifts that presumed competence creates? Here are some ways:

- Focus on who your students are becoming, not what they are doing. It is the process, not the product.
- Consider that every interaction has the possibility of being the "*a-ha!*" moment.
- Give the gift of assuming intentionality in communication.
- Even if you are wrong in your assumption, you will teach intentionality by responding as if the action was intentional (pure application of behavior analysis there).
- See strengths: What can they do? How can you shape what they can do? How can you better understand why they do what they do within the assumption of competence?
- Wait. Then wait more.
- Patience makes things possible (allow processing time).
- Rushing is no path to discovering abilities.
- Puzzle out possibilities.
- Think critically about your students and how to reach them.
- Treat writing evaluations and IEPs as an opportunity to better understand the individual and share that understanding with others.
- Use the right tools for the job.
- Introduce and teach assistive technology (AT).
- Always work towards the next step in using assistive technology. (Don't be satisfied with cause and effect: keep trying for something more.)

Ignore the nay-sayers and negative people who see every student action through the lens of the lowest possible level of understanding and imply your presumption of competence is no more than your projection of your wishes for the child.

You can do no harm by making the least dangerous assumption. And you might even change the world.

> Never give up.
>
> Even when everyone else has.
>
> Especially when the student has.

References
Donnellan, Anne. "The Criterion of the Least Dangerous Assumption."

Behavioral Disorders 9(2) (February 1984): 141-50 (print copy not available).

Rossetti, Zach, and Carol Tashie. "Outing the prejudice: Making the least dangerous assumption." *The Communicator: Newsletter of the Autism National Committee* (2002). Downloaded from *inclusivelife.files.wordpress.com/2007/09/least-dangerous-assumption.pdf* on June 30, 2010.

Note: A further discussion of the "Least Dangerous Assumption" concept is Jorgensen, Carol. "The Least Dangerous Assumption: A Challenge to Create a New Paradigm." *Disability Solutions* 6(3) (Fall 2005). Downloaded from *www.disabilitysolutions.org/newsletters/files/six/6-3.pdf* on June 30 2010.

—

A version of this essay was originally published at TeachingLearnersWithMultipleNeeds.blogspot.com.

Special Ed 101

Kristina Chew

Prior to my son Charlie's diagnosis of autism in July of 1999, I knew even less about special education than I did about autism. I literally didn't know anyone—family members or friends—who had ever been in special ed. I had less than zero idea if any of the public schools I had attended back in the 1970s and 1980s in California had special ed classes. I'm sure they did; to say that I was ignorant is an understatement.

Now I realize that my lack of experience and knowledge about special education back then speaks to a general attitude about special ed, a sense that it's great that our society provides it, but best not talk to about it; that special ed is for "those kids" who don't do well in school, or have behavior problems, and so forth.

So here is a bit of a primer about what special education is and about how to navigate your way through getting services and an education for your child and dealing with the provider of those, your school district.

Note: There are many, many available websites and books about special ed. I've only highlighted web resources in this essay as I prefer to concentrate on a few quite comprehensive sites; it's very easy to be overwhelmed by all the information out there.

What Is Special Education?

Special education refers to the services and accommodations needed by children who are not able to be educated in a "regular" classroom, due to their learning needs and disabilities. Special education services are provided for children ages three to twenty-one by your school district, under federal law.

The IEP and IDEA

IEP stands for Individual Education Plan; IDEA is the Individuals with Disabilities Education Act of 1997, a federal law. IDEA's predecessor, the Education of All Handicapped Children Act (EAHCA), was signed into law in 1975 following the passage of the Education of Handicapped Children Act of 1974.

The IEP is a combination contract—it is a legal document—and guide for a child's education. The IEP spells not only what services your child is to receive, but the educational goals—the curriculum—for your child's schooling.

In reference to the IEP and your child's actual education, this is the exact wording of the law about what an IEP must contain:

(4) A statement of the special education and related services and supplementary aids and services, based on peer-reviewed research to the extent practicable, to be provided to the child, or on behalf of the child, and a statement of the program modifications or supports for school personnel that will be provided to enable the child—

(i) To advance appropriately toward attaining the annual goals;

(ii) To be involved in and make progress in the general education curriculum in accordance with paragraph (a)(1) of this section, and to participate in extracurricular and other nonacademic activities; and

(iii) To be educated and participate with other children with disabilities and nondisabled children in the activities described in this section. [§300.320(a)(4)]

IDEA was made possible by the Americans With Disabilities Act of 1990.

Education for students like Charlie is a federal and civil right. It wasn't always so: prior to IDEA, families were on their own to educate their children and to get what help they might, or rather might not, from school districts. It is only fairly recently that public school districts started educating autistic students, or felt—or were legally mandated under IDEA—that they must do so. My son has been educated either in special education classrooms in local public schools or (as has been the case since November of 2009) in an autism center (a "non-public school" that is not a private school) with tuition and transportation provided by our school district. As the school district is not able to provide an appropriate classroom/educational setting for Charlie, it is legally required to have him placed in a school that is able to do so.

More information on IEPs is available at the Wrightslaw website and also at the National Dissemination Center for Children With Disabilities (NICHCY) website. For regular reports about special ed law, see the Special Education Law Blog by Charles Fox.

More on the history of special education and IDEA and on congressional intent by Jennifer Parker and also at through the Council of Parent Attorneys and Advocates (COPAA).

How It Works: Getting Started Getting Services

Charlie was in a daycare center in St. Paul, Minnesota, when his teachers noticed that he was developmentally delayed, back in the autumn and winter of 1998 and 1999. We were given information about developmental disabilities and services and encouraged to have Charlie evaluated. We didn't do so for some months as we were in shock that Charlie might have delays. In retrospect, I'm very glad that Charlie's delays were identified as early as they were. While I remember some incredibly painful and strained interactions with the daycare teachers, I thank them today for noting that Charlie was not developing speech, social interaction, play, and other skills like the other children, and insisting on having him evaluated.

It might be your child's pediatrician or you yourself who has concerns about your child not developing; not developing language is one early autism sign (it was one of a couple of signs in Charlie's case). In some states, you will be referred to your state's Early Intervention program, which (in New Jersey) is overseen by the Department of Developmental Disabilities. You may also be advised to set up an appointment with a specialist such as a developmental pediatrician or a neurologist, or a speech therapist or psychologist, to further evaluate your child. In St. Paul, early intervention services are overseen by the public schools. So Charlie's Individual Family Service Plan (IFSP) was put together by a Child Study Team from the St. Paul school district.

To qualify for special education services, you will need proof in the form of evaluations and reports that your child needs them, usually provided by reports from doctors and/or therapists. The school district may wish to further evaluate your child to determine what services he or she is eligible for.

You will be referred to a Child Study Team and assigned a case manager (usually a school psychologist, social worker, or learning consultant) who will handle the administrative responsibilities for your child. Your case manager is your basic contact person to find out about scheduling evaluations, writing the IEP, and organizing IEP meetings. This team will include your case manager, your child's teacher, a regular education teacher, speech therapist, occupational therapist, physical therapist, and—very, if not most, importantly—you as the parents.

Kinds of Special Ed Services

What services your child needs will first be based on the evaluations of your child. Once your child has started receiving services, there should be clearly stated criteria about accessing your child's learning and provisions made for what to do when your child is *not* progressing.

Services can include:

• Placement (general education classroom placement; special ed placement with part-time inclusion; self-contained special education placement)

• Resource Room

• "Related services" including therapies (speech, occupational, physical)

- Aides (in special ed classrooms; as a support for your child if he or she is mainstreamed—partially or fully; on the bus)
- Assistive technology such as an augmentative communication device

When requesting a therapy or services, frame your request in regard to how they will help your child reach his or her IEP goals, rather than because your child "needs" such, or because you've found a research study saying that such and such a therapy achieves such and such results for children with your child's diagnosis. It is certainly a good idea to stay up to date with current knowledge about autistic children's learning, but you always need to explain how a teaching method, for example, will assist in your child achieving her or his IEP goals and objectives.

IEP Meetings

In theory, IEP meetings should be thoughtful, hopeful conversations about your child's needs, abilities, and how best to foster his or her learning. In practice, IEPs can be combative sessions in which, with the tape recorders (yours and the school district's) running, you argue about the services your child should receive—a 1:1 aide, placement at a specific out-of-district placement that you know offers the best and most appropriate education for your child—and how these are to be delivered.

You have the right to bring someone else with you. The same goes for the school district. However, who attends an IEP meeting should be determined in advance of the meeting and all parties informed. If the Assistant Special Education Director shows up at your IEP meeting, and her or his name was not on the list of people you signed off on to be at the meeting, you should at least point this out, and then request that that person leave or (if he or she will not) that the meeting be rescheduled with only the persons present who everyone knows, in advance, have been approved.

This is serious stuff and may it sounds excessive. But once you make it clear to the school district that you are not going to be "messed around" with, things will be easier. You are not there to be friends with administrators. It might be better to think of the IEP in terms of a business meeting because in some ways that's what it is to the school district. Call me cynical, but it's budgetary needs that often ultimately drive decisions made by school districts, though no one is going to say that.

It's a cliché but the squeaky wheel does get the grease: you can never make too many phone calls, leave too many voice messages, ask too many questions, write too many emails (email is actually a very good way to communicate with your school district as you have an automatic written record of your communication, or attempt to communicate with the school district). It's been said many a time but you the parent are truly your child's best advocate and must represent him or her as you know you need to. IDEA is the reason that Charlie is able to live with us and to lead what I like to call a "good life," being a member of the community and living among friends and family. School districts and personnel can get preoccupied with numbers, budgets, and protocols; it's your task as a parent to remind them that, for a child like Charlie, school isn't just about learning the three Rs. It is the preparation for his whole life.

Some suggestions on preparing for an IEP meeting by developing a "positive student profile" can be found here via the websites. of the National Dissemination Center for Children with Disabilities (NICHCY). Advocates for Special Kids has more information about advocates and their role.

The Ten Steps of Special Ed

These are the Ten Steps of Special Education according to the NICHCY:

1. Identification of a disability in a child—this might be by a parent or family member or perhaps by a professional such as a pediatrician.

2. Evaluation of the child to determine what diagnosis he or she has, by a developmental pediatrician or neurologist; other professionals, including some from a school district (such as a school psychologist, social workers, or speech therapists) might also make a diagnosis of your child (but you may need to seek out a diagnosis from a medical professional to qualify for services).

3. Deliberation and determination of eligibility for services by the Child Study Team assigned to your child by the school district (this will include a case manager/school psychologist, special education teacher, speech therapist, occupational therapist, and others).

4. Decision that a child is eligible for services. Within 30 calendar days after a child's eligibility is determined, the IEP team must write an IEP for a child.

5. Scheduling of an IEP meeting by the case manager.

6. The actual IEP meeting being held and the writing of the IEP, usually by the case manager. Know that as a parent you can *always* provide input at *every* stage of the process. I suggest always writing a statement to be included in your child's IEP, so that the IEP always contains your own perspective about your child. You can write this prior to the meeting and share it at the meeting; I usually revise my statement after the meeting and then submit it to the case manager. I tend to get rather passionate at IEP meetings (especially when my son has been having difficulties, a not-infrequent occurrence) and have found it helpful to read from my prepared statement.

7. The actual providing of services (ranging from, perhaps, sessions of speech therapy to placement in a full-day special education classroom).

8. Gathering of data on child's progress towards meeting the goals of the IEP and reporting of this (to you, and to the Child Study Team) with a view towards assessment: are the services a child is receiving appropriate—-is the child learning and moving towards the goals and objectives specified in the IEP?

9. Reviewing of the IEP; this usually occurs annually but can certainly occur more frequently if your child is not progressing in his or her placement.

10. Reevaluation of your child to determine if he or she is still in need of services, and/or if the services the child is currently receiving are appropriate.

Special ed was terra incognita when Charlie was diagnosed, and while there's been a lot of trial, error, sweat, tears, and frustration, we've been able to get Charlie placements in classrooms and schools and the services and supports that he has needed. He loves going to school and is anxious during vacations. Year-round school with breaks of no more than two weeks (if not one week) maximum would better suit his learning needs.

"Will my child always need special ed?"

In the case of my son, yes. Charlie has never been in anything but a classroom or school for autistic children. He attended "specials" (library and music) with "typical" children for a brief period in elementary school with an aide but he struggled a lot and we had to conclude that these were not appropriate for him. He has needed speech therapy, occupational therapy, and teachers and aides specially trained to teach autistic children for all of his years in school and will continue to do so until he finishes school.

Not every child who starts in an early intervention program or requires special education classrooms, speech therapy, and the like as a preschooler will need all this throughout their lives. Indeed, the hope is that thanks to all of those services, a child might progress to the point that he or she would not need any more "special" services and be "just another typical" schoolchild—though one should be careful, lest a school district deem your child "too high-functioning" for any services at all with the result that your child might be placed in a "regular" classroom without any supports at all—and flounder.

It would have been hard to hear that Charlie would always need special ed when he was a preschooler. When he was in elementary school, I used to drop him off and pick him up from school and felt a great deal of bitter-sweetness at those moments: intense love and pride to see him with his backpack drooping from his shoulders, and a pang that he was in a "special" class and could only join in the regular activities of the school (assemblies, Halloween parade) with extra assistance, and sometimes not at all. It's hard to hear your child referred to as "classified" and that he or she is "different;" to hear other parents say to you (as one parent once said to me) that they feel "sorry for what you have to go through."

Those are the moments when I remind myself how it is Charlie's civil right to be in school and to have an education provided for him, just as it is for students who don't need special ed. In a sense, there's nothing so "special" about special ed. Schools need to teach students, need to teach all of our children.

Choosing a School for Children on the Autism Spectrum

Kristina Chew

My son Charlie has been in both public and private placements. He is thirteen years old now; he started attending school—a special education preschool classroom in the St. Paul Public School District—when he was just around two years old. Looking back, he's been through most every kind of placement, from special education classrooms located in a public elementary or middle school, to a small private school only for autistic children, to a large public center for some 200 children with autism and other disabilities.

Again and again, we have found ourselves looking for a school for Charlie. Too often, we have thought we have found "it"—a school, a school district where the right program and supports and staff seem to be in place, and then things started to seem not so good, and then to fall apart. At no point have we simply found a school and been able to say "this is it," though we've come close to such in regard to his current placement at the large public center. We initially felt a lot of hesitation to choose a separate placement for Charlie, where all the students have disabilities and many are on the autism spectrum and there are no opportunities for interacting with "typical" children. As it has turned out, Charlie has (so far) seemed quite content at the center, a reminder to me that the best criterion for knowing if a school is right is based on how your child responds.

Please note: While some aspects of what follows are particular to our state of New Jersey, I am hopeful that much of what I've noted here about choosing and assessing schools may be more generally applied.

Schools for Children on the Autism Spectrum

You've gotten past the "early intervention" stage and it's time for your child to start going to school. Indeed, you sense that it's time for your child to be in a school setting in addition to, or rather than, a home program, so that he or she may have opportunities for interacting with other children and be more independent, and because it's just time for your child to be in school, with other children. Perhaps your school district has a special ed preschool program that, from what you're told and what you've read, uses the same sort of teaching methodology (perhaps Applied Behavior Analysis—"ABA"—which is pretty much the norm for autism programs in New Jersey where we live) and provides speech therapy and occupational therapy.

But, in doing your research, you've heard about this other school, a private one, that uses ABA too and is directed by someone whose name you recognize from some articles you've read and they're holding an open house and you have this feeling, you must check it out.

Your local autism organization is one source to start with, to identify school programs. Also helpful are other parents of children with disabilities—indeed, I've often found them the best sources of information, especially as regards getting a feel of what different schools are like.

School Types:

In-district

Your child attends school in a school in your public school district. Depending on your child's needs, this school may or may not be your "neighborhood" school; the district may have a program that suits your child's educational needs that is out of your "zone." Transportation is provided under the Individuals with Disabilities Education Act (IDEA) regardless of how far (or close) you live from the school.

Out-of-district

Your child attends a school that is not in your town. Such placements may be public (such as "centers" run by a consortium of districts, or a county) or private schools.

Public

Your child attends a program that is run by your local school district and located in one of its schools.

Private

Your child attends a private school for children on the autism spectrum. Teachers and other staff members are employed by the school, rather than being employees of the school district. The school staff decides which children will be accepted into the school. Often, the school has places for only a specific number of students.

Non-Public Schools (NPS)

These are not, strictly speaking, private schools; a child can attend a NPS only when funded by your school district of origin. Acceptance is based on need, and the number of places is (or is supposed to be) dependent on the number of children who need such a placement.

Charter Schools

Some charter schools have also been created for children on the autism spectrum. Besides ABA, other methodologies that schools might use include DIR-Floortime, Verbal Behavior, and RDI (Relationship Development Intervention).

It's imperative to see the classroom, program, and school that your child will be in. Like many things, this is easier said than done.

(Caveat: Here in New Jersey, you have to live in the district before you can see a public school program. You can't check out a program and then decide to move into a school district. This makes sense from the school district's perspective—programs ought only to be for residents of a town. But, before one makes the huge decision to pack up and move, of course, one would like to know what a program is like, rather than simply relying on word of mouth.)

When you look at a school, it's important to try to set your philosophical and political views aside, or at least to keep them under wraps, and focus on the people who will be teaching your child. How are the teachers interacting with the children? What is the "feel" of the school? What is the noise/sound level at the school? A noisy school is not necessarily a bad one, and a very quiet one (where you could hear a literal pin drop) is not necessarily the best, even for a child with sound sensitivities (who may prefer some "background noise"). The question to be answered is, is this a good school in and of itself? A place where students are educated, are respected and accepted for who they are; a place where teachers seek to teach students based on their individual needs and not according to some unwavering predetermined methodology and curriculum?

Private schools here in New Jersey have monthly open houses during the school year. Some of these schools are the ones that, according to a May 6, 2000, *New York Times* article, people come from Greece, Italy, and Israel to have their children attend; getting one's child a spot in one of those schools has been said to be harder than getting into Harvard. Going to one of these open houses can be something of a tense experience, with everyone feeling that they're trying to be on their "best behavior" to garner a spot for their child.

Introductory sessions at the numerous private autism schools I visited all follow a general format, with a lecture/presentation by (usually) the school's director followed by a tour. Given that these schools all had the teaching methodology and staffing that we were looking for—plus some of the schools are housed in some very nice facilities—what differentiated one from another?

It's the atmosphere, the mood in the air that—after all those school visits and after all the different placements Charlie has been in—I've learned to look for. In visiting a school, I put out my sensor for a combination of acceptance merged with hope, with the sense that students are students and people first, for an aura of kindliness and caring.

I did feel this at one (quite famous) autism school. It was definitely an ABA school; the atmosphere was welcoming and warm. Other ABA schools I've visited seem more (if I may use the word) sterile, with most of an emphasis on having the students adhere to strict criteria for behaviors at all times. The introduction at the former school was highly informative and clearly indicated the experience of the director; still, there was a casual tone and an openness that was carried over to a tour of the school. Rather than lead us from classroom to classroom, visitors were allowed to go to whichever classrooms they wished, on their own. The director noted that we might see students upset and having tantrums and that this was routine; that students there had behavior challenges and the staff could deal with it, and in a humane way.

At the other school, and generally at most schools, visitors were required to stay together and visit rooms on a schedule so there was much more a feeling of the visit being controlled, as if to make sure that we didn't see anything we oughtn't.

For us, the right school has nothing to hide, and is open about you visiting, asking questions, and making inquiries and even suggestions.

A Checklist

The first things most people think about in considering schools is the academic program and the training of teachers. But other factors need to be taken into account, in particular:

- How are "behaviors" handled?
- How open is the school? What is the visiting/observation policy? Is there a limit on how often you can visit? Can you simply drop in to see your child in his or her classroom?
- How will the school communicate with you? A communication notebook? Email? Will there be a note every day regarding your child's activities? Or fewer times? How will you get reports from the speech therapist, OT, PT, as well as the adapted physical education (APE) teachers and music and art teachers?
- What is the nurse's training in addressing the health and medical needs of children on the autism spectrum?
- How are staff supported? What kind of staff development is offered?
- What is the policy for substitute instructors, when a head teacher, aide, or therapist is absent?
- Do you sense that the staff really wants to have your child there?

The building/physical setting of a school also needs to be taken into account. Once upon a time, I didn't think this was important, but recent experiences have shown me how significant the physical setting can indeed be. First, many children on the spectrum, my son included, have sensory issues: Charlie is hyper-sensitive to sound and can hear noises in a neighboring classroom or down the hall or up in the sky and may have behavior problems as a result; due to his limited language, he is not able to explain that he has such problems. This sound sensitivity was an extra challenge for Charlie when he was in a public school autism program, with his classroom located in a large middle school. Also, being able to walk and move around has been crucial to help my son "manage" his behaviors. In a public school, my son's access to places to walk was severely limited. There were of course many children throughout the school in classrooms, and Charlie crying or some such was quite noticeable and, for middle school students, not the usual sort of way to express frustration.

A separate school means severely reduced opportunities for interactions with other children. On the other hand, he has access to lots of places to walk and even, if need to be, to lie down (Charlie's sleep habits are sometimes irregular and he will be up very early or go to sleep very late, and still get up very early). There is a gym, a track, and a swimming pool. The school is in a huge building designed somewhat like a shopping mall, with open space at the center and classrooms around the edges in a circle. It's an open layout that seems reassuring for him (Charlie seems less comfortable in small and confined spaces, though when he was younger he sometimes sought these out).

Teachers, Therapists, and Training

I've included teachers and their training in a separate section, as in our experience, it is the teachers and the aides who spend the majority of the school day with your child who are key—are the most important.

- What is the training and educational background of the teachers?
- How long have they been teaching and in what sorts of settings and programs?
- What kinds of supports and supervision do they receive?
- What kinds of professional development have they had, or are they planning?

That said, sometimes the best teachers my son has had have not come out of a "traditional" educational course in school. Just because someone has an educational degree, or even one in special education, does not necessarily mean he or she will be a good teacher. Teachers and aides might have majored in psychology or history or other fields. A very young teacher may have the credentials and "book knowledge," but there's no replacement for actual experience. On the other hand, an older teacher may not have the same energy and enthusiasm as someone who is starting out.

The Issue of "Appropriate" Placement

Ideally, the school that your child attends will be the one that you have determined to be the most appropriate for her or his educational needs. There are a few potential obstacles, however:

- The school may have a restricted number of spots.
- Your school district may not agree on the placement.

A school district may disagree about a placement on the grounds that it is not "appropriate" for your child. In many cases, the reason for the objection may well be, ultimately, economic: The school district may have its own in-district program in mind that, on paper, may have the sort of educational and therapeutic methodologies that you may be seeking for your child, but you may find that it is actually not the right setting for your child, due to the ratio of staff to students, or the physical location and set-up of the classroom, or other factors. Plus, who oversees the program that your child will be in and provides training for the aides and teachers? Is there a behaviorist on staff or does the district have an outside consultant? And how was this consultant chosen? How are behavioral issues addressed? What is the district's policy on the use of restraints and seclusion?

Also, a school district may well object to an out-of-district placement at a private center due to the costs: if that placement is approved, the school district is required under the Individuals with Disabilities Act (IDEA) to finance both the tuition and transportation. The latter can be a significant part of the bill, and more so if the private placement is not located near your residence.

If, after having seen the in-district program offered by your school district, you do not deem it appropriate for your child, and if you have found a placement that you think *is* appropriate, you will have to prove to your school district why the placement you have found is appropriate. This might be a point at which you decide to retain the services of an advocate and/or a lawyer who specializes in special education law, as you may face a legal battle with your school district over what is "appropriate" for your child. If you and your Child Study Team do not agree about the placement, you may have to go into mediation, with a hearing officer learning about your side and that of the school district. If no decision results from that, you may have to go into due process and face a legal battle and, in some cases, even go to court.

Ideally, this will not happen, everyone will agree that they need to "do the right thing" for your child, and you can focus not on legal issues, but the real heart of the matter—making sure that your child has the education she or he needs to achieve her or his full potential, to learn and to grow, and to lead a good life.

Autism, An Equal Opportunity Disorder

Frances Vega-Costas

Autism is a very complicated disorder and not only affects each individual differently, it can happen anywhere in the world. Never in my life would I imagine that I would be a special education advocate nor that would I use the "A" word almost on a daily basis. Almost ten years ago the "A" word moved into my house and it has been a very interesting relationship with its ups and downs but as any regular couple we learned to live with each other in peace, accepting each other as we are.

My son was diagnosed at almost four with Persistent Developmental Delay–Not Otherwise Specified (PDD-NOS), which by that time I did have an understanding of, and to be honest for me is a fancy label for "we don't know in what part of the ASD Spectrum your son is." When he was eighteen months old we began to see that something was wrong with our only son, and due to the lack of resources in my native country, Puerto Rico, it took a lot of time to find out why he lost his speech, lost his sleep, and was lining blocks for hours every day. Autism spectrum, it could not be. Why was this is happening to us? We decided to get help and look for services.

Then he was too old for Early Intervention services (there is a long waiting list), Head Start did not let us register him because we did not qualify because of our income (yeah, right!), we had a few horror stories with a private school supposedly for children with disabilities, and then we finally decided to put him in the public school system—there is Individuals with Disabilities Education Act (IDEA) 2004, why should I worry? (How naïve and trusting I was back then!)

I will spare you the two years of complaints, meeting, fights, and the nightmare of trying to make the agencies understand that you are just asking what for what your son needs to have a better future. We became frustrated with the system, and decided to move to United States. Because of my frustration and because the teachers kept complaining that there was almost no information about autism in Spanish, I decided to gather all information about autism in Spanish and make a website. And in March 2006 *Viviendo en otra dimension* was born.[1] Meanwhile we were making the arrangements to leave our country, and moved to Michigan in the fall of 2006.

The two weeks after I registered my son in school, they did that Individual Education Plan (IEP) meeting to match the services I had in Puerto Rico, they had somebody translate it, and we were so excited; finally the kid was going to get what he needed. So, after two months of our first winter ever, the school did an emergency meeting to discuss placements because things were not working out. It took me a little bit more than a year and a Special Education Advocate to make the school district understand my son's needs and design an appropriate IEP and behavior plan for him, and right now things are great. Now inclusion is a possibility and he has made gigantic progress.

But it made me realize that I was lucky—I was fluent in English and yet I had to use translators. The cultural differences made things more difficult and sometimes complicated. I never felt more alone in my life. My family and friends were miles away, and I live in a city where there are almost no Hispanics. That's the reason why now, as a special education advocate, I do cultural competency presentations for school districts and agencies. So I am going to share a few tips on how to reach Hispanic families:

Not all Hispanics are Mexicans. Hispanic is not a race but an ethnic distinction. Hispanics come from all races and physical traits. Hispanic describes cultures or countries that were once under Spanish rule (Mexico, Central America, and parts of South America where Spanish is the primary language). Hispanics share a common language, but their cultures, values, and beliefs are unique. To assume that all Hispanic cultures are the same is a critical mistake.

When you are working with a Hispanic family, use the family's preferred language. Find a fully bilingual interpreter, even if the family is fluent in English. Imagine you are in a meeting with fifteen people you don't know who are making decisions about your kid's future and you are so nervous you are having trouble speaking, and then imagine doing that in a language that is not your native one. And it doesn't hurt to learn some basic Spanish words, like greetings; those details make such a big difference.

Make sure your materials are not only in Spanish but culturally relevant; use artwork or pictures that reflect the Hispanic culture. "Invite" and encourage involvement from the very beginning. Be aware of a general distrust of American/Anglo culture and outside influences.

Don't forget that the traditional Hispanic family is patriarchal so that means the father usually has final say in making decisions. Don't be surprised if in an IEP meeting the Hispanic mother doesn't want to sign documents until her husband reads them and gives his approval.

Disability is still a taboo topic for most of the Hispanic cultures. And that is one of the biggest challenges for the providers. Autism is still perceived as an emotional illness not a developmental disability in most of these countries. And to add to it, sometimes autism is used as an adjective to refer to egoistical individuals or bad politicians, and that's something that parents with kids diagnosed on the ASD spectrum in Latin America are fighting against. As a provider, reinforce that autism is a developmental disability and that the earlier the interventions, the better the outcome.

Remember that to understand different cultural beliefs and practices requires flexibility and a respect for others' viewpoints. Be sincere and firm, but not condescending.

Quite simply, providers who are respectful of and responsive to the beliefs, practices, and cultural and linguistic needs of diverse consumers can help bring more positive outcomes.

"Diversity is not about how we differ. Diversity is about embracing one another's uniqueness." —Ola Joseph

And that is one of the best lessons autism has taught me: to love and respect life as it is.

---

[1] www.viviendoenotradimension.com

As of Summer 2011, the National Dissemination Center for Children with Disabilities (NICHCY) has a complete Spanish-language website: www.nichcy.org/espanol/publicaciones.

Writing Effective IEP Goals and Objectives: Suggestions for Teachers and Parents

Daniel Dage

I have not attended many Individual Education Plan (IEP) meetings where the goals and objectives were actually the subject of enough scrutiny by the attendees. Most of the time, the biggest issue of contention is during the discussion of placement.

What most parents (and an embarrassing number of teachers) don't realize is that goals and objectives are what are going to drive the students' placement and services during the coming school year. While a Behavioral Intervention Plan (BIP) is the most abused part of the IEP, the goals and objectives are among the most neglected. My youngest, Percy, just had his IEP, and while the objectives are different, the criteria for mastery and method of evaluation are all exactly the same; three out of four opportunities, and teacher observation. All the way down. Most teachers simply mark in 75 to 80% all the way down for criteria. This pretty much renders the objectives as written in the IEP as useless. Because when progress reports come out, teachers are going to eyeball the objective's progress and make it up out of the air as they go.

Let's take a sample goal of increasing academic skills and the supporting objective of reading sight words. "Thomas will read ten sight words." The criterion is at 80% and the method of evaluation is teacher observation/data collection.

What direction does this give Thomas' teacher next year? All it says is that he will read ten words with 80% accuracy. So does he master the objective the first time he reads eight out of ten? And how is the teacher teaching and tracking this?

Let's turn this ugly duckling around. Thomas is still going to read ten words, but now the criteria for mastery is to read eight of ten words over five consecutive sessions. Now I have a much better idea of what mastery really looks like. And I'm going to evaluate progress using discrete trial data. Now when it comes time to teach this, I know discrete trial is the format of choice. My objective now has the components of a basic lesson plan and Thomas's next teacher can have a clearer idea of what is to be taught and how to do it.

How about a different goal: Thomas will remain on task for twenty minutes. His caseload manager will put in 80% and have "data collection/teacher observation" as the way to evaluate progress. That objective is all but useless. I have absolutely no way to tell whether he has mastered this or made progress or gotten worse. And there's no hint of how to teach him to stay on task. The teacher is simply going to pull something out of their butt in order to say he has mastered this by the end of the year. It is a crock of crap.

If you are a parent, look at your child's goals and objectives in their IEP. If they all have the same criteria and have the same method of evaluation, you are being sold a worthless bill of goods. If they all have a mastery criteria of 80% and nothing else, the goals are rubbish. "Teacher observation" is shorthand for "pulling results out of my posterior." "Data collection" is shorthand for "pulling a pencil out of my posterior and using it as a magic wand to make results appear by magic." If you are a special education teacher and trying to skate by on this, you are wasting your time. It may seem easier to do this, but in the long run you are going to pay dearly. You can not teach from this, much less evaluate how your teaching is working. It's better to have a few well-thought-out objectives than a dozen haphazard ones.

So how can we redeem this objective? Certainly, staying on task and attending are worthy goals if a student has difficulty with this. Think. How long are they attending now? Chances are, you don't really know. It varies, depending on the task. A student may attend for hours on the computer or video game, but not be able to remain on-task for five minutes for written seat work. So let's concentrate on seat work. Okay, you've already improved your goal by defining the conditions in which you plan on observing and teaching it!

"Thomas will remain on-task during independent written seat work." Now you know when to observe. Not during circle time or recess, but during those times he has to be sitting down and writing something. Now let's keep going and improve it more. Is twenty minutes too long? For younger students, it might be. If he is having serious problems, five minutes might be more realistic. But we're going to find out. How are you going to figure out how well he is doing now? You are probably going to want to time him. Think again. Take a five-minute session and divide it into thirty-second intervals. During each thirty-second interval, he is either sitting and writing, or he is off-task. Track how many intervals he is on-task versus off-task. Let's say he is off task for half of those intervals. You now have a good idea of how to write this goal. We can still use 80%, but we need to be more precise. Think about how you will get him from 50% to 80%.

"Thomas will remain on-task for five minutes with nonverbal prompts and cues." The criteria will be 80% of intervals over five sessions and the evaluation method will be using interval data. Now when you revisit that IEP three or four months from now you not only know what to teach but have some idea of how you teach and measure it. Making mastery over several sessions gives a better indication of true mastery rather than a whim. If he does master this, you can either extend the length of time or up the criteria from 80% to 90%.

Teaching special education involves a high level of sophistication and expertise. Some knowledge of data collection and precise teaching methods is crucial to writing meaningful goals and objectives.

Parents, much of this may seem like Greek to you. But if I present you with an Microsoft Excel graph of your child's progress, you will be able to see how your child is doing, and anyone can see how quickly or slowly your child is getting it. Success is everyone's goal, but monitoring and measuring it is the job of the teacher. That's why the good folks in the county pay us what they do.

You also see why I don't like too much vagueness. This is why we end up with these senseless tests and calls for accountability from the Feds, because of sloppiness that serves no one. The problem with these tests is that they do not measure ongoing progress. If they fail a test in third grade, they will be tested next in fifth grade after two years and after being handed off to two different teachers. But at least the tests give some degree of accuracy at a given point in time. In special education, the process needs to be continuous with some degree of accuracy. And those new teachers who are being pulled off the street with no training have no idea of how to do it.

Unfortunately, most parents do not have the level of expertise necessary to correct sloppy objectives, much less write good ones of their own. But what they can do is demand accountability. When mastery of previous goals is discussed, ask to see supporting data, such as data sheets and/or a graph. Better still, you might consider asking for these during progress report time. A teacher making stuff up will be forced to either fly right or they will have to make even more stuff up. And making up data is not as easy as it sounds. You will probably be classified as a "problem parent" and might not get a Christmas card from your child's case manager. But you will end up with a better IEP.

As a teacher (or teacher wannabe), putting this extra thought and effort in the IEP today will help you teach better in the fall. You reap what you sow, and sowing crap in the spring will yield more crap in the fall. One other reason to put this level of work into your objectives is that all of them will comply with alternate assessment criteria. They are supposed to be well-defined and measurable. *All* of them need to be measurable, and thinking about how to measure them will help write a better goal.

I want to add one more note to any teachers who might be reading this: do not try writing meaningful goals the night before the meeting. It simply cannot and will not happen. Goal drafts can be started as early as the first progress report when you look at goal mastery and revise it as the year goes on. By the time of the annual review, you should already have an idea of where the student is and where they should be going. You can help yourself and the rest of the committee by submitting both a copy of the goal drafts and a copy of the previous year's mastery to parents up to a week ahead of the meeting. This gives parents enough time to think about the goals, review them, and then add their own suggestions. If parents have suggestions, they can send the draft back, you revise and then send it home again. In just a few rounds, you may end up with goals both parties agree to and you can simply ratify the goals and objectives at the meeting. An added benefit is that it can help parents participate and buy into it. If the student is old enough, don't forget to include him or her in this phase as well. Bringing both parents and students into the process during the drafting process can lessen anxiety for everyone as it minimizes surprises.

Writing IEPs is a difficult process. I'm not trying to make them more difficult as much as making them more meaningful. Right now, the way most objectives are written, they are rubbish and an absolute waste of time.

—

A version of this essay was originally published at
www.specialed.wordpress.com

Rotten Food, Lousy Service: Dodge the Restaurant Mentality to Get Your Kids the Services They Need

Carol Ann Greenburg

Sometimes I feel like getting services for my autistic son is like trying to dine at the world's worst restaurant. You can't afford the best eatery in the city, who could? You're still really hungry so you walk into some local dive and the wait staff, whose entire job it is to feed you, is standing around staring blankly at the many obvious health-code violations. They're clearly offended by the interruption when you ask for a menu. You're the one who is hungry after all, why can't you come in knowing what you plan to eat? Finally someone ambles over with a menu, drops it on your table like they're doing you a favor, and you realize there's nothing even remotely edible on it. Specials, substitutions? Forget about it! After you wait an unholy amount of time, someone brings you the wrong order. Cold. You complain, and in their very first efficient move of the day, the staff coalesces to kick you out unfed because they reserve the right to deny service to anyone for any reason.

Our kids' minds and spirits need appropriate, completely individualized services just as urgently as their bodies need food. A bounty of services should lie at their sweet little fingertips. No family in our position should have to wait for, fight for, or make do with inappropriate services, because a child needs something that's "not on the menu." Unfortunately, however, the truism that Life-Is-Unfair is even truer for us, so we must use a combination of persistence and creativity to score resources that should be, but aren't, easy to access.

So let's start with two "P" words: Prioritizing and Persistence (note P also stands for Politeness and Patience). Prioritizing means: draw a line down the middle of a piece of paper and write "Needs" at the head of one column and "Wants" at the head of the other. My seven-year-old singing, dancing, sports-loving attention magnet is severely language delayed. So while music therapy and swimming lessons are of great benefit to him, speech therapy is at the top of our Needs list. That doesn't mean our family should forget all about music therapy or swimming, but when push comes to shove, it is speech first, music second. Assuming we're battling with the folks who are supposed to pay for the service, which we unfortunately often are, it's always easier to fight on a single front than on multiple ones.

Now that we've figured out the top priority, we have to tap the most logical source of funding. When it comes to speech therapy, an obviously academic need, we will naturally go first to the board of education. By law, all kids are entitled to FAPE (a free appropriate public education), so if we get lucky, the district will immediately offer all the speech that is required. This does happen sometimes. No one gets into the field of special ed to make their first million by time they're twenty-five. Many school staff and district personnel care deeply about your child's education, but their departments are not well funded, so they have to make hard decisions about who gets what.

This is where the second "P" word comes in. Persistence. Persistence does not entail screaming over the phone at one bureaucrat after another who would like to help, but can't because their boss's boss just wrote a memo about the need for tighter purse strings. Persistence is about writing detailed polite letters to the leader of the IEP team, letters that simultaneously acknowledge their expertise and your full membership in said IEP team. Persistence means following up with polite phone calls, during which you inquire if they might need any more information from you, so everyone reaches an agreement you can all live with. Persistence means taking detailed notes on every single conversation, with as many exact quotes as you can write down. If there are raised voices and unhelpful attitudes, they'd better not be yours, but they'd also better be objectively and accurately documented by you. In the end, this strategy gives you the best chance of getting your child's needs met.

Now what about their wants? Or your wants? Or your other children's wants? This is where creativity comes in. As I mentioned before, my son loves music therapy and we want him to have it. He's an only child, so we don't have to worry about other kids' soccer games or cheerleading practices, which I hear are inevitably held in the opposite direction. Music therapy isn't cheap, but with help from generous relatives we've managed to pay for it. The conservatory is a fairly short drive and we have two cars, so in the end we can fulfill that particular wish. Now, I'm sure my son would also enjoy skiing in the Alps, but that would be a little more than our family can handle, in terms of time, money, and energy. In a perfect world, our limitless wealth would provide for his every desire and he'd be chauffeured to each delightful treat while we sat eating delicious but calorie-free bon-bons on the couch. (If anyone knows of such a perfect world, by the way, please email me the location.) In this world however, the choices we make for our autistic child really have to work for the whole family, which requires some creativity.

Funding is the first issue you have to approach with an open mind. It can become almost automatic to hold out your hand to the Board of Ed for any service, because so much of what you want for your child has educational implications, direct or indirect. If, however, the service is more of a Want than an absolute Need, and particularly if it can be interpreted as, say, more recreational than immediately educational, think of other sources before you go to your local school district. I could reasonably argue that my son's music therapy has an impact on his education, for example, but the district could counter that music therapy is an extracurricular activity more appropriately covered by Medicaid, or a corporate charity, or a local nonprofit organization. Casting a wide net financially makes everyone happier—you're more likely to get the money you need from the school district because it's eternally strapped for cash, and from the corporation, foundation, or other nonprofit, because they need to demonstrate that someone needs their services to justify their next grant application.

The next challenge to your creativity comes in the form of a phrase quoted reverently, and justifiably, by any decent disability rights advocate: "Person-first thinking" is vital here. All autistic people, my son and myself included, have what the neurotypical world calls "obsessions" and what we autistic folk often refer to as "special interests." When I was twelve, I started teaching myself Japanese. That may not sound so unusual to today's parents, but back then, most Americans had never heard of Manga or Anime, there was no such thing as a Japanese language class in any East Coast middle or high school. And services? Please. There was no working Asperger's diagnosis back in the seventies, much less any services geared towards verbal people on the spectrum like me. Luckily I had good parents who encouraged my interests, however odd, and what I like to refer to as not so much the symptom of, but the Autistic Superpower of, perseveration. Even if we had the Internet back then, I'm quite convinced no Google search for "East Asian Language Instruction for Autistic Preteens" would have yielded useful resources. So I started learning words from the one English/Japanese dictionary I could find, stalking and practicing on commuter trains filled with unsuspecting Japanese business people, and adjusting the antenna of my ancient black-and-white TV to find obscure channels where people spoke Japanese. An unusual approach to be sure, but for outside-the-box thinking it's best to go to someone so autistic they can't even see the box.

Back to the present, to My Son the Jock, who unlike me had an early and clear diagnosis, good services—and at least so far—less esoteric special interests. Thank goodness most of us now have some sort of access to the Internet, so it's pretty easy to look up his sport du jour. My husband noticed his fascination with TV shows about obstacle courses. Forgetting myself and putting disability first, I looked under "Obstacle courses, autistic children." Luck smiled upon me and I actually did find something. In Colorado. We live in Brooklyn, New York. He has a twelve-month school year, and the chances of finding the one obstacle course clinic specifically designed for autistic children that fit into his school schedule— well, I don't have to tell you how successful that effort wasn't. I'm sure you've been there too.

Putting him, his individual interests, and personality first was not only more respectful, it was more useful. Just looking under "Obstacle Course, Kids" I found a few. They weren't right around the corner, but New Jersey is a lot closer to us than Colorado. So say we do decide to pursue this further in our family's copious spare time. When you think about it, it actually doesn't take a gargantuan effort for me to email or call whomever is in charge of the program explaining that our child, who most importantly loves obstacle courses and by the way also happens to be autistic, might like to participate.

I know even five years ago, the program coordinator might have muttered something not completely intelligible, but clearly negative. We live in a different and I think better world now, though, thanks to greater autism awareness. The rising rate of autism has created an atmosphere in which geek is chic, so it's rare to meet anyone who doesn't at least know someone who knows someone with a kid on the spectrum. A world that I believe is gradually evolving into a less fearful, more accommodating place for all human beings.

I regret that I couldn't get a diagnosis for myself until I was 44, and that I personally never got the kind of services I can now access for my son and children like him. But I also rejoice that he has been diagnosed in time to get those services when they can most help him. Like any mother, I worry about his future, but on my better days, I believe the world is his oyster. Great. So what's next on his list, pearl diving?

The "R" Word Revisited

Brian R. King, LCSW

Recent headlines about the epidemic of bullying, unfortunately point to school systems overall that appear either indifferent to bullying, referring to it in some cases as "a rite of passage that children must endure as a means of building character" (one school administrator actually said this in an Individual Education Plan [IEP] meeting I attended), or they minimize it as a misunderstanding. Others exercise willful ignorance under the guise that "We didn't see it"— as though the bully is supposed to say, "Teacher, looky here! I'm going to treat Johnny like crap now." Give me a break! If a child bullies another student out of the view of a teacher, it's still bullying and not an opportunity to evade responsibility because the bully is savvy enough to know when you aren't looking.

Bullying is not a simple problem of the playground tough guy establishing his dominance while teachers are preoccupied. This problem isn't caused by school or teachers looking the other way. It's a larger social problem that we all bear responsibility for creating, allowing, and exacerbating.

That surge in bullying news has also opened up a lot of old wounds from my own childhood. That and today's incident with my son reminded me of an incident when he was younger. An incident which brought me out of my shell in a big way, and opened the door for the self-advocate I have become. I'm revisiting the article I wrote about it back then, because it is still an issue that is out of control. This needs to stop as fast as a bird slamming into a window (for you bird lovers, I was just looking for a concrete metaphor to drive my point home).

It was about five years ago. We lived in another town then. My son came to me and informed me that there was a neighborhood bully who was targeting him. Even worse, the bullying often took place in front of other parents, who didn't intervene. Once I heard that, my papa bear instincts reared up. It terrified me that I couldn't look to my neighbors to be role models to their own kids or others when they were so clearly out of line.

I admit that, at the time, my neighbors were not that familiar with me. I am not a social being, and their tendency to assemble in groups was enough to keep me indoors. So when my son told me what happened, I struggled with reaching out, as I didn't have a rapport with any of them.

I decided to write a letter that would allow me to organize my thoughts, choose my words carefully, and eliminate the possibility of becoming nervous and tongue-tied during a face-to-face interaction. Below in italics is the letter I constructed.

Hi Neighbor,

My name is Brian King. My wife and I live at (address omitted). You may be familiar with our older son, Zachary.

The reason I'm writing this letter is to introduce Zach to you, and help clarify some misunderstandings. Zachary has been diagnosed with a form of Autism called Asperger syndrome. This often causes him difficulty when interacting with your children, as first and foremost Autism Spectrum issues make it difficult for Zachary to socialize in a conventional way.

Zachary is a very sweet and honest boy. Unfortunately, his enthusiasm and self-assuredness can come off as pushy, and sometimes controlling. Zachary can be very talkative and I understand that he can sometimes require a lot of energy to be around.

I apologize for not having made an effort to meet you, but as they say the apple doesn't fall far from the tree, and my boys inherited their autistic features from me. Thus, I am shy to new people and am anxious around groups of people. Make no mistake, I am eager to get to know you.

Most importantly, I am writing this because I want to extend myself in every way to help support you in supporting your children, and mine, as they try to form friendships in the neighborhood. Zach has a clumsy social style, due to his Autism Spectrum challenges, and your children, no doubt, find him frustrating to deal with, at times. I don't expect your children to understand this about him because, how could they.

Unfortunately, a problem has arisen that compelled me to write this letter. One boy on this street has taken to routinely calling Zachary a "retard." In the special needs community this is the equivalent of calling an African American the "N" word. For a child who knows he is challenged and is trying his best, this word cuts deeper than you can imagine.

Though we may not have met, I would love to meet you and support you as you support my son in his efforts to make friends in the neighborhood. He will no doubt have challenges his entire life in socializing and being understood. I would hate to see his neighbors turn their backs on him.

I am here to support you, and your child's efforts, in getting to know Zach. Please, by all means, feel free to let me know when he has pushed one too many of your buttons and I'll gladly come get him. I'd rather him continue to be welcome at your home than to be a consistent source of aggravation. I am here whenever you need to talk.

Thank you so much,

Brian King

That's the letter that was hand-delivered, by Zach, to the parents of each child he played with. Zach was allowed to read the letter before he delivered it and was comfortable with doing so. I am happy to say that the response to the letter was extremely positive.

The first parent to receive the letter came over immediately and thanked me for it. He had experienced Zach's intensity firsthand and had experienced the frustration addressed in the letter. He told me of the difficulty he had at times knowing how to interact with Zach, and was at a loss over how to address it with parents he'd never met. This letter not only gave him the insight he needed into Zach's unique behavior, but also in how to approach me. He also offered to more closely monitor the social interactions of the neighborhood kids and to introduce me to the other parents when I was ready.

The second parent to come to the house was the mother of the unnamed bully in the letter. She said she knew upon reading the letter that it was him and that this has been an ongoing issue with him. She explained that he too has social awkwardness, is bullied at school, and often resorts to taking it out on others.

She further stated that upon reading the letter she called a family meeting and had her son read the letter to the family and had a discussion about the impact of bullying. After that discussion the boy who'd called Zach "retard" asked if he could come over and apologize to Zach.

In all honesty, I did have reservations about sending out this letter in the first place, as I quietly feared that my neighbors wouldn't care, because so many stood by while the bullying took place. It would seem that the letter instilled a little self-awareness and accountability in the parents without specifically pointing fingers.

If you feel the need to write a similar letter to your neighbors and fear it will result in negative consequences, I, unfortunately, cannot promise you that it won't. I was very fortunate in the response I received. However, I assure you, it is far more damaging to have your child be excluded and bullied because you've allowed the neighbors to remain uninformed and ill-equipped to interact with your child. Please don't underestimate your neighbors.

If you want to stop bulling, start in your home, your neighborhood, and your community. Begin the dialogue and continue the dialogue until bullying stops.

What Is an Appropriate Education for Autistic Children?

Katharine Beals, Ph.D.

The problem of reading comprehension

Autism manifests differently as our children mature. One area where students with autism may struggle is with reading comprehension. This can pose significant problems for students who are mainstreamed and whose teachers may not understand their struggles with comprehension. Consider the following two passages:

> Nobody gave The Treatment like Farquar. Palmer knew a kid who had his arm in a sling for a week after. Yet Farquar himself was maddeningly unpredictable. Some birthday boys he seemed to totally ignore, passing them on the street as he usually did, as if they were dog doo. On the other hand, he had been known to walk halfway across town, knock on a door and say sweetly to a surprised parent, "I hear there's a birthday boy in here."

> Some kids turned into quivering zombies. They kept their birthdays as secrets as possible. In school, if their teacher announced their birthday, they denied it, claiming that it was a mistake. They refused to have parties. They stayed inside their house for a month so they would not bump into Farquar.

> But there was another side to it. There was the honor. There was the respect you got from other kids, the kind of respect that comes to soldiers who survive great battles... (From *The Wringer*, by Jerry Spinelli.)

> —

> Instead of fighting with weapons, Gandhi and the Congress Party began to use other methods of resisting the British. They taught the Indians to resist with "noncooperation"—meaning that Indians simply refused to pay taxes to the British government. They encouraged Indians to "boycott" British goods (refuse to buy anything made in Great Britain). Gandhi told his followers to make their own handmade cloth for their clothes, rather than buying British cotton. When the British put a tax on salt, Gandhi led his followers on a march of 240 miles to go collect salt from the sea, rather than buying the taxed salt. He started with seventy-eight people. By the end of the march, thousands of people were following him.

Gandhi told Indians to take their children out of British schools. He asked them to give up privileges given to them by the British. He himself sent back a medal that the British government had given him for his work in South Africa. When a factory refused to give its workers enough money to live on, Gandhi went on a hunger strike. He refused to eat until the factory owners agreed to the raise. It took three days for the factory owners to give in and agree. They didn't want to be responsible for Gandhi starving to death! (From *The Story of the World, Volume IV*, by Susan Wise Bauer.)

Both *The Wringer* and *The Story of the World* are intended for the nine- to twelve-year-old age range (approximately third to sixth grade). And according to the usual measures—vocabulary, sentence length, and sentence complexity—the second passage is unequivocally the more difficult of the two.

But in terms of the work the student must do to fill in the gaps in literal content to make sense of the text, the first passage is much more challenging. In particular, nowhere is it stated that Farquar beats kids up on their birthdays. If you don't infer this, you then won't understand why kids try to keep their birthdays a secret. And without this, and a grasp of the social meaning of "honor," you'll be completely baffled by the second paragraph of the excerpt.

In the second passage, on the other hand, much more is spelled out. The explanatory asides, while they contribute to the length and complexity of the sentences, offer useful definitions of key terms ("noncooperation" and "boycott"). In general, much less filling-in is necessary to understand the connections between sentences.

These differences between texts make sense when we consider their different settings. One is set close to home, and centers on schoolboy dynamics with which most neurotypical children are familiar. Because of this, it can leave many things unstated and still make sense to most readers. The other text, on the other hand, is set in a faraway time and place, and involves issues that nine-to-twelve-year-olds cannot be assumed to be familiar with. Thus, much more needs to be made explicit. For children with autism, many of whom have difficulty detecting social dynamics in everyday life, this has the effect of leveling the playing field.

Because of this phenomenon, readings centering on other times, places, and issues tend to be much more accessible to those with autism than readings centering on everyday life. Unfortunately, however, in their zeal to make everything "relevant" to students' purported "personal lives," today's educators are biasing their reading selections more and more towards realistic texts about everyday life.

Such readings not only assume background knowledge in which autistic children tend to be deficient, but, as with fiction in general, involve social features that autistic children may find baffling. Any parent who spends any time reading with their autistic child sees how their social deficits impede their understanding of characters, relationships, dialogue, tone, author's intent, and the emotional effects of literary devices. But too few of those who teach autistic children in school settings—be they regular-ed or special-ed teachers—have either the training or the one-on-one reading support experience to understand how autism affects these subtle aspects of reading comprehension.

What should autistic children read?

When I watch my thirteen-year-old, seventh-grade autistic son struggle through *The Wringer* and other fourth grade reading level novels, getting almost nothing out of them, I wonder how reasonable it is to insist, as J's teachers do, that someone like him read fiction.

Here's a child who readily reads technical manuals, does pretty well with grade-level science texts and with fourth-grade-level history books, but who misses most of what matters in all but the most simple, basic, character-driven fiction.

On the one hand, carefully chosen fiction might help him with his social reasoning skills by giving him opportunities to see characters interacting. To this end, however, I generally prefer movies and TV shows: audio-video media capture many more of the cues of real-life social interaction than does printed text (though we keep this channel open as well, with captions turned on for extra feedback).

But if the goal is the "well-rounded" liberal arts education that comes from appreciating literature, I'm not sure it's a realistic one when it comes to those children whose social deficits are as extreme as J's.

I'm all in favor of a well-rounded education for most kids, and wary of underestimating potential and prematurely shutting off opportunities for academic development. With this in mind, it's important to recognize the vast array of subjects that don't involve the social subtleties and complexities of fiction. In terms of reading in particular, here are just a few suggestions for autistic students who can read nonfiction at least a fourth-grade level: straight-forward history texts, like Susan Wise Bauer's *The Story of the World* series (we're currently on volume 4, excerpted above); how things work books, like David Macaulay's *The Way Things Work*; the *Eyewitness Books* series, like *Great Scientists* or *Robot*; straight-up science texts on anything from anatomy to cosmology to electronics to ecology. Next on our list is *The Way Life Works: The Science Lover's Illustrated Guide to How Life Grows, Develops, Reproduces, and Gets Along.*

Mainstreaming environments: some neglected areas

As the mother of a mainstreamed autistic middle school child, and as the designer of an online course on high-functioning autistic students in mainstreaming environments, I spend many of my waking hours thinking about how best to accommodate students with autism in regular-ed classrooms. The article "Leveling the Field: Inclusion Program Readies Autistic Students for High School," featuring an Asperger/autism inclusion middle school teacher by the name of Cherie Fowler, caught my eye.

According to the article, Ms. Fowler's goals are to teach her students to express themselves better so they are successful academically in general education classes in middle school and beyond. The article credits Ms. Fowler with five specific strategies:

- Allowing autistic students to type assignments others would have to write by hand
- Allowing them to use other assistive devices
- Shortening some of the assignments
- Allowing them one class period that is designed just for them
- Educating each general-education class about what Asperger's/autism is

Laudable goals, and very much in line with what the eminently practical Asperger's expert Tony Attwood recommends in his *Complete Guide to Asperger's Syndrome*.

However, this list left me wishing for more.

In terms of reading, in light of what I discussed above, middle school teachers may want to consider the benefits of severely reducing or eliminating fictional works from the required reading lists for their ASD (Autism Spectrum Disorder) students in favor of non-fiction or technical literature. The costs to the student of comprehending fiction may outweigh the benefits. In particular, it would free up time for activities specifically targeted to improve social skills.

When it comes to writing, ASD students often languish when asked to write about their personal lives and personal feelings, or to produce realistic fiction. When the topic is science or fantasy, on the other hand, they are often much more inspired and have much more to say.

In math, ASD students often do complicated problems in their heads and aren't able to explain their answers verbally. They should be exempted from having to give such explanations, and should receive full credit for correct answers that lack verbal explanations.

When it comes to large, interdisciplinary/multimedia/open-ended projects, ASD students are often so overwhelmed by the breadth of material that they don't even know where to begin. In lieu of such projects, they should be given a larger number of shorter, more structured assignments that offer the same degree of academic challenge.

ASD students also flounder when required to work in groups. While group activities specifically targeted at improving their social skills, run by an expert in ASD, are fruitful, group activities centering on learning tasks should be replaced by independent learning opportunities.

Finally, ASD students are often way ahead of their peers in certain subjects and need to be allowed to progress at their own rates.

What ASD children need, in other words, are not just supports for and modifications of existing assignments, but a wholesale replacement of many of these assignments by alternative assignments and learning opportunities that are specifically tailored to their strengths and weaknesses.

Inclusion: Make It an Open Classroom Discussion

Diane Levinthal

Sensitivity and compassion can result from having kids with autism and social challenges included in regular education classrooms. It is also likely that there will be no choice other than inclusion, financially, in the future. Classrooms will have to accept differences (and I write this knowing that every child is "different"). How do we make inclusion positive for everyone involved?

I taught in a district autism spectrum inclusion project, have worked in speech for twenty-five years, and have a middle school child with PDD/ADHD. In my experience, what is important and overlooked is that regular education peers are not given good information. The teachers are trained (supposedly) as is the rest of the staff, but the kids themselves are told little besides "Do unto others as you would have them do unto you."

It has been my observation that in kindergarten and early elementary school, most kids are either fairly supportive of an included classmate and may try to help them out in the classroom, or—more often—politely ignore them. But once they hit the last half of third grade, all children are aware when a classmate is significantly different.

One of the most helpful things I was able to do for my son and his classmates in an included setting (and for the other included peer in that same class) was to talk with them all about social, organizational, attentional, and sensory "challenges" and "how to handle this as a peer." Students were absolutely astounded and relieved to find that it would be okay, for example, to tell a socially challenged peer that they were tired of listening and now it would be their turn to speak. Yes! It's okay to be direct and spell out the rules for "social"! Please do! Kids need to know that included classmates are not "out of step on purpose"! Regular education peers need roadmaps and information, and their included classmates can provide them.

Regular education peers are more helpful and more understanding when they know what the heck is going on with a classmate. After I spoke about social challenges in my son's fourth grade class, his peers not only started coming up with helpful solutions that the staff hadn't thought of, but they asked better questions about things they needed to know. Their parents showed up afterward to learn more about the "workshop" that held their child's interest and developed more understanding of social challenges.

My presentation was effective not because I am a wonderful speaker, but because I had information that classmates wanted, and I shared it in a very practical way. All parents of special needs kids have this information and can share this information with their children's classmates. The object is to demystify and share practical strategies which allow peers and classmates to help themselves, and which end up helping our kids.

On a social level, it's the other students who have to deal with our kids 99 percent of the time, not the staff. We tell siblings what's going on; why not the regular education classmates? I think they deserve that much and can handle it. This is nothing like pointing out who does and doesn't have challenges in a particular classroom—it is just about understanding and learning to cope with something that they are going to see during each year of school.

And that's what I told my son's classmates: "There are certain learning challenges on the rise and you will deal with this in your families, in class, and in the community." As I wrote, kids know who has social challenges— no one needs to use names or point fingers. I found that the two kids in the class who were on the autism spectrum welcomed a discussion, and ended up sharing out loud what life is like for them. The regular education peers were absolutely glued to their seats, listening and learning. They got it, and at a deep level.

After the workshop one regular education fourth grader said, "I really don't know what this autism thing is (and I never used the word "autism"!), but I just know that if it didn't exist, there is a lot I would not have in my life." This was a kid who had two friends on the autism spectrum who could deal with his "ADHD-ish" challenges without teasing him or making him feel weird. Lovely. Again, everyone has "differences" in a classroom. One of the kids with autism wrote me a letter saying, "Thank you for telling people that it's okay to tell me what I should do—I am so scared when people just yell at me."

So, if you have a child with autism who is included in a regular education classroom, think about going into your child's class and sharing some specific yet age-appropriate information, especially if you plan on having your child stay in that school for several years. An added benefit is that if aides or teachers are present during your talk, they may learn more about the realities of children with autism and social challenges than they would at a teacher in-service training, and they can also feel freer to ask questions about challenges "on behalf of the children."

The Inclusion Dance

Susan Etlinger

It's official: I'm a bitch. By which I mean I've moved past that initial flush of optimism and teamwork and wanting everyone to feel good about themselves to disappointment, confrontation, detente, anger and now—inevitably—relentlessness.

And it is relentless—for reasons bureaucratic, cultural, personal, possibly gender-determined, and sometimes inexplicable.

The day starts with a clamor of children in the big yard. It's an expansive space—too much for the kindergartners, much less any child with sensory issues—and children whiz around, hollering, bumping into each other, a chaotic, moving mass of kidness.

Isaac refuses to set foot in the yard. This full frontal assault first thing in the morning is unbearable. He makes a beeline for the library, and insists we sit and read a book. He falls apart when I tell him it's time to go to the classroom. "Nooooo," he wails, sinking boneless to the floor. "Come on, Isaac," says one of the administrators as she briskly picks her way around him. "You'll be late."

We are on another planet, I think. One where there is no word for "late."

In my most philosophical moments, I realize that it's not their fault. This is a foreign language, and they are struggling to learn even the most basic syntax. If he melts down right after lunch (a hasty affair in the multipurpose room, where the echoes are too much even for me), they ascribe it to stubbornness or poor impulse control. They don't ask about what happened right before. That's not the point for them; his behavior is the point.

And so, like a detective, I try to sift through the scraps of information I glean from time to time to find the answer: What was he doing when he got upset? What was the class doing? Where was he? They think I'm making excuses, but I'm looking for a pattern. Was it noise? Did something upset him?

It's exhausting, for them and for me, but mostly for him. "He's so smart," they'll say. "He knows he'll get a reaction. What do you do to discipline him at home?" "Well," I respond, gathering what is left of my wits, "It depends on the situation. If he's dysregulated, I help him collect himself and vocalize how he feels. If he's just being five, we set limits, give choices, the usual. It's annoying, but developmentally it's actually really great." And I chuckle weakly. But no one is interested in an impromptu lesson on theory of mind.

What they don't realize is that Isaac is starting to become aware of his differences. His father and I know this because we see how hard he works to keep it together throughout the day. By the afternoon he's clinging to regulation like a shipwreck survivor to a fragment of driftwood. They're not seeing that his nerves are fraying. And when he lets go and hurls a book at the wall in frustration, it's back to the question of discipline.

What they should do instead: tell him how proud they are that he kept it together this long, soothe him, help him understand what he needs and a better way to ask for it. I worry, more than ever, that his self-esteem is at stake, that he's learning the worst lesson of all: to internalize his feelings.

And yet there are amazing moments, too: hearing that the other children in the class ask him to help with their spelling, or that he loves his social speech group; seeing him stand up with his class at the Thanksgiving pageant.

Inevitably, my crusade to explicate my son is impossible without a fundamental understanding of how his wiring works, and that is in short supply. It's not just that the autism experts in our district are too understaffed and overstressed, it's that they are starting from square one; they have to make up for years of inertia. It's true, he's a complicated kid, and I don't expect anyone to care as much as his father and I do, but—he, and the other kids like him, deserve better.

This was my saddest lesson of the year: being nice doesn't help. I hoped it would. I was empathetic, I sent links to articles, I offered to bring in experts. But, as one of our therapists said to us, they just don't know what to do with the bumpy kids. So I became that mom: the one whose calls the administrators dread.

When Isaac was just about to graduate from his amazing inclusion preschool, a panel of parents of some older children came to share their experiences. There was one woman who told a story of how she had put her son, a "high-functioning" boy, into inclusion because she couldn't bear the thought of sending him to a school for kids with special needs. But after a year of struggle, she decided that this decision was more about her self-image than it was about what he needed. It was a disservice to him, she felt, and they changed schools.

That story depressed the hell out of me at the time, but it also felt oddly liberating. What if we were in a place where the natural response to a meltdown was joint compression and heavy work rather than yet another pullout? Or where multiple modes of communicating—verbally, visually— were routine ? What if we were with our people?

But there is no workable option here, and at the end of the day, he's back in the rest of the world, which is not filled with wiggle chairs and chewies and people who appreciate his quirks. And we have to teach him to live in the world we live in, not the world we wish we lived in. It breaks my heart.

So we include, even though the inclusion experience feels like a kind of noblesse oblige. We wake up, we get dressed, we go to school, and we crash the neurotypical party every single day. And it hurts, but we do it anyway, in the hope that, if only by our sheer relentlessness, our sheer bovine refusal to disappear, we'll clear a space for him, and, more importantly, help him clear a space for himself.

—

The above essay was written during my son's Kindergarten year. Would it surprise you to learn that first grade, and, so far, second, have been an entirely different experience for us? Isaac has a more appropriate support system, and, as importantly, has matured to a point where some of the earlier sensory challenges have smoothed out somewhat. He still requires continual support, but is thriving and happy—and very much part of his class.

It's not perfect—we still fight the good fight—but we've entered a new phase. We're no longer in an active war; it's more of, well, let's call it ongoing diplomatic engagement. We don't expect this phase to be permanent—nothing ever is—but we're appreciating it while it lasts.

—

"The Inclusion Dance" originally appeared in "Parent and Sibling Roundtable: Neurodiversity and Caregiving," Disability Studies Quarterly 30, no. 1.

Creating a Special Education PTA

Jennifer Byde Myers

Community is critical for parents of children with special needs. Community gives us emotional support and provides information about our kids' therapeutic, medical, and educational choices. Our communities have the experience and knowledge to weigh in on our decisions; its members empathize and help us keep going when times are hard, and they rejoice with us in our children's accomplishments.

It's not always easy to connect with parents like us. These kids we love so much are vulnerable, they need us – and the demands of our extra-intense parenting can leave us feeling drained and isolated. But if you can muster a burst of energy and round up a few like-minded individuals, then you can create your own community: by forming a Special Education Parent Teacher Association, or SEPTA. That is what we did when we helped found SEPTAR, the Special Education PTA of the Redwood City (California) School District.

Most traditional PTAs are attached to a single school. We found that this model didn't work for us, as most campuses in our district had only one or two special day classes, or a few students in full inclusion. So we made SEPTAR district-wide, including any family with a child with special needs, from Early Start (age three) through eighth grade. We also reached out to teachers, therapists, staff psychologists, and community leaders.

As parents, we already had a vision of support, education and community. Forming a new PTA also takes resolve, district support, and a lot of attention to detail (at least in the beginning). But it was worth it. SEPTAR is now in our fifth year. We have become a go-to resource for our special education families, with a parent support group, a speaker series, and social events such as weekly park playdates and "Break from Winter Break" jump house parties.

We have the full support of our District leaders, and put a lot of effort into maintaining open communication, in working with administration rather than against it. And our special education teachers feel supported; we provide grants to help our educators go to seminars, or get our kids the equipment they need. We host conferences for parents and professionals on topics that include social skills development, and technology and communication—to help parents get informed, and contribute to our children's educators' professional development.

Our name is out in the community now: we hand out business cards, and we attend the local Education Foundation events. During a recent election cycle we even hosted a moderated debate by the school board candidates.

Below is a basic how-to for starting a SEPTA. It may look daunting, but we somehow managed to do all this in less than six weeks:

- Find at least five people who share a common vision, and are willing to pay dues plus meet together many, many times. You can find these people in your children's classrooms, or on local email parenting boards. Ask your child's teacher, OT, PT, and behavior specialist too!

- Contact your district's head of Special Education and ask how they would like to be involved. You could also contact someone from the Board of Education.

- Select a secretary and a chairperson from among this first group to undertake responsibilities until officers can be elected.

- Organize temporary bylaws and nominations committees (we recommend organizing a communications committee as well).

- Have your chairperson contact the local district PTA president, or a state representative—easily done by going online and searching for your city name and "District PTA President."

- Draft bylaws, working with the local state PTA representative the district PTA president helped you locate. This person will ensure that you follow state PTA guidelines.

- Determine officers, meeting times, and dues amounts.

- Set a date for the organizational meeting to actually form and charter the new PTA unit.

- Have the nominating committee draft a slate of officers for the new PTA board. This might happen quickly, or it might take a while if you need to search for people to fill certain positions. At the very least, you must have a president, secretary, and treasurer.

- Get the information about the organizational meeting to as many parents as possible. This is why you want to have a communications committee, which can determine the best channels for communicating to your community. We announced our first meeting in the local paper, via flyers and emails to the schools, and via email to local special needs parenting groups.

- At the organization meeting, follow parliamentary procedure. The original committee chairperson should call the meeting to order and state that the reason for the meeting is to organize a new PTA. Then a motion to start a new PTA is made and a vote is taken. If the motion passes (and we're sure it will), a break in the meeting is taken and those present at the meeting join the PTA.

- After the break, the newly formed PTA elects officers.

- The new PTA president takes over the meeting, presents the bylaws, and has the association vote on adopting them.

- The new president may then add other items to the agenda.

- When the meeting is over, the new president needs to sign a few papers, which make the new charter official.

When the paperwork is complete, the state representative who guided you through the process will call the State PTA to get the official Employee Identification number (EIN) so the new PTA can open a bank account and begin the actual work of the PTA—making a difference for your local special needs community.

At every SEPTAR association meeting, we have parents lingering, talking, conspiring, connecting—taking part in a community that understands them and their kids, and wants to support them fully. With a little organized structure, our PTA provides resources, camaraderie, and the opportunity to come together as one community.

Please keep in mind that PTAs are non-profits, which must meet certain criteria to maintain their non-profit status—so please check with your State PTA before randomly filing taxes and signing checks!

—

More information can be found at www.pta.org

National PTA Information Center: 800.307.4782, or info@pta.org.

10 Resources

Books

Adults With Autism

- *Be Different* by John Elder Robison
- *Born on a Blue Day* by Daniel Tammett
- *Look Me in the Eye* by John Elder Robison
- *Thinking in Pictures* (or indeed any book) by Temple Grandin
- *The Uncharted Path* by Rachel Cohen-Rottenberg

Approaches and Advice

- *Ask and Tell: Self-Advocacy and Disclosure for People on the Autism Spectrum* by Stephen Shore
- *The Autism Mom's Survival Guide* by Susan Senator
- *Behavioral Intervention for Young Children With Autism: A Manual for Parents and Professionals* by Catherine Maurice
- *Coloring Outside Autism's Lines: 50+ Activities, Adventures, and Celebrations for Families with Children with Autism* by Susan Walton
- *Managing Meltdowns: Using the S.C.A.R.E.D. Calming Technique With Children and Adults With Autism* by Deb Lipsky

Historical and Cultural Contexts

- *The Horse Boy* by Rupert Isaacson
- *Not Even Wrong* by Paul Collins
- *Unstrange Minds* by Roy Richard Grinker

For Kids With Autism

- *A is for "All Aboard"* by Paula Kluth and Victoria Kluth
- *All Cats Have Asperger Syndrome* by Kathy Hoopman

Parenting Perspectives

- *Cowboy and Wills* by Monica Holloway
- *Gravity Pulls You In: Perspectives on Parenting Children on the Autism Spectrum*, edited by Kyra Anderson and Vicki Forman
- *Making Peace With Autism* by Susan Senator
- *My Baby Rides the Short Bus*, edited by Yantra Bertelli, Jen Silverman, and Sarah Talbot
- *Not My Boy! A Father, A Son, and One Family's Journey With Autism* by Rodney Peete

- *A Regular Guy: Growing Up With Autism* by Laura Shumaker

For Siblings of Kids With Autism

- *My Brother Charlie* by Holly Robinson Peete and Ryan Elizabeth Peete
- *Ian's Walk* by Laurie Lears
- *Andy and His Yellow Frisbee* by Mary Thompson

Movies

We appreciate movies in which people with autism do more than inspire neurotypical characters' self-discovery arcs. Keep this in mind when watching the following movies about people with autism:

- *Adam*
- *Loving Lampposts*
- *Mozart and the Whale*
- *Rain Man*
- *Temple Grandin*
- *Snowcake*

Online Resources

Accessibility

- *Institute for Human Centered Design:* www.adaptenv.org

Advocacy, Community Building, and Visibility

- *The Autism Acceptance Project*: www.taaproject.com
- *Autism Society of America*: www.autism-society.org Improving the lives of all affected by autism.
- *The Autistic Self Advocacy Network* (ASAN): www.autisticadvocacy.org The Autistic Self Advocacy Network seeks to advance the principles of the disability rights movement in the world of autism.)
- *Best Buddies:* www.bestbuddies.org/best-buddies A global volunteer movement that creates opportunities for one-to-one friendships, integrated employment, and leadership development for people with intellectual and developmental disabilities.
- *Disability.gov*: www.disability.gov Connecting the Disability Community to Information and Opportunities.
- *MyAutismTeam*: www.myautismteam.com A searchable database with over 30,000 providers. Exchange tips and advice about favorite autism providers, write reviews, recommend autism-friendly businesses.

Advocacy and Rights

- *A Special Advocate*: www.aspecialadvocate.com
- *New York Special Needs Consulting*: www.nyspecialneedsconsulting.com We want to help all kids like we helped our own.
- *Special Education Advisor*: www.SpecialEducationAdvisor.com An IEP and special education social network.
- *The Social Security and Disability Resource Center*: www.ssdrc.com
- *TASH*: www.tash.org. Equity, opportunities, and inclusion for people with disabilities since 1975.
- *Wrightslaw*: www.wrightslaw.com Accurate, reliable information about special education law, education law, and advocacy for children with disabilities.
- *Yellow Pages for Kids With Disabilities*: www.yellowpagesforkids.com A Wrightslaw site where you can search for disability-related resources by state.

Art and Music

- *Artism*: The Art of Autism: www.artismtoday.com
- *Artists and Autism*: www.facebook.com/ArtistsandAutism
- *Developmental Rhythms*: www.developmentalrhythms.com
- *Online Interactive Drum Kit*: www.kenbrashear.com
- *VSA: The International Organization on Arts and Disability*: www.vsarts.org

Assistive Technology, iPads, iDevices, Apps, Software

- *Apps for Children With Special Needs*: www.a4cwsn.com
- *The Family Center on Technology and Disability*: www.fctd.info
- *Dynamic Therapy Associates, Inc.*: www.mydynamictherapy.com. A Speech Language therapy practice that focuses on work with assistive technology
- *Geek SLP*: www.geekslp.com
- *Hacking Autism*: www.hackingautism.org
- *Speech-Language Pathology Sharing*: slpsharing.com
- *Squidalicious.com iPads and Autism resource page*: www.squidalicious.com/p/on-ipads.html

Bullying

- *AbilityPath*: Disable Bullying: www.abilitypath.org/areas-of-development/learning--schools/bullying

Communities

- *5 minutes for Special Needs*: www.5minutesforspecialneeds.com Where mothers of children with special needs can find inspiration and connect.

- *Aspies Central*: www.aspiescentral.com Community for Asperger's, Autism, and Associates.

- *Autism.About.Com*: an archive of over 400 researched articles and links on every aspect of autism.

- *Autism Blogs Directory*: www.autismblogsdirectory.blogspot.com We are a community; we share common bonds and common ground.

- *Autism Women's Network*: www.autismwomensnetwork.org Provides effective supports to autistic females of all ages through a sense of community, advocacy, and resources.

- *Autistics.org*: The real voice of autism.

- *The Coffee Klatch*: www.thecoffeeklatch.com A cup of coffee with parents of special needs children; meet, share, laugh, and take a little time for yourself.

- *Hopeful Parents*: www.hopefulparents.org Grassroots support for parents of children with special needs.

- *WrongPlanet.net*: www.wrongplanet.net Online resources and community for those with Asperger's.

Employment

- *Adult Autism and Employment*: www.dps.missouri.edu/Autism.html A guide for vocational rehabilitation professionals.

- *APSE*: www.apse.org. A growing national non-profit membership. organization, founded in 1988 as the Association for Persons in Supported Employment, now known as APSE.

- *The Transition Coalition* www.transitioncoalition.org/transition/index.php Mission: Providing online information, support, and professional development on topics related to the transition from school to adult life for youth with disabilities.

Español

- *iAutism*: www.iautism.info

- *National Dissemination Center for Children With Disabilities: Nuestros Publicaciones*: www.nichcy.org/espanol/publicaciones

- *Viviendo en otra Dimensión: Descubre el mundo del Autismo*: www.viviendoenotradimension.com

Foundations

- *Autism Science Foundation:* www.autismsciencefoundation.org

- *HollyRod Foundation:* www.hollyrod.org

Inclusion and Social Skills

- *Inclusive Connections*: www.inclusiveconnections.com. To further the social objective of inclusion in our schools, spiritual and religious communities, on the playground, in the neighborhoods and in children's everyday lives.

- *Michelle Garcia Winner*: www.socialthinking.com

- *Paula Kluth*: www.paulakluth.com/autism.html Toward more inclusive classrooms and communities.

- *Diane Levinthal*: Social Strides: www.socialstrides.com Pragmatic language and social skills

Journals

- *Disability Studies Quarterly*: www.dsq-sds.org
- *Shift: Journal of Alternatives: Neurodiversity and Social Change*: www.shiftjournal.com

News

- *Autism News Beat*: www.autism-news-beat.com
- *Kristina Chew at Care2.com*: www.care2.com/causes/author/autismvox
- *LeftBrainRightBrain*: leftbrainrightbrain.co.uk

Portals

- *Autism Hangout*: www.autismhangout.com

Religion and Faith

- *Blue Hijab Day*: www.facebook.com/bluehijabday Support and resources for Muslim families dealing with Autism Spectrum Disorders.

- *Friendship Circle*: www.friendshipcircle.com. Each independent Friendship Circle is operated by its local Chabad Lubavitch Center, and entirely supported by each local community to benefit local children with special needs.

- *Interfaith Disability Network*: www.interfaithdisability.org

- *Snappin' Ministries*: www.snappin.org We plug parents into a wide variety of financial, spiritual, respite, and social resources.

Safety

- *California Peace Office Standards and Training: Autism Recognition and Response Video*: senweb03.senate.ca.gov/autism/post2.htm

- *Dennis Debbaudt's Autism Risk Management*: www.autismriskmanagement.com

- *MedicAlert*: www.medicalert.org

- *Oneida Medical Jewelry*: www.oneida-medical-jewelry.com

- *SafetyTat*: www.safetytat.com

Sensory Processing

- *SPD Blogger Network*: www.spdbloggernetwork.com
- *Sensory Processing Disorder Foundation*: www.spdfoundation.net

Stories and Interviews

- *American Public Media,* "Being: Being Autistic, Being Human," being.publicradio.org/programs/beingautistic, Paul Collins and Jennifer Elder, interviewed by Krista Tippet.
- *Disney Channel,* "The Time I Realized My Brother Was Different," youtu.be/vgU-ImoAyKQ
- *NPR,* "Autism Gives Woman an 'Alien' View of Social Brains," www.npr.org/templates/story/story.php?storyId=129379866. Lisa Daxer says she doesn't want a typical brain; her autism is part of who she is.
- *Radiolab,* "Diagnosis: The Frowners," www.radiolab.org/2008/dec/29/the-frowners. Emanuel Frowner was diagnosed with Asperger syndrome as a young adult. Would it have helped or hindered him to get that diagnosis earlier in life?
- *SnagFilms,* "Refrigerator Mothers," www.snagfilms.com/films/title/refrigerator_mothers. Mothers of autistic children in the 1950s and 1960s are blamed for their child's illness.
- *StoryCorps*
    - o   "Q and A," storycorps.org/animation/q-and-a. 12-year-old Joshua Littman, who has Asperger syndrome, interviews his mother, Sarah.
    - o   "Does It Bother You to Think of Home?" storycorps.org/listen/stories/sarah-and-joshua-littman-2. Sarah Littman interviews her son, Joshua, who has Asperger syndrome, about his first semester at college.
- *This American Life,* "Hit Me With Your Best Shot" www.thisamericanlife.org/radio-archives/episode/317/unconditional-love. Dave Royko talks about the decision he and his wife faced about his autistic son's future.
- *This American Life,* "Wary Home Companions," www.thisamericanlife.org/radio-archives/episode/420/neighborhood-watch. A woman goes to her neighbors with an incredible request—to help care for her son [with autism] after she dies.
- *What You Ought To Know from The Brothers Winn,* "Autism," www.whatyououghttoknow.com/show/2008/07/18/autism.

Supplies, Materials, and Gear

- *Affordable Weighted Blankets*: affordableweightedblankets.com.
- *Beyond Play*: www.beyondplay.com. Early intervention products for young children with special needs.

- *Chewelry*: www.chewelry.ca.
- *Ozmo*: www.ozmofun.com. Autism toys, relaxers, and rewards.
- *Office Playground*: www.officeplayground.com. Source for stim toys.
- *PECS for All*: www.pecsforall.com. Free visual supports.
- *Sure Grip Bendable Utensils*: www.cooksdirect.com/product/13738/eating-aids.

Therapeutic Activities, Resources, and Toolkits

- *Autism Games*: sites.google.com/site/autismgames.
- *The Hanen Center: More Than Words*: www.hanen.org/web/home/HanenPrograms/MoreThanWords/tabid/78/Default.aspx. More Than Words is a family-focused program that gives parents of children with Autism Spectrum Disorder (ASD) and related social communication difficulties, practical tools to help their children communicate.
- *The Interdisciplinary Council on Developmental and Learning Disorders*: www.icdl.com.
- *The Motor Story*: www.themotorstory.com. The Motor Story lists activities for children to enjoy with explanations of how these tasks nurture development.
- *Rethink Autism*: www.rethinkautism.com. Online behavioral instruction and support; community.

YouTube Channels

- *WrongPlanet*: www.youtube.com/user/theWrongPlanet. Online resources and community for those with Asperger's.
- *Autism Science Foundation's YouTube Channel*: www.youtube.com/user/AutismScienceFdn

Blogs

Autistics and People with Autism

- *Clay Adams*: cometscorner-clay.blogspot.com
- *Aspie Rhetor*: aspierhetor.com
- *Aspie Teacher*: www.aspieteacher.com
- *Amanda Baggs*: ballastexistenz.autistics.org
- *Julia Bascom*: juststimming.wordpress.com
- *Corina Becker*: nostereotypeshere.blogspot.com
- *Landon Bryce at ThAutcast*: thautcast.com
- *Rachel Cohen-Rottenberg*: www.journeyswithautism.com
- *Matt at Dude, I'm an Aspie*: dudeimanaspie.blogspot.com

- *Kassiane at Radical Neurodivergence Speaking*: timetolisten.blogspot.com
- *LastCrazyHorn*: lastcrazyhorn.wordpress.com
- *Lindsey Nebeker at Naked Brain Ink*: www.nakedbrainink.com
- *Nicole Nicholson*: womanwithaspergers.wordpress.com
- *Rory Patton*: springingtiger.wordpress.com
- *John Elder Robison*: jerobison.blogspot.com
- *Square 8*: aspergersquare8.blogspot.com
- *Amanda Forest Vivian*: adeepercountry.blogspot.com
- *Zoe*: illusionofcompetence.blogspot.com

Education and Advocacy

- *Liz Ditz: I Speak of Dreams*: lizditz.typepad.com
- *Liz Ditz: Academic Remediation*: lizditz.typepad.com/academic_remediation

Neurodiversity Journalism

- *Steve Silberman*: blogs.plos.org/neurotribes

Parenting

- *Anybody Want a Peanut?*: www.wantapeanut.com
- *Elise Ronan, aka aspergers2mom*: asd2mom.blogspot.com
- *Both Hands and a Flashlight*: www.bothhandsandaflashlight.com
- *Kristina Chew: We Go With Him*: autism.typepad.com/autism
- *Christa Dahlstrom*: hyperlexicon.blogspot.com
- *Kitaiska Sandwich*: www.kitaiskasandwich.com
- *Mama Be Good*: mamabegood.blogspot.com
- *Meredith: The Ryan Files*: notanaffliction.blogspot.com
- *Mir Kamin*: www.wouldashoulda.com
- *Sarah Low*: planetjosh.squarespace.com
- *Jennifer Byde Myers at Into the Woods, Living Deliberately*: www.jennyalice.com
- *Jennifer Byde Myers at Have Autism, Will Travel*: haveautismwilltravel.blogspot.com
- *Shannon Des Roches Rosa at Squidalicious*: www.squidalicious.com
- *Shannon Des Roches Rosa as BlogHer contributing editor, parenting kids with special needs*: www.blogher.com/blog/shannon-des-roches-rosa
- *Susan Senator*: www.susansenator.com
- *Amy Sheridan*: aspergerninja.blogspot.com
- *Kristen Spina*: kristenspina.wordpress.com

- *Squillo*: confutata.wordpress.com
- *The Tumultuous Truth*: sharon-theawfultruth.blogspot.com
- *Frances Vega-Costas: Mundo Autismo*: dimensionautismo.blogspot.com
- *Emily Willingham : A Life Less Ordinary*: daisymayfattypants.blogspot.com
- *Kim Wombles*: www.scientificblogging.com/science_autism_spectrum_disorders

Professionals

- *The Autism Blog at Seattle Children's Hospital*: theautismblog.seattlechildrens.org
- *Barbara Boucher at TherExtras*: www.therextras.com
- *Tahrireh Bushey at Autism Games*: autismgames.blogspot.com
- *Brian R. King at Spectrum Mentor*: spectrummentor.com
- *Jordan Sadler at Communication Therapy*: communicationtherapy.wordpress.com
- *Stephen Shore*: autismasperger.net

Research

- *Dr. Jon Brock at Cracking the Enigma*: crackingtheenigma.blogspot.com

For additional resources, including a list of resources by region, please visit www.thinkingautismguide.com/p/resources.html.

11 Editor & Contributor Bios

Editors

Shannon Des Roches Rosa has opined about autism, parenting, advocacy, evidence-based approaches, iPads, and geekery at The New York Times, The Wall Street Journal, Bill and Melinda Gates Foundation, Redbook, Parents Magazine, KQED Forum, and PBS Parents. Her personal blog is www.squidalicious.com, and she is also BlogHer.com's contributing editor for parenting kids with special needs. She also gets a kick out speaking at conferences, giving iPad workshops, editing anthologies, and contributing to books like the award-winning *My Baby Rides the Short Bus*. She, her handsome husband, and their three capricious children live near San Francisco, California. She is trying to be a better listener. Trying.

Jennifer Byde Myers left a cubicled life in management at a Fortune 100 company in 2000, and has since been chronicling her family's journey from diagnosis to daily living with her son's special needs at www.jennyalice.com. Her essays have also appeared online at Salon.com, and in several books including the award-winning *My Baby Rides the Short Bus*. She is a featured blogger at goDandelion.com, a special needs parenting website, and is a Parenting.com Must-Read Mom. She lives on the San Francisco peninsula with her supportive husband Shawn, their two wily children Jack and Kate, and a dog named Gus. Follow her on Twitter @jennyalice.

Liz Ditz is a dyslexia and handwriting consultant and advocate for struggling students on the San Francisco peninsula. She has had a long and varied career in publishing and nonprofit organizations. She started her blog, I Speak of Dreams, in December 2003, writing on a wide range of issues. She has consistently published on science- and research-based approaches to education and for autism and other learning challenges. Her blog for struggling students' issues is Academic Remediation.

Emily Willingham earned her doctorate in biological sciences after realizing that a B.A. in English was not the moneymaker she'd anticipated. Upon completing a postdoctoral fellowship in pediatric urology, she turned to teaching and writing full time, authoring *The Complete Idiot's Guide to College Biology* and blogging at both *A Life Less Ordinary* and *The Complete Idiot's Blog for College Biology*. Living the life of a writer, teacher, and editor up to her ears in science, Emily cannot believe her good fortune, which she shares with a direct descendant of the Vikings and their three sons, all of whom show similar tendencies to a love of all things biology.

Carol Greenburg, executive director of New York Special Needs Consulting, is a special education consultant and lay advocate in private practice serving the five boroughs of New York City and beyond. Her unique perspective as an adult with Asperger syndrome and as the mother of a severely language-delayed autistic child informs all of her work. In September 2010, she was appointed the East Coast Regional Director of Autism Women's Network (www.autismwomensnetwork.com). A frequent speaker at national conferences and area universities, parent support groups, and community-based organizations, she is a member in good standing of Council of Parents Attorneys and Advocates (COPAA). Carol lives in Brooklyn with two humans: her magnificent husband and son, as well as two cats (which species outranks which should be obvious to those in a similar position).

Contributor Bios

Kate Ahern, M.S.Ed., is a teacher of learners with multiple or significant special needs. She has been working with youngsters who have developmental disabilities since she was fourteen years old. Her professional interests are diverse and include the impact of presumed competence, integrating assistive technology in the classroom, and alternative and augmentative communication and positive behavior supports as a framework for implementing application of behavior analysis. She blogs at Teaching Learners with Multiple Special Needs, teachinglearnerswithmultipleneeds.blogspot.com.

Kyra Anderson is a homeschooling mom and writer who systematically neglects her blog, This Mom dot com. She co-edited the anthology *Gravity Pulls You In* (Woodbine, 2010) and is currently at work on a memoir. Kyra lives in western Massachusetts with her husband, children's book writer and illustrator David Milgrim, and their son, whom she refers to on her website by the dubious nickname Fluffy.

Asperger Ninja is the way Amy Sheridan decodes and interprets life with Asperger's and ADHD, through the experiences she has with her son, Nate. Amy works with children on and off the Spectrum, through the YMCA and the Northeast ARC. She is pursuing her degree in Mental Health Counseling at North Shore Community College. She loves her amazing child, Diet Coke, chocolate, sleeping, and My Little Pony.

Katharine Beals, Ph.D., is the creator of the GrammarTrainer, an interactive, multi-level, English-teaching software program for children with autism, and the author of *Raising a Left-Brain Child in a Right-Brain World: Strategies for Helping Bright, Quirky, Socially Awkward Children to Thrive at Home and at School*. She is also a lecturer at the University of Pennsylvania Graduate School of Education and an adjunct professor at the Drexel University School of Education. Both her teaching and her research focus on the education of children on the autistic spectrum. Her book, her blog, and her various education articles expand this focus to include a much wider variety of socially quirky children.

Corina Lynn Becker is an autistic adult with a B.A. in English who is currently studying Disability Studies at Ryerson University. She is a writer and artist, and is a contributor to the *Perspectives* anthology. Corina has been sharing her experiences as an autistic since 2005, and is involved with the leadership of various autism organizations, including the Autism Women's Network, www.autismwomensnetwork.org. She writes at www.nostereotypeshere.blogspot.com, and publishes comics at www.nekomics.com. She can also be found at twitter.com/CorinaBecker.

Barbara H. Boucher, OT, Ph.D., PT, has focused her therapy career on children and the needs of their parents. Her career is meshed with her personal roles as a wife and mother. She is a specialist in the treatment of movement disorders and developmental problems. Dr. Boucher has clinical experience in rehabilitation hospitals, neonatal intensive care units, private homes, and public schools. She was a university faculty member and taught graduate students in physical therapy for six years. She blogs at www.TherExtras.com.

Liane Kupferberg Carter writes frequently about autism. Her articles and essays have appeared in numerous publications, including the *New York Times Motherlode* blog, the *Huffington Post*, the *Chicago Tribune*, *Parents*, *McCall's*, *Skirt!*, *Babble, Literary Mama,* and many newspapers and journals. She is a 2009 winner of the Memoir Journal Prize for her essay "Love Is Like This," and is writing a memoir about raising a child with autism. You can follow her on Twitter @LianeCarter and on Facebook at on.fb.me/lnKzH1.

Sara Chapman is an educational and DIR® consultant in private practice in the San Francisco Bay Area. She specializes in working with young children with special needs and their families, primarily in home and community-based settings. She believes in capitalizing on each child's unique strengths, individual differences, and specific learning styles to support growth, development, and learning potential. Sara holds a master's and teaching credential in early childhood special education. She is a graduate of the DIR® Institute, completing the DIR®/Floortime certificate through the Interdisciplinary Council for Learning and Developmental Disorders (ICDL)), and now trains others in the model as a tutor and DIR® Facilitator. Sara is a member of ICDL, the Profectum Foundation, and the National Association for the Education of Young Children (NAEYC).

Kristina Chew is an Associate Professor of Classics at Saint Peter's College in Jersey City, New Jersey. She has published a number of articles about autism, disability studies, and literature, most recently "The Disabled Speech of Asian Americans" in *Disability Studies Quarterly* (volume 30), for which she won the 2010 Tyler Rigg Award. Since 2005, she has been blogging about autism at websites including *Autism Vox* and *Change.org;*

she currently writes about life with her son, Charlie, at *We Go With Him* (autism.typepad.com) and also blogs for *Care2.com*. She is working on a translation of the Roman poet Virgil's Eclogues and has also published a translation of Virgil's Georgics (2002).

Clay writes, "There wasn't any word for it when I was a kid. There was 'sissy,' there was 'big baby,' (one of my sister's favorite words for me), there was 'queer,' (meant with either of the connotations), and of course, there was 'ostracism.' My parents didn't much notice, they had divorced when I was four, and when they weren't tearing each other down, they were drinking. My three older sisters were only jealous of me, because I was the son my father always wanted—except that I wasn't. He wanted another son, someone he could call 'Butch.' I clearly didn't live up to his expectations."

Rachel Cohen-Rottenberg is a wife, mother, writer, and artist who was diagnosed with Asperger's syndrome at the age of 50. She holds a bachelor's degree and a master's degree in English from the University of California, Berkeley, where she worked as a graduate student instructor in English composition and literature. After many years as a technical writer and homeschooling mother, she now lives a quiet life in rural Vermont, where she writes and publishes the blog www.journeyswithautism.com and the site *Autism and Empathy: Dispelling Myths and Breaking Stereotypes* (www.autismandempathy.com). She is also the author of three books; her latest work, *Blazing My Trail: Living and Thriving with Autism,* is a sequel to her memoir *The Uncharted Path.*

Daniel Dage has been teaching and serving individuals with various disabilities for over fifteen years. He received his bachelor's degree in Agriculture Education from Iowa State University in 1987 and his master's degree in Special Education from Georgia State University in 1996. He also has done coursework and research in Applied Behavior Analysis. He and his wife and two sons live near Atlanta, Georgia. Other interests include open source technology, twenty-first-century learning, and home gardening.

Christa Dahlstrom lives in Oakland, California with her husband, Chris, and their son. Shortly after her son was diagnosed with ASD and hyperlexia at age three, Christa created a blog called Hyperlexicon (hyperlexicon.blogspot.com), where she publishes reflections on raising an extraordinary child. In her professional life, Christa is a writer and designer the field of corporate training and learning design. She is also the creator of Flummox and Friends (www.flummoxandfriends.com), an off-beat, live-action video series for kids and families that teaches social skills.

Michael V. Drejer is thirty-three years old, and was diagnosed with Asperger syndrome at age twenty-five. He lives in Aarhus, Denmark, with his cat, Lucius. The company he works for, which specializes in hiring people with a diagnosis on the autism spectrum, is called BOAS Specialister. You can follow him on Twitter @maialideth.

Judy Endow MSW, maintains a private practice in Madison, Wisconsin, providing consultation for families, school districts, and other agencies. Besides having autism herself, she is the parent of a grown son with ASD. Judy presents internationally, is part of the Wisconsin DPI Statewide Autism Training Team, and is a board member of both the Autism Society of America, Wisconsin Chapter, and the Autism National Committee. In addition, Judy works with Autistic Global Initiative (AGI), a program of the Autism Research Institute that is self-run by autistic adults working in the autism fields. Her book Paper Words, Discovering and Living with My Autism (AAPC, 2009) was 2010 International Book Award Finalist in Autobiographies/Memoirs. Judy has also received the 2010 Autism Society Media Excellence Award for her DVD The Power of Words: How *We Talk About P*eople with *Autism Spectrum Disorders Matters!* (AAPC, 2009). Practical Solutions for Stabilizing Students With Classic Autism to Be Ready to Learn: Getting to Go (AAPC, 2011) is Judy's most recent book. Please see Judy's website, www.judyendow.com, for a complete listing of publications.

Susan Etlinger began writing about autism and special needs both to document her family's experience and to offer practical resources for families, teachers, therapists, and friends of children on the autism spectrum. She was recently named one of Parenting Magazine's "Must-Read Moms" for her blog, The Family Room (www.familyroomblog.com). She lives in San Francisco with her husband and eight-year-old son.

Shawn C. Graves is dating the mother of an autistic child. It has been rewarding, challenging, and frustrating. He is always seeking to learn more about autism. The more he learns, the more he realizes he needs to learn. He has two children of his own who are not autistic. Tree has challenged everything he knows about kids, autism, and communication. He is just an outsider, observing what few people will ever experience.

Prather Harrell is the proud mother of four boys, two of whom are on the autism spectrum (one diagnosed with ADHD and PDD-NOS, the other diagnosed with high-functioning autism). She was a board member and community relations director for African-American Autism Support Services of Arizona, and has worked as a center liaison and family advocate for Lauren's Institute for Education (L.I.F.E., www.laurensinstitute.org) where her son receives therapy and habilitation services. When she is not working to further the cause of getting the voice of autism heard, or volunteering at her sons' schools, she spends her time with her husband and four children, living, loving, and celebrating God and life.

Michelle Hecht is an educational and behavioral consultant and a Board Certified Behavior Analyst. She has worked for over twenty years in special education, and for over ten years with clients with autism, ages eighteen months through adulthood. Michelle provides behavioral consultation and ABA program supervision to private clients, school districts, and agencies for adults in the San Francisco Bay Area. She conducts agency staff training and parent education through local parent support organizations for families of children with disabilities. Michelle received her B.A. in psychology from Vassar College, and M.A. and Ed.S. in Educational Psychology from the University of Minnesota.

Jess is the mother of two beautiful little girls: "Katie," a typically a-typical fifth grader, and "Brooke," an anything-but-typical third grader diagnosed with PDD-NOS. Jess relishes the privilege of mothering these two incredible creatures. She writes about her family's journey at www.adiaryofamom.wordpress.com.

Jillsmo lives in Berkeley, California, with her husband and two boys, one of whom is nine and has autism; the other is six and is king of all he surveys. When she's not doing her children's laundry or driving her children from one location to the next, she is volunteering for her children's school, blogging about life with autism and kids in Berkeley at *yeahgoodtimes.blogspot.com* and attempting to make a living as a bookkeeper. Follow her on twitter @jillsmo.

JoyMama describes herself as "mom (two daughters), wife, data librarian, musician (hand bells), artist (wheat straw), autism advocate, blogger, voracious reader, tired!" Her cheerful, energetic daughter Joy has several developmental diagnoses, including epilepsy and autism. JoyMama blogs pseudonymously at Elvis Sightings, *elvis-sightings.blogspot.com.*

Mir Kamin is a mom, writer, wife, and spoiled dog wrangler who lives with her family outside of Atlanta. She's pretty sure that she's completely awesome, because they say the universe never gives you more than you can handle, and she has both a hormonal teenage daughter and a son with Asperger's. She is planning to try that whole leaping-tall-buildings-in-a-single-bound thing once she's caught up on everything else and has a nap. In the meantime, she's equivocating over her life at her personal blog, Woulda Coulda Shoulda (wouldashoulda.com).

Brian R. King LCSW, is the founder of SpectrumMentor and is an international consultant on the topics of confidence building and win-win relationship strategies. He is also known for his work with developmental disabilities including the autism spectrum. Brian and his three sons are all on the autism spectrum. Through his books, website, mentoring programs, and interactive workshops, Brian has become known worldwide for his focus on abilities and his belief in the potential of all people to develop the skills they need to live their dreams. As Brian says, "I am defined by my dreams and my commitment to achieving them and not by any label that tries to tell me otherwise."

Estée Klar is founder and executive director of The Autism Acceptance Project (www.taaproject.com) and blogger at *Joy of Autism* now located at *www.esteeklar.com*. She is the mother of a young autistic son named Adam and writes about autism and art for publication. While currently completing her graduate degree in Critical Disability Studies at York University in Toronto, Estée continues to work as a curator of art and has organized major exhibitions of "outsider art" to promote a discourse about how we think about, regard, and treat autistic citizens. Estée also lectures on Autism and Representation at universities across North America.

Judy McCrary Koeppen M.S., CCC-SLP is a forty-something gal who lives on the San Francisco Peninsula with her husband, two kids, and a plethora of pets. She is the parent of a child with PDD-NOS, ADHD, SPD, and some other things that don't have such cool acronyms. Judy was a founding member and the charter president of the Special Education PTA of Redwood City, California (SEPTAR). Judy's private speech therapy practice, Sage Therapy, is also located in Redwood City. She specializes in early intervention, problem eaters, difficult feeders (those having motor control issues), and other regular speech therapy stuff. She incorporates her therapy dog, Izabelle, into her therapy sessions. In her spare time Judy enjoys family and friends and her continual quest for fine chocolate and good coffee.

Devon Koren Alley is a devoted mother, a freelance writer, a talent specialist, and a human laugh track. Her daughter was diagnosed with autism at the age of two and has been receiving various therapies and special services ever since. Devon resides in the foothills of East Tennessee with her daughter, Aisling, her husband, Thomas, their cat, Pantoufle, and their puppy, Pippin.

Kev Leitch is a web developer from Oxfordshire, United Kingdom. He blogs about autism at leftbrainrightbrain.co.uk and is dad to three children, of whom one is autistic; and step-dad to three children, of whom one is autistic.

Kim Leaird (aka KAL) is a graphic designer and writer living in the D.C. metro area. In 2006, when her identical twin boys were both diagnosed on the autism spectrum at the age of two, she began chronicling their story on her blog, *Autism Twins*. As a mom to two extraordinary boys, she now knows far more about the Sesame Street oeuvre, cloud formations, and Greek mythology than she ever dreamed possible. Her days are never boring, and she wouldn't have it any other way.

Diane Levinthal M.A. CCC-SLP, is the owner of Social Strides Therapies in Redwood City, California and an MGWinner/Think Social certified mentor. She runs social thinking groups for students of all ages and lives in Redwood City with her husband and their three children, one of whom was diagnosed with social language challenges in 1999.

Sarah Low is a former nurse practitioner, now a stay-at-home mom, living and writing in the Pacific Northwest with her two boys, Zach fifteen, and Josh, thirteen. Sarah maintains a personal blog, Planet Josh, which is an uncensored look at life with her boys—primarily Josh, who is profoundly autistic. She has also been a guest blogger for Momversation.com.

J. Lorraine Martin is a graduate of the University of Florida and mother to three children, one of whom has autism. When her autistic son suffered a regression, she was asked to stay within five minutes of his school in case he needed the early pick-up. A freelance writing career was launched in a nearby coffee shop as a means to navigate through the pain of the journey. Her work has been featured in the Huffington Post, Home by Three, Autism Speaks, and Age of Autism. She hopes to use her voice to help educate the public on the unusual challenges and hard-fought-for rewards found within the mercurial world of autism. No matter the obstacle, she always hopes to find a laugh along the way.

Lindsey Nebeker is a pianist, songwriter, consultant, and speaker who lives and works in the metro Washington D.C., area. She was diagnosed with autism at the age of two, and began to speak around age four. She grew up in Tokyo, Japan, with her younger brother, who shares the same diagnosis, but who faces a lot more challenges. She attended special education programs until kindergarten, when mainstreaming into a typical classroom environment ensued. She earned a bachelor of arts degree in music technology from the College of Santa Fe in 2004. Since then, she has been highly active in the conference speaking circuit along with her boyfriend, Dave (who also has autism). She is especially interested in the topic of ASDs and sexuality, and incorporates it into her workshops and on her blog, Naked Brain Ink (nakedbrainink.com). She is a graduate of the Partners in Policymaking program, and she is currently serving on the board of directors. She is also the Washington, D.C. liaison for the Autism Women's Network. Lindsey has been featured in *Glamour* magazine, ABC's Good Morning America, IPC Media (UK), and appeared on the cover of *Autism Spectrum Quarterly*.

Kristin Neff got her Ph.D. at the University of California, Berkeley in 1997, and is now an associate professor at the University of Texas at Austin. Her main research focus is on self-compassion, a field which she pioneered: www.self-compassion.org. She teaches workshops on self-compassion, and is the author of the book *Self-Compassion: Stop Beating Yourself Up and Leave Insecurity Behind* (William Morrow, 2011). Kristin lives in the countryside in Elgin, Texas, with her husband, Rupert Isaacson—an author and human rights activist—and with their son Rowan, who is autistic. She and her family were featured in the film and book *The Horse Boy:* www.HorseBoyMovie.com.

Rory Patton knew very little about autism until a friend of his wife's said some of his behavior was "like other people with Asperger's." Prompted by this he found out enough to realize the comment was not without foundation and had himself assessed. He is married, a grandfather, and in full-time employment. When not working he is trying to give the world a realistic view of autism, or messing about with his PC, his camera, or in his garden. He spends a lot of his time trying to calculate how it must feel to have a "Theory of Mind." You can follow him on Twitter at twitter.com/springingtiger.

Holly Robinson Peete is an actress, author, activist, and philanthropist. With her husband, Rodney, Robinson Peete created the HollyRod Foundation, inspired by her father's battle with Parkinson's disease. Inspired by their son, they expanded their mission to include Autism. With her daughter Ryan, Robinson Peete published her second book, *My Brother Charlie*, examining autism from a sibling's perspective.

Pia Prenevost is the mom to one beautiful and wicked smart boy who fits somewhere on that wide, wide autism spectrum. She is a fierce protector, fiery advocate, and in desperate need of a nap. She happens to have a Ph.D. in Developmental Psychology, works as an NICU nurse, and dreams of the day she can discuss Voltaire with her little man. Or even Curious George. She isn't picky. Some days she dreams about becoming a writer, but then she remembers that bills have to get paid. You can find her honing her storytelling skills on her blog *The Crack and the Light.*

Brenda Rothman is a writer, public speaker, and political activist with a background in information technology, writing, and health law. She is a parent to a child diagnosed with autism. Brenda blogs at *Mama Be Good* and contributes to the *Thinking Person's Guide to Autism* blog and the *Sensory Processing Disorder Blogger's Network*. Her essay about race and autism was featured on *My Brown Baby's* blog and at Parenting.com. Brenda was interviewed by *Atlanta Parent* and *The Lime* magazines. She has advocated for autism insurance reform and autism support in front of legislators, insurance representatives, medical professionals, and the autism community. She lives in Atlanta with her husband and son.

Jordan Sadler, M.S., CCC-SLP, is the director of Communication Therapy, P.C., in Chicago, Illinois. Jordan enjoys helping each child develop to his or her full potential by working with the whole family within natural environments, and has been recognized for her work in private practice, and public and private schools. In her clinical practice, Jordan draws from the SCERTS Model, DIR/Floortime, and the Hanen program, and is enthusiastically working on a variety of projects designed to improve the lives of those with autism through the use of technology and media.

Susan Senator is the mother of three young men, the oldest of whom has a fairly severe form of autism. She is the author of *Making Peace with Autism: One Family's Story of Struggle, Discovery, and Unexpected Gifts* (Trumpeter, 2006) and *The Autism Mom's Survival Guide: Creating a Balanced and Happy Life While Raising a Child with Autism* (Trumpeter, 2010). A speaker, blogger, writer, and English professor, she has had work published in the *New York Times*, the *Washington Post*, the *Boston Globe*, and *Education Week*, among other places. Her website is www.susansenator.com.

Laura Shumaker is the author of *A Regular Guy: Growing Up With Autism*. She writes a nationally recognized autism blog for the *San Francisco Chronicle* and has contributed to several anthologies, including *Voices of Autism* and *Gravity Pulls You In*. Laura's essays have appeared in the *New York Times*, the *San Francisco Chronicle*, *Literary Mama*, *The Autism Advocate* and on CNN.com. Laura speaks regularly to schools, book groups, and disability organizations.

Kristen Spina is a freelance writer living in New York whose writing has appeared in numerous trade and consumer publications, as well as the anthology *Gravity Pulls You In: Perspectives on Parenting Children on the Autism Spectrum*. She is currently at work on a novel.

Squillo is a former person, on hiatus while she raises her two children. Her son has PDD-NOS, and her daughter is just nuts in the typical way. Both children have inherited their father's intelligence and her teeth, for which she is profoundly grateful. She is not an expert in much of anything. She has an opinion anyway.

Mike Stanton lives and works in the United Kingdom, where he teaches children with severe cognitive disabilities, many of whom are autistic. His adult son is diagnosed with Asperger syndrome. Stanton is a member of the United Kingdom's National Autistic Society. He speaks and writes on autism. His book *Learning to Live with High Functioning Autism* is also available in a Spanish translation, *Convivir con el Autismo.* He has also contributed a chapter to *Asperger Syndrome in Adolescence,* edited by Liane Holliday Willey.

Mike's website and blog, *Action for Autism* (actionforautism.co.uk), was named as a reaction against names like Action Against Autism and Defeat Autism Now! Names like these suggest to autistic people that we are against them as people. You may not mean that. But if you care about autism, you ought to care about the feelings of autistic people and not use language that makes them angry or upset. If you disregard the feelings of autistic people, do not be surprised if you are disregarded.

Hartley Steiner lives in the Seattle area with her three sons. She is the award winning author of the SPD Children's book *This is Gabriel Making Sense of School* and *Sensational Journeys,* as well as the founder of the SPD Blogger Network (*www.spdbloggernetwork.com*). She is a contributing writer for the *SPD Foundation*'s blog, *S.I. Focus Magazine,* and *Autism Spectrum Quarterly,* among dozens of other online websites and blogs. You can find her chronicling the never-ending chaos that is her life on her personal blog, Hartley's Life With 3 Boys (*www.hartleysboys.com*) and on Twitter as @ParentingSPD. When she isn't writing, or dealing with a meltdown, she enjoys spending time in the company of other adults preferably with good food and even better wine.

Frances Vega-Costas is the mother of an eleven-year-old boy diagnosed with PDD-NOS. She has created a website about autism in Spanish (www.viviendoenotradimension.com) and writes articles for Hispanic blogs and online magazines. She is Puerto Rican and currently works as a special education advocate for a nonprofit called Community Advocates (*communityadvocates.org*), for people with developmental disabilities, in Kalamazoo, Michigan. She is involved with several non-profit organizations in her area.

Susan Walton is the author of *Coloring Outside Autism's Lines* (Sourcebooks), a practical book about ways to have fun at home, with friends, in the community, during holidays, and on vacation. She has three children, and her eldest son is autistic. Her two girls are twins and quite simply the best sisters a brother could have. The whole Walton family is passionate about finding excitement and new ways to enjoy being together. She is on the board of the Best Day Foundation, a non-profit organization that gives kids with special needs memorable days of outdoor adventure with surfing and downhill snow sports. She blogs at *Even More Outside Autism's Lines* at susanwalton.blogspot.com, and can be found on Twitter as @swalton47.

Jean Winegardner lives in the D.C. Metro area with her husband and three wonderful children: Sam, Jack, and Quinn. Her middle child, Jack, was diagnosed with PDD-NOS shortly before he turned five. Passionate about creating a positive view of special needs children and adults, Jean writes often on her blog, *Stimeyland*; runs an autism-events website for Montgomery County, Maryland, called *AutMont*; and writes *Autism Unexpected*, a column in the *Washington Times Communities*. Through her writing, Jean hopes to help dispel the idea that autism is a terrifying tragedy and to encourage acceptance of autistic individuals. She is also a firm believer that when you have a choice between laughing and crying, you should always try to laugh. Although sometimes you may have to do both.

Kim Wombles is an instructor of English (and occasionally psychology) at a community college in Texas. She is mother to three wonderful children on the spectrum, and wife to a pretty swell guy. In her spare time, she writes several blogs, some of which are snarky, some of which are sweet, and some of which are science-based. Occasionally, all three combine in one place. You can find her at science20.com/countering_tackling_woo for the science-based snark-free stuff.

Sandy Yim, M.S.Ed., is a writer and consultant with Asperger syndrome and Auditory Processing disorder. She is passionate about working with companies and organizations to bridge mainstream practices with the needs of autistic individuals.

12 Index

We would like to thank every volunteer who contributed their time to the production of Thinking Person's Guide to Autism. This book wouldn't be here without your expertise, passion, and hard work.

Our copy editors were Amber Ayers, Stacey Becker, Jenny Benson, Anita Carey, Rivka Iacullo, and Bobbi Sheahan. Our logo was artwork was created by Will Hornaday of Hornaday Designs. Our cover design is by Amy Freels. Sincere gratitude to John Ordover for his publishing insights and guidance.

—

It was not possible to include all the essays we posted online since Thinking Person's Guide to Autism was founded in June 2010. Please visit our website www.ThinkingAutismGuide.com for regularly updated autism essays, resources, and other information from autistics, parents, and professionals.

For autism news, articles, and information, follow @ThinkingAutism. For inspiring and enriching conversation, please join our Facebook community at www.Facebook.com/ThinkingPersonsGuideToAutism. If you would like to contribute an essay or suggest a resource, please contact us at ThinkingAutism@gmail.com.

Made in the USA
Middletown, DE
26 June 2018